This insightful work is unique for it provides a multi-disciplinary approach to innovation that is firmly grounded and well documented, while being insightful and applicable in a series of carefully planned, easy to follow steps. This innovative approach to integrated innovation will, I believe, help students, researchers and professionals engaged in the volatile and tumultuous high tech environment.

Prof. George Haramis, University of Macedonia, Thessaloniki, Greece

This monograph serves a two-fold goal: it aims to provide a succinct yet engaging and thought-provoking review of the literature on integration for (high tech) innovation. It approaches and presents it as a unified whole and not isolated attempt. It also builds and expands on this research by proposing a firmly grounded model to render innovation affordable and attainable in today's volatile high tech environment.

Prof. George Tsiotras, University of Macedonia, Thessaloniki, Greece

Dr. Fotiadis's monograph includes a thorough survey of the literature while the proposed methodology and model are fairly easy to implement, well-grounded and documented and may prove potentially very useful for High Tech enterprises.

George J. Siomkos, Professor of Marketing & Dean, School of Business, Athens University of Economics & Business, Greece

Strategic Marketing for High Technology Products

In order for High Technology (HT) companies to tackle contemporary demanding market challenges, they frequently deploy time-reduction strategies with respect to product launch. Marketing of technology-related products – and especially cutting-edge ones – involves a complex and multidimensional bundle of specific and unique characteristics, such as the complexity of products, the intensity of the competition, confusion and/or fear of adoption among consumers, fast pacing changes in the external environment. The very nature of the interrelations that evolve as part of the dynamic process of strategy formulation contributes further to the formulation of a very challenging environment which is described as tumultuous, volatile and turbulent. These specific features, qualities and characteristics constitute the core of the innate need for an integrated approach that requires and depends on the cooperation and coordination of specific functional competencies. This book employs a systemic approach that accommodates the integration of specialized departmental capabilities as a fundamental prerequisite and a cornerstone for the successful navigation of high-tech organizations in their extremely competitive environments.

It provides a solid and extant context of compact and consistent cognitive background that is specific to the HT strategic marketing field, and a strategic tool that utilizes, relies and is built on the turbulent environment of HT rather than just overlooking, avoiding or ignoring it, and that assumes a proactive point of view, capitalizing on characteristics specific to this field, through the provision of a strategic managerial and marketing model that is overlaid onto a reliably assessed foundation of dynamic qualities, with a long-term orientation and scope, albeit one that would be easy to apply and which will generate immediate results.

Thomas Fotiadis is Associate Professor of Marketing and is Director of the Marketing Lab, Department of Production and Management Engineering, Democritus University of Thrace in Greece.

Routledge Studies in Innovation, Organizations and Technology

Dynamics of Knowledge-Intensive Entrepreneurship
Business Strategy and Public Policy
Edited by Franco Malerba, Yannis Caloghirou, Maureen McKelvey and Slavo Radosevic

Collaborative Innovation
Developing Health Support Ecosystems
Edited by Mitsuru Kodama

Innovation Drivers and Regional Innovation Strategies
Edited by Mario Davide Parrilli, Rune Dahl-Fitjar, and Andrés Rodríguez-Pose

Information Theft Prevention
Theory and Practice
Romanus Izuchukwu Okeke and Mahmood Hussain Shah

The New Production of Users
Changing Innovation Collectives and Involvement Strategies
Edited by Sampsa Hyysalo, Torben Elgaard Jensen, and Nelly Oudshoorn

Foundations of Information Systems
Research and Practice
Andrew Basden

Social Inclusion and Usability of ICT-Enabled Services
Edited by Jyoti Choudrie, Panayiota Tsatsou and Sherah Kurnia

Strategic Marketing for High Technology Products
An Integrated Approach
Thomas Fotiadis

For a full list of titles in this series, please visit www.routledge.com/Routledge-Studies-in-Innovation-Organizations-and-Technology/book-series/RIOT

Strategic Marketing for High Technology Products

An Integrated Approach

Thomas Fotiadis

Routledge
Taylor & Francis Group

LONDON AND NEW YORK

First published 2018
by Routledge

2 Park Square, Milton Park, Abingdon, Oxfordshire OX14 4RN
52 Vanderbilt Avenue, New York, NY 10017

Routledge is an imprint of the Taylor & Francis Group, an informa business

First issued in paperback 2020

British Library Cataloguing-in-Publication Data
A catalogue record for this book is available from the British Library

Library of Congress Cataloging-in-Publication Data
A catalog record for this book has been requested

ISBN: 978-1-138-55928-8 (hbk)
ISBN: 978-0-367-59111-3 (pbk)

Typeset in Times New Roman
by Apex CoVantage, LLC

It is customary for dedications to refer to persons or events that exert a unique shaping power on one's life. Mine refers to the one – which upon arrival – will constitute a groundbreaking game-changer – a unique provider of meaning in life.

Contents

Illustrations

Figures

Tables

Acknowledgments

The author expresses his deep gratitude to the members of the doctoral dissertation scientific advisory/supervising committee for their valuable comments and unfailing support on the forerunner of this work.

The author would also like to thank Mr. Panos Stogiannos for his assistance with the translation and editing of the manuscript. The author would also like to acknowledge the input and valuable contribution of Mr. Efthymios Kokmotos, PhD student in the Department of Production and Management Engineering of the Polytechnic School of Democritus University of Thrace, who read the manuscript and made insightful comments and suggestions.

1   The environment

1.1 High Technology: definitions, characteristics, environment, importance

Before somebody can venture into the specific cognitive subject of High Technology (HT), it is deemed purposeful and useful for them to satisfactorily familiarize themselves with the wider framework within which HT is incorporated and from which it follows – the notion of technology.

Technology is derived from the Greek word τέχνη, meaning "art". Its connection to its root implies a set of techniques or methods which may be employed in order to manufacture, produce, or "build" something. Should one expand the meaning of the word, then what it, essentially, means is "that which men use to control their environment" or, otherwise, "the way by which men dominate their natural environment".

Depending on the adopted viewpoint, there is a multitude of approaches utilized in order to conceptually define the word *technology*:

- In case the approach takes place under the light of the dimension offered by Economic Sciences, then Technology is indissolubly intertwined with the efficiency that may be attained by adopting it. It essentially is a toolbox focused approach to the relationship between men and technology, whose value and contribution are assessed based on the economic benefit that may ensue from the application of technology toward the improvement of the efficiency of the productive process. Consequently, it is regarded not only as a founding stone and vital support of economic development but also as a necessary ingredient of personal economic prosperity, because of its fundamental influence on living standards.
- Despite the fact that the economic orientation for delimiting technology is the most common one, it is not, however, the only one; neither is it axiomatically the most important one. An integrated approach toward the concept emphatically dictates the consideration of other dimensions as well, dimensions which, in most cases, do not cancel one another but function complementarily in order to facilitate a multidimensional understanding of the concept.

In this context, one must not forget that the "economic science" employed in order to outline the term earlier, is a subset of the sociological framework wherein (economically active) individuals, structures and the relations amongst them subsist. Through this framework the needs and demands of individuals, as well as of the economy itself, emerge and are satisfied. It suffices for someone to consider the economic and social framework as inextricable constituent parts of a directly inter-affected dynamic system, each element of which feeding and being fed by the other (even if with some time lag), in order to apprehend the "greater" picture: From a sociological viewpoint, technology is an interrelated system of knowledge, processes, methods and apperceptions which stands as the necessary and sufficient convention in order to make the satisfaction of human needs feasible, an integral part of which are also social ones.

Finally, a common constituent of the approaches, from a philosophical standpoint, is to treat technology as a basic pillar from the evolution of the known civilization. The subject of controversial criticism, technology is at times considered as the catalyst for integration and self-realization while, at other times, as a contributing factor for the alienation and maladjustment of people.

Whichever viewpoint one has adopted and whatever cognitive subject filter is employed as an interpretative tool, it is important to approach technology in the context of the role it plays with respect to the satisfaction of human needs in their entirety.

It is also important to underline that technology is a human activity, the subject of which is the well-being and comfort of people.

1.1.2 Technology

Technology is a transformation force. It is something much wider than a system set of tools which probe or are extensions of our bodily movements. It not only constitutes a sturdy and reliable material for technical achievements and economic accomplishments but also functions as a vehicle for the manifestation of perceptions subsumed to the sphere of social and cultural intricacies. It is a human cognitive intervention which pervades, grows, jaunts and outflows to and from the world surrounding us; shapes it; but is also shaped by it. It would amount to no hyperbole for someone to suggest that Technology is closely interrelated with almost any form of human activity – that is it essentially constitutes an intrinsic variable thereof. Moreover, to possess it, even on a rudimentary level, is nowadays an elementary condition for someone to be harmoniously and functionally included in the social, economic, cultural and working processes.

Technology and humans have a bidirectional so close that one could define it as one, particularly resistant to time, system, while the substance of its parts is in a direct and dynamic interrelation. The double identity borne by each constituent part of this system – namely, its simultaneous identity as a subject and the object of the shaping influences from and toward the other part – largely defines the entirety of the expressions not only of each fold related to humans but also of the "imprint", the mark humans leave.

Technology emerged as the most effective approach by a rational and creative being in order to function as the vehicle that would allow this being to shape the coordinates defining its existence. As the medium for the satisfaction of man's multidimensional needs, technology depends on humans. On the other hand, humans depend on technology, since technology – via its penetration and diffusion – constitutes the basic pillar/carrier for the satisfaction of human needs.

What is cited earlier only serves to accentuate what Pythagoras proclaimed, namely, that humans are, throughout the eons, the measure for all things. The skeptics of the utility or even the purposefulness of the existence of this relation, where humans are the measure, the creators as well as the subjects of the influence of technology, advocate that the artificial extension of their capabilities frequently fashions a false picture of personal happiness and self-fulfillment. They criticize technology on the basis that beyond its contribution to the survival of our species, it, ultimately, became the measure of its progress. That it frequently becomes an end in itself and the field of its own evolution, leading humans to something alien to their nature.

The expansive discourse that has been developed throughout the ages and the literally countless dimensions via which one can approach the concept of technology are the main reasons for the existence of many – and frequently ragtag – definitions. One, be the person a disputant or apologist of a greater or lesser emphasis on viewpoints stressing the anthropocentric hue, or driven by a background oriented/ influenced by a philosophical, or sociological or economic basis may adopt some other, different approach as the most firmly grounded.

Fischer and Pry (1971) emphasize the role and contribution of Technology in catering for needs, as such, are defined and delimited by the overall value system on each occasion. It grants power to those who control it and control its applications. It includes our efforts to shape, control, morph and ever impose our will on our environment, via the involvement of technology on the use and exploitation of resources.

Technology is connected to the effectiveness of the application of our skill to "do" things.

The aforementioned, as the statement of a definition, could be further particularized – and, correspondingly, be subjected to the entailed limitations of a more specific approach – should Technology be defined as a toolbox – a set of methods, processes, structured approaches and techniques which operates catalytically, systemically and collaboratively with the other productive factors, assisting them toward the objectives posed in the context of the productive process (Papageorgiou, 1990).

A similarly oriented (with respect to the productive process) approach attempts to signify that an integral part with an almost universal participation in the quiver of Technology is the knowledge that is applicable to the productive process. It may take the form of technical information relating to aspects or the whole of the production process, or the products, or it may be expressed in the context of the transformation of the production factors to tangible products or services. It may even include the cognitive background of Managerial science which participates both horizontally and vertically in the organization, management, planning and control of the productive process.

In its more expanded version, the definition of *technology* shall cover both specific technological systems, as well as the economic-production system, but also manifestations of social structures and practices (Vakalios, 2002).

In the context of a broader delimitation of the term, Technology could be viewed as a unified and complex system of material elements and processes that are necessary for the integration of some functional action. A founding stone in this set of heterogeneous elements (machinery; design, calculation and control methodologies, processes and techniques) are also the thinking and theory schema that set and document the aforementioned system.

Besides, however, of the system via which needs are satisfied, minimized or staved, Galbraith introduces another dimension of technology, by involving science and underlining in parallel the role of scientific-organized knowledge: by technology one also refers to the systematic application of scientific or other structured knowledge, in order to facilitate practical purposes.

The United Nations Educational, Scientific and Cultural Organization's (UNESCO's) *Dictionary of Social Sciences* (Gould and Kolb, 1964) attempts to include and incorporate the principal points of the preceding approaches: Technology is considered the whole or an organized part of the knowledge that exists and regards science, the discoveries that have taken place, the productive processes of the present as well as those of the past, the energy resources and reserves, but also circulation and information, that are associated with the improvement of the production of tangible and intangible products. The same source approaches the concept from a socio-anthropological background (thus limiting the scope of the approach) and cites that technology is defined as the sum of available knowledge for the production of tools and all kinds of artifacts which are aimed at the exercise of technical and manual activities and extraction and collection of materials.

Independently from the origins of thought, or the predispositions of any kind which shape the orientation of perception and the interpretative framework, or even the temporal circumstances or cognitive background, the following may be considered as the less contested and more objective pylons for delimiting the concept of technology:

- Technology is a mighty force of transformation bringing a reformational force of leverage not only on the economic, social, political, cultural and anthropological level but also one that is evidently and almost axiomatically involved in every manifestation of human activity and/or of the results thereof.
- Technology influences and frequently forms perception, apperceptions, the bio-theory, and the system of values of the "initiated", but at the same time it is being affected by, formed, shaped and evolves because of their existence and in parallel to these. It constitutes a complex, multileveled and dynamic system (an integral ingredient of which are humans), the constituents of which are at a continuous dialectic interrelation and exchange of influences.
- Technology is composed, grows together, is produced, expressed, produces and requires a broad set of elements, material and immaterial, of an intellectual or not process and substance, the degree of participation and involvement of which is ever changing.

- Since its birth, the objective aim of Technology has always been to facilitate humans. More specifically, the probing and expansion of humans' abilities (physical strength, skills and dexterities, senses, communication, cognitive skills, thinking, science, creativity, etc.) and the acquirement of new ones in order to improve living quality.
- Its almost universal participation in human activities constitutes the principal reason for this extraordinary breadth of inter-temporally possible and different approaches. The different viewpoints may rest on heterogeneous bases with ambiguous and possibly contrasting orientations, correspondingly producing heterogeneous (and perhaps even mutually exclusive) conclusions with respect to the delimitation and the sign of the participation of this concept to the welfare of man.

1.1.3 Technology and science

There are very close ties between Technology and Science, but this should not lead one to the misconception that they are two absolutely overlapping or synonymous concepts. And while the average Joe considers technology to be the applied implementation and practical application of steadfast, commonly accepted and documented scientific knowledge, however, the array of influences exchanged between technology and science is bidirectional in nature and governed by complexity.

In reality, technology has historically appeared several hundred years before science, since its first recoded emergence of the latter dates back some four centuries. Furthermore, across the entire spectrum of their historical common course, Technology has been to a large extend ahead of Science, given that the forcefulness that drives technological changes precedes the full, documented and structured understanding of the "asocial" systematic and detailed scientific knowledge and interpretation.

And while science is a body of systematically structured and organized knowledge, which is composed systematically from parts of organized material (Karvounis, 1995), Technology is a body of knowledge pertaining to specific activities, processes, methods and techniques, which produce specific and practical results, act in specified manners and produce specific effects (even if the "fastidious" science has not yet been able to decode their causes).

It would be extremely shortsighted and limiting to adopt the viewpoint of causality, directed from science to technology. As Fischer and Pry (1971) observe, approaching the concept of technology solely as an excipient of applied science, which is just a subset of the breadth of connections between Science and Technology. If Technology were limited only to the spectrum of what can be scientifically explained, then the human race would have followed a very different course. The definition of Technology offered by Fischer as the set of ways envisioned by men to improve their lives, implies, on one hand, the existence of purposefulness which is manifested in a positivist manner. Of course, Technology makes frequent use of scientific knowledge in order to be further developed. Consequently, when one refers to the development of new technology, there are two variables functioning as its pillars: existing technology and existing science.

That which needs to be emphatically stressed with respect to the nature and degree of equality on the level of influences in the relation between science and technology is that the latter does not trail behind; it is not a follower or a passive receiver of the configuring schema of the first.

Technology affects science as the provider of an immense magnitude of empirical knowledge which science then organizes and structures, while based on it, science shapes, tests, checks and amends its theories in order to understand and interpret in an objective manner the real world and the causality relations that govern it.

Additionally, Technology, by means of its dynamically evolutionary nature, acts as a tracer for the orientation of where science will place its emphasis and the outlining of future fields of its action and application. It was cited earlier that technological progress depends on science, and, consequently, the expansion of the limits of understanding signifies the conditions for technological progress.

And while the earlier reasoning appears to be more self-catering in the framework of an equal relation, one, however, must not forget the purposefulness to which we referred previously. Technological discoveries signify significant improvements in the levels of social and economic utility. This, in itself, can be considered as an adequate and sufficient criterion for a deeper scientific interpretation and understanding.

Finally, technology is very frequently considered as the provider of tools for science, tools that function as aides for its further development and promotion.

1.2 Definitions of High Technology by (inter)national organizations and its delimitation vis-à-vis its distinguishing features

1.2.1 High Technology: definitions and features attributed to it by national/international organizations

It is true, to a degree, that the "definitions" pursuing to offer a reference framework for High Technology are roughly "as many as the people who study High Technology". For example, the definition of *High Tech industry* offered by the Office of Technology Assessment of the US Congress in 1982 defines it as that "which is involved in the design, development and launching of new products or/and innovative production procedures, via the systematic implementation and application of scientific and technical knowledge".

The majority of the descriptions/definitions of High Technology may be grouped into two categories. One category includes definitions/descriptions provided by government sources or international organizations, while the other includes those definitions employed and adopted by researchers.

With respect to the first category, one may observe that the High Tech sector is classified based on specific criteria, such as the number of technical staff, the magnitude of the research undertaken, development plans or and the number of standards that have taken place in an industry. For example, the US Bureau of

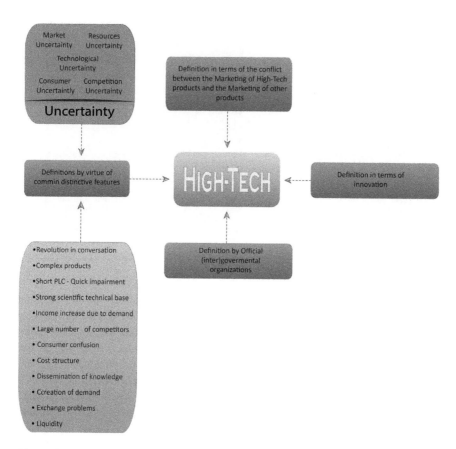

Figure 1.1 Summary of approaches to defining *High Technology*

Labor Statistics classifies industrial sectors based on the ratio of employment for the Research & Development (R&D) department. The Organisation for Economic Co-operation and Development (OECD) uses a similar definition, defining High Tech in terms of the ratio of R&D department expenditures with respect to the added value of each specific industry, while the American National Science Foundation assesses the intensity or the ratio of R&D expenses to net sales.

Of course, there has been criticism of such kinds of classifications due to the inherent ambiguities they include. Luker Jr. and Lyons (1997) consider the definition offered by the US Bureau of Labor Statistics to be too broad, meaning that it includes, on account of its breadth, certain industries the products of which have been only marginally amended (e.g., the tobacco industry) and with respect to which a technological leap has not occurred for several years. Such a kind of classification may also include of industries which attain large volumes of production while employing a fairly unskilled workforce and standardized procedures.

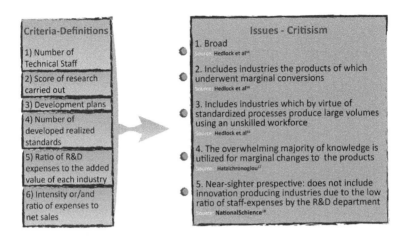

Figure 1.2 Description of HT sector by official government sources and international
organizations.

Despite the fact that the ratio of scientific-technical personnel may be such that
justifies its characterization as "High Technology", the overwhelming majority
of knowledge, however, is utilized, as Mohr, Sengupta and Slater (2005) point
out, to marginally change the features of established products in slowly evolv-
ing and intensely targeted by advertising markets. On the other hand, Richard
Lipkin (1996) observes that despite the fact that the aforementioned definition is
quite broad, the classification employed may, simultaneously, be so shortsighted
so as to exclude the development of new products or processes by employees
possessing knowledge simply and only due to the fact that the sector where such
employees belong may not possess the necessary and sufficient ratio to be characterized as High Technology. Finally, the fact that many PC manufacturers mass
produce components, also using production routines, and, in many cases, employ
a minimum number of technical personnel, accentuates another inherent defect
in this kind of definition: These industries are classified as high tech, due to the
fact that they exhibit high capital-to-labor ratio and require labor of a fairly low
scientific level.

To avoid the implicit weaknesses of these type of definitions, which approach
High Tech based on an industrial viewpoint, many researchers provide definitions
based on the underlying common features.

1.2.2 High Technology: delimiting High Technology by virtue of its distinctive features

1.2.2.1 Common characteristics of High Technology markets

Regis McKenna (1991) considers the HT market sector to be characterized by
complex products, a large number of competing enterprises, consumer confusion
and fast change.

Shanklin and Ryans (1984) term as High Tech any company participating in a process which exhibits High Technology features: "The company requires a sound scientific technical base, new technology can fast render older ones obsolete and, since as new technologies emerge their applications either create demand or revolutionize demand".

Other common features shared by HT markets include, according to John George, Allen Weiss and Shantanu Dutta (1999), the following:

a   Cost/unit: Cost structure applicable in HT markets when the technical know-how enclosed in a product/service represents a significant part of the value of the product or service is, usually, as follows: Production costs for the first unit are very high compared to the cost for reproduction (the production of the next units).
b   Increase revenues due to demand (or network externalities or bandwagon effect): This feature refers to the increase in the value of the product stemming from the increase of the adoption of its use by consumers. In other words, the usefulness of a product – innovation is a function of the number of its users. As soon as the market share representing the critical mass of consumers is attained, the value increases exponentially.
c   Exchange problems: When knowledge represents a major part of a product's value, the exchange between the seller and the buyer transforms into an intellectual property transaction. Exchange problems emerge when it is difficult to ascribe a value to knowledge, especially when such knowledge is implicit and nested in both people and organizational routines.
d   Dissemination of knowledge: It refers to the collaborations during the creation and transmission of knowledge, resulting in the further increase of the existing knowledge depository. In simple terms, every innovation shapes the conditions for a greater number of innovations to flourish. In other words, the building of knowledge on knowledge.

Gardner, Johnson, Lee and Wilkinson (2000) observe that ultimately, and following intense and in-depth research, the definition of High Technology (what they see as a term in wide use) is a very tough job. They conclude that the superficially easy task of coming up with a definition that may be generalized does not exist either in the technical or the managerial bibliography.

Rexroad (1983) attempts to define *High Technology* as follows: "the segment of technology considered to be nearer to the leading edge or the state of art of a particular field. It is that technology inherent in emerging from the laboratory into practical application". Grunenwald and Vernon (1988) define High Tech products/services "as those devices, procedures, techniques or sciences that are characterised by state-of-the-art development and have typically short and volatile lives".

Link (1987) comments that High Technology, due to its intrinsic transitivity, defines itself almost self-deterministically. He observes that it is a moving "label" which must be detached from old products and be ascribed to a continuously expanding set of complex business activities.

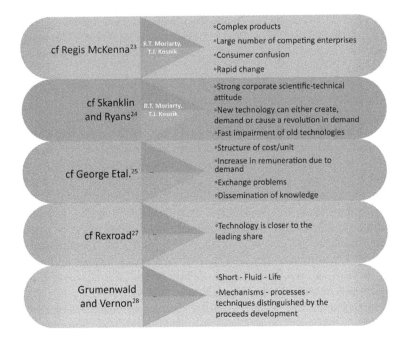

Figure 1.3 Summary of the common features of HT markets

Samili and Wills (1986) consider that High Technology comprises of a sector of industries which goes beyond computers to a multitude of research industries, such as biotechnology, pharmaceutics, chemistry and aerodynamics.

Rosen, Schroeder and Purinton (1988) adopt the view that there are features in High Technology markets which are able to differentiate these products from other product categories. Besides, even under Porter's (1980) view on emerging industries, it follows that marketing strategy for High Tech must be different.

Gardner, Johnson, Lee and Willkinson (2000) propose for the purposes of their research work an approach that follows from the combination of the technological levels with the view that consumers have of innovation. This viewpoint is consistent with Veryzer's (1998) approach, according to which the innovation of a product is deemed to lie between dimensions which reflect the changes in the utility gained from the product, its technological capabilities and the usage standards for its consumption. The definition that follows from the aforementioned interaction for High Technology products is

> High Technology products are those products which result from "turbulent, volatile and voluptuous" technology and which presuppose significant changes to the behavior of at least one part of the product-use channel.

Economists also strived to find some acceptable definition for High Technology. But the general emphasis on innovative inflow measures, on innovative product outflow and industrial development, that initially rested on statistical data, is not useful for defining High Technology products.

Should one wish to escape the confines of the academic field, then one will observe that High Technology becomes the subject of definitions based on a somewhat different dimension. In the context of such a logic, "people dedicated to action" (e.g., the heads of marketing) approach a different delimitation of what High Technology is. The field of High Technology is crystallized for them via the features manifested by its products.

Such a feature is that they are being developed and replaced at fast rates. Moore's Law, named after the founder of Inter, characteristically cites that the number of transistors per memory circuit doubles every 18 months.

1.2.2.2 Uncertainty

High Tech products require a lot of resources to be invested in research and development.

Moriarty and Kosnik (1989) combine the definitions provided by Regis McKenna and the US Bureau of Labor Statistics, that considers that any sector where the number of technical staff employed and the R&D expenses are double than that of the average of other sectors can be termed as a High Tech sector, thus finding to common dimensions which they ultimately feel that characterize High Technology markets:

a   Market uncertainty
b   Technology uncertainty

With respect to the first dimension, it suggests that market uncertainty can be identified with the type and limit for which customers' needs may be satisfied by technology. It cites the difference between the marketer and the salesperson, pursuant to the principle formulated by Ted Levitt, as a response to the previous issue, suggesting that the marketer views the entire productive process as a sequence where the effort to discover, create and satisfy any of the consumer's needs has been fully integrated.

The entire issue is posed through the viewpoint of understanding and satisfying customer needs that is adopted by this fully customer-centric philosophy. And this is so, since in High Tech markets, potential clients are not in a position where they could "articulate" their needs. Market uncertainty is, therefore, composed as the constituent of five main causes:

1   What needs will be satisfied by a new technology?
2   How will needs change in the future?
3   Will the market adopt the standards of the industry?
4   How fast will new technology proliferate?
5   How large is the potential market?

With respect to the first question it is very possible for consumers not to fully realize which of their needs will be satisfied by new technology. With respect to the second, and provided the needs are clarified, it is possible for them to be the subjects of fast and unexpected changes, as the result of chain reactions to the swift changes to the environment. Furthermore, there is still the question if the market will ultimately adopt the new standards, so as for the products that cover such needs to enjoy a degree of compatibility with their auxiliary products. The growth and spread of new technology are very difficult to predict and ultimately – also as the result of the preceding four concerns – it is extremely difficult to predict the size of the potential market.

Moore (1991) very insightfully summarizes all the preceding to an acronym: FUD: Fear, Uncertainty and Doubt. He employs the FUD factor to describe the fear, uncertainty and doubt overcoming consumers with respect to what problems will be solved or what needs will be covered by new technology, as well as with respect to how well it will perform with respect to these. The bewilderment ensuing from such emotions means that potential customers may postpone adopting an innovation, that they may demand a high degree of education and information on an innovation and that they require post-purchase affirmation and empowering, which will eradicate all doubts. Ketteringham and White (1984) define technology as an industrial application that requires scientific or technical knowledge. The process of technological innovation may be considered as a process for decreasing uncertainty or, alternatively, a process for the collection and processing of data, where uncertainty is defined as a difference in the volume of data required in order to complete a specific objective and the volume of data already existing in the enterprise's depository of knowledge. Information, as adopted as a concept in this instance, is verbally codified knowledge. And knowledge, according to Glaser, Abelson and Garrison (1983), includes (1) facts, truths or principles; (2) the understanding that naturally follows from experience; (3) practices; (4) ideas or processes certified with respect to their validity by prior testing; and (5) the findings of valid research.

According to the viewpoint adopted by Souder and Moenaert (1992), the view that the process of technological innovation may be also considered as those data processing activities that aim to decrease uncertainty is commonly accepted. With respect to technological uncertainty, Rowland, Moriartiy and Kosnik (1989) observe that it results from five factors:

The uncertainty of whether the new product will function as expected
The uncertainty if it is going to be consistent with its predesignated delivery time
The uncertainty of whether the supplier will manage to cater for post-purchase service issues
The uncertainty emerging from the existence of possible collateral impacts caused by the product or service
And, finally, the uncertainty of whether this new technology will render the existing technology obsolete and decommissioned

According to Rowland et al. (1989), uncertain is the technology which ensues from the fact that we do not know if the technology – or the company that will provide it, will be true to its promise that it will cover these specific needs, provided, of course, if said needs have been articulated.

The first constituent of uncertainty deals with the lack of information regarding the operating performance of the product – whether it will actually do what the salesperson promises it will, while the second one reflects delays by producers to have the product ready by the pre-designated date – a fact that is the rule rather than the exception. The third constituent of technological uncertainty is associated with the lack of "experience" relating to the performance of a product in the market – it is not tested as mature technologies are – and whether maintenance problems will, ultimately, be dealt with expediently and effectively.

With respect to Greece and the computer systems market, research carried out in 26 enterprises and organizations gave clear indications on the upgraded and now reinforced role that maintenance is now called to play, with respect to the behavior of potential customers for computer systems. Service and maintenance gather greater weighted gravity both with respect to the cost for the purchase of a computer system, as well as from the supplier's reputation.

This can be principally attributed to the fact that enterprises-buyers of computer systems have had bad experiences from the non-timely, deficient support from suppliers and the realization of the burdensome financial and business consequences it entails.

Rendered as a figure, what is suggested by Rowland et al. (1989) as ultimately differentiating High Tech markets may be condensed as shown in Figure 1.4.

Moreover, the authors attempt to classify (in a matrix) the potential cases that marketing will be called to address, depending on the degree of the participation of technological uncertainty and market uncertainty and possible combinations thereof.

Using this matrix, the authors attempt to define High Tech marketing by juxtaposing it to its other three kinds. Where there is a low degree of both kinds of uncertainty, it regards the application of a known/mature technology to known needs. Where there is high technological uncertainty and low market uncertainty, a new technology appears, coming to satisfy an existing need, which is conscious and existing on the side of the consumer. In a case where there is high market uncertainty and simultaneously low technology uncertainty, technology changes relatively slowly, but it is difficult to predict consumer needs. The coexistence of a high degree of uncertainty both with respect to market and technology is also the landmark for the activation of the existence of High Tech marketing.

Gardner (1990) adds a third to these two dimensions of uncertainty, considering it as the common characteristic of HT markets: the intensity of competition. The intensity of competition refers to changes taking place in the competitive environment, namely, as to who the competitors are, what their product offers are and which are the tools they use to compete.

Jakkie Mohr (2005) cites three sources for the intensity of competition which contribute, in a chain-reaction fashion, to the increase of the degree of uncertainty.

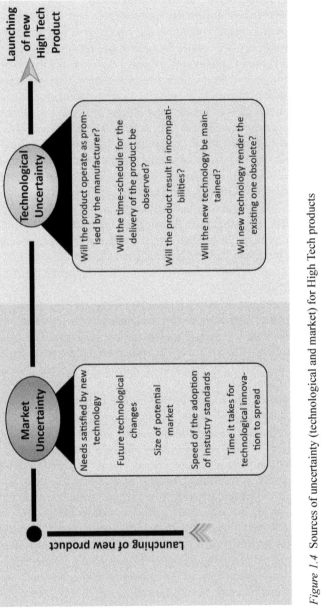

Figure 1.4 Sources of uncertainty (technological and market) for High Tech products

The first uncertainty follows from the fact that one does not know which companies are the potential future competitors, while the fact that in the majority of cases new technologies are introduced and commercialized by "parachuting" companies renders HT markets a treacherous and inhospitable environment.

Mohr (2005) considers the second kind of uncertainty to be created by the tactics mentioned earlier and which are employed by outsiders. Their competitive tactics may be known to their natural field of activity, but they are unknown in the HT field they infiltrate and create confusion in the players already existing in this field. Hamel (1997) suggests that ultimately it is these new players that shape the rules, changing the profile of the market for all players engaged in it.

Finally, the new competition emerges in the guise of a new product platform or the new ways for satisfying customer needs or resolving their problems. To give an example, one of the greatest sources of uncertainty that the personal computer sector was called to address in 2000 was the new "informational devices", which could be used to access the Internet. Hewlett Packard decided to simultaneously focus on PCs and informational devices.

Jakkie Mohr (2005) considers this intersection of the three sources of uncertainty as defining the area where High Tech subsists. Indeed, she advocates that the simultaneous coexistence of all three factors is that which renders such uniqueness to this environment.

With respect to uncertainty, Souder and Moenaert (1992) observe that one may distinguish among three categories of uncertainty: the uncertainty stemming from consumers (namely, the uncertainty with respect to their needs), technological uncertainty (namely, uncertainty with respect to the optimal technology that must be adopted) and, finally, competitive uncertainty (namely, uncertainty with respect to the competition). Each one of these three sources of uncertainty, Katz and Kahn (1996) suggest, originates from that is considered, by general systems theory, as external environment. These factors may interact, but this is by no means necessary. For example, the uncertainty associated with consumers may fluctuate independently of technological uncertainty. But both contribute to a large extent in determining competition uncertainty. As Abell (1980) puts it, if a company is uncertain with respect to the constituents of its customers and its consuming groups or/and alternative technologies, then it follows that it will also be uncertain with respect to its competitive placement in the sector.

Despite all the preceding discussion, all organizations must decrease their competitive, technological and market (consumer) uncertainty, and this is a prerequisite in order for them to develop successful innovations. The basic means an organization possesses for the collection of data for each one of the three uncertainties are the sources. Thus, it should come as no surprise that research has shown that the degree of an enterprise's effectiveness to allocate its resources among the human, financial and technological sectors is greatly associated with the success of the innovation.

The fact that the same resources must be allocated so as to decrease uncertainty introduces a fourth type of uncertainty, resources uncertainty.

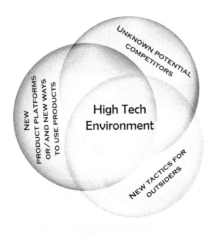

Figure 1.5 Uncertainty under Jakkie Mohr's viewpoint

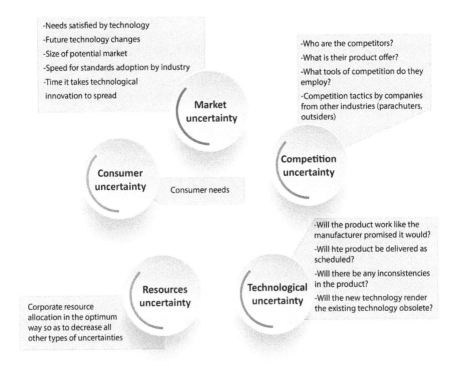

Figure 1.6 Summary of the kinds of uncertainty existing in HT markets and their constituents

The greater the uncertainty with respect to competition, technology and customers (market) is, the greater the uncertainty with respect to the type and magnitude of the resources the company needs becomes.

A different school of thought emphasizes potential uncertainties between the market, technology and competition ones. Clark (1985) emphasizes the competitive side, considering that since competition frequently aims at the same market share with the same or similar products and by utilizing alternative technologies or strategies, this will affect both the survivability and the success of the organization's innovation process.

1.2.2.3 Innovation

Another feature of a High Tech product is the qualitative magnitude of the innovation it exemplifies. It is considered that it shall bear changes to its market and that it, consequently, will spearhead the relegating of other products.

High Technology, as can been seen from the definition and the description of its environment so far, is associated with innovation, either directly or indirectly. Innovation is the outflow of High Technology, and High Technology is the natural setting for the creation of innovation. In other words, in most cases, High Technology is the "vehicle", tool or medium via and in which an innovation will be developed. While even in those cases where the conception of an innovation was not assisted, at its inception, by High Technology, it is almost given that High Technology will play the role of the helper and facilitator for its development and transubstantiation into a product.

According to Jakkie Mohr (2005), there are two kinds of innovation, which are determined from the intensity by which innovation participates in the product and the degree of innovation, that is, ascribed to the product.

Radical innovation is something so different that it cannot be compared with some existing and utilized practice or even conception. These kinds of innovation employ High Technology and establish new markets. They shape changes in the way things are perceived which "make history". In marketing terminology they are referred to as discontinuous innovations. Others, such as Abernathy and Utterback (1978), refer to such innovations using the term *revolutionary*. Shanklin and Ryans (1984) consider such innovations to be developed by the side of the offer, namely, by enterprises aiming to commercialize the findings of the company's R&D department, since innovations are developed by this department, which will then give the stimulus to the marketing department to seek and find the appropriate conversion of innovation into a commercialized product. This, namely, is that kind of innovation that is developed without the preexistence of the underwriting of its conversion to something useful and without the process for its creation to depend on the possible applications of said innovation in products. On the other hand, a radical innovation may be developed as a response to some existing need or as a way to tackle an emerging one.

The fact, however, remains that irrespective of whether radical innovation originates as the product of scientific research that then finds ways of useful application (on the side of offer) or is an effective means created to offer a more integrated, modern and effective solution to some (existing or emerging) problem, innovation by itself creates a new market.

The second kind of innovation is incremental innovation. In sharp contrast to the term *discontinuous* which is used for radical innovation, this innovation is distinguished by its duration. It emerges gradually and essentially is an extension – a marginal evolution of methods and practices already in use. In direct contrast with the term *revolutionary*, such innovation could be coined "arising". The products ensuing from them will, according to Rangan, Kasturi and Bartus (1995), by close substitutes of already existing products and both consumers and producers will clearly realize the limits of their capabilities. Incremental innovations, indeed, relate to markets the products of which have clearly established features and to consumers who can describe their needs. They originate and emerge, therefore, as pointed out by Shanklin and Ryans (1984), from the side of demand.

Of course, the proviso must be underlined that the earlier descriptions regard those uncompounded cases where there is a full concurrence of opinions between producers and consumers on the type of innovation. Rangan, Kasturi and Bartus (1995) recommend a matrix which includes, besides commonly characterized innovations, the combinations of cases, for which there is no agreement. Where companies perceive of an innovation as radical, while consumers feel it is an incremental/marginal innovation, we have delusionary products. The same authors characterize the opposite case as shadow products.

According to Chandy and Tellis (1998), innovation can be rendered the protagonist in a "David and Goliath" scenario.

Foster (1986) and Tushman and Anderson (1986) suggest that radical innovations are able to destroy company assets. Difficult to acquire, clients may desert a company with which they collaborated until now as soon as an innovation used by some other company increases the performance per dollar paid. Thus, high-cost investments and abilities become obsolete and the company is rendered non-competitive. On the other hand, Wind and Mahajan (1997) deem that a radically innovative product may be the source of a competitive advantage for the company introducing it to the market. According to Geroski, Machin and Reene (1993), the results of innovation may be of great magnitude, positive and long lasting.

It is considered by many scholars, such as Wesley (1995), that the bulk of the bibliography has focused on the size of a company as the key organizational variable that affects radical product innovation. Other authors have proposed different variables:

Damanpour (1991) underlines that the way a company is organized may play an important role in its performance with respect to radically innovative products. Olson, Orville, Walker and Ruekert (1995) feel that high level of autonomy inside the company shape an environment that favors the development of innovations, while Ettlie, Bridges and O'Keefe (1984) underline the role of "champion products" in promoting innovation. Moorman and Miner (1997) acknowledge the results of organizational information flows and organizational memory on the new product creation level. Having said this, Kleinschmidt and Cooper (1991)

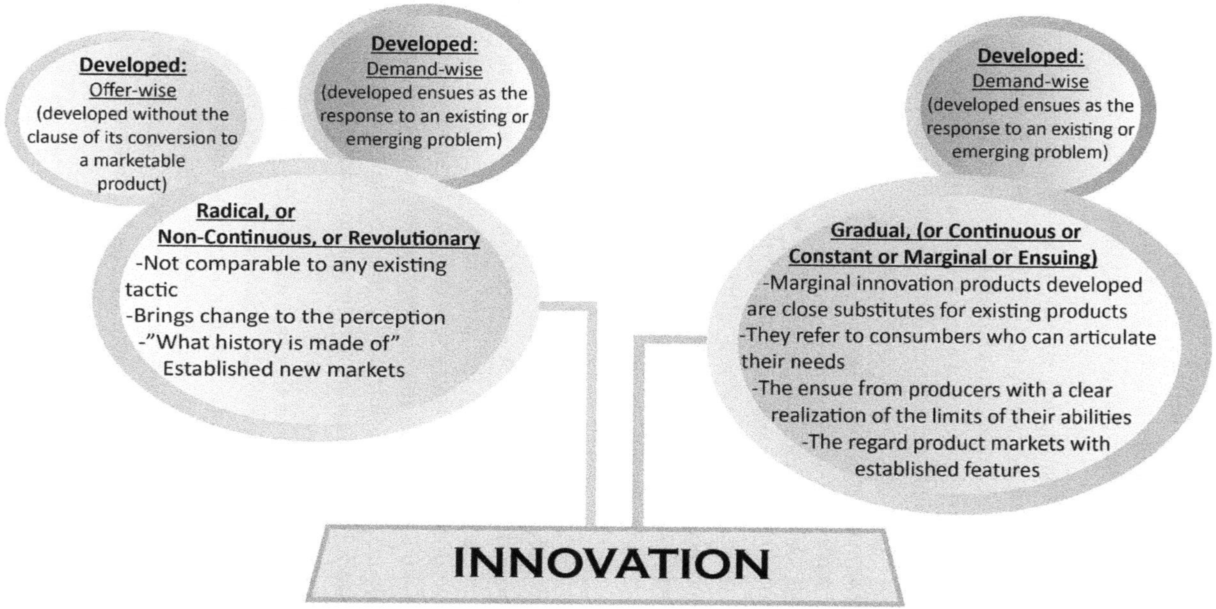

Developed:
Demand-wise
(developed ensues as the response to an existing or emerging problem)

Gradual, (or Continuous or Constant or Marginal or Ensuing)
-Marginal innovation products developed are close substitutes for existing products
-They refer to consumers who can articulate their needs
-The ensue from producers with a clear realization of the limits of their abilities
-The regard product markets with established features

Developed:
Demand-wise
(developed ensues as the response to an existing or emerging problem)

Developed:
Offer-wise
(developed without the clause of its conversion to a marketable product)

Radical, or Non-Continuous, or Revolutionary
-Not comparable to any existing tactic
-Brings change to the perception
-"What history is made of"
Established new markets

INNOVATION

Figure 1.7 Levels of innovation and delimitation of their development

consider research in this field to be limited, noncontinuous and lacking. There is, that is, no integrated framework to adequately and sufficiently explain how organizational factors affect radical product innovation.

Technological innovation is delimited by technological innovation as any product, process or entity would be delimited, the development of which presupposes that the initiating entity invests human, monetary and technical resources so as to acquire new or unknown technologies or to combine already known ones but in a novel and new way.

A school of thought considering innovation as a processing for bridging the information gap between user needs and opportunities of a technological nature. People and groups trap, connect and exploit the reservoir of knowledge in order to tackle uncertainties with respect to needs and requirements users are conscious of and with respect to both existing products but also to potential technological solutions.

The bibliographical survey by Chandy and Tellis (1998) proposes two dimensions common across all definitions offered on innovation. The first dimension is technology. This factor determines the extend by which the technology involved in a product differs from previous technologies. The second dimension – market – determines the degree by which a new product satisfies key-needs of consumers in a better way than already existing products. The research they undertook led them to consider two levels for each factor (high and low), namely, four types (combining innovation with products):

Incremental (marginal) product innovation: This is, namely, the combination of fairly low technological differentiation (compared to already-existing technologies), with a relevantly low contribution to the satisfaction of the consumer's needs (compared to the satisfaction that the consumer would have enjoyed from already existing products of an already-tested technology).

Market Revolution: Despite the fact that in this case technology continues to be only marginally differentiated, the ensuing product, however, offers considerably higher levels of satisfaction to consumers compared to the already-existing ones.

Technological Revolution: In this case and despite the fact that the adopted technology differs fundamentally from the already used one, it is not capable of improving the satisfaction return for consumers.

Radical innovation: This is the combination of high levels for both dimensions, which implies the simultaneous existence of spectacularly greater levels of satisfaction which ensues from the use of a fundamentally new technology. It must be noted that the authors define the satisfaction the customer enjoys always in relation to the monetary units the customer pays to acquire it.

Foster (1986) and Utterback (1994), observe that these four different types of innovation are interrelated by a significant dynamic, curves (S) of technological innovation (Figure 1.4). Technology curves are S-shaped due to the fact that a given technology (e.g., T_1) initially improves consumer satisfaction at an increased rate when it is first introduced, while during its maturity the rate decreases and its gradient changes. During the course of the life of such a technology, a new technology emerges. When it appears it is at a disadvantage compared to T_1 with respect to the satisfaction it offers to consumers. It is precisely this phase when one talks of Technological Revolution. By the passage of time and due to intense research, the new technology, T_2, begins to increase the levels of satisfaction it offers at an accelerated rate and thus to mark its own positive inclination. At the next phase it has completely superseded both technology T_1, as well as the advantages it offers to consumers satisfaction-wise compared to T_1. It is precisely at this point that the product which incorporates this technology moves to the sphere of radical innovation. Golder and Tellis (1993) support, via empirical research, that it is precisely this point that signifies a change in sales behavior.

The users of T_1, threatened by T_2, strive to improve on the benefits offered by T_1. An incremental innovation may ensue from such efforts or even a market revolution. Having said this, marginal improvements move at much lesser rates than T_2, and therefore, T_1 is unavoidably replaced by T_2, which is now designated as the dominant technology. Of course, and in due time, T_2 will also run the same course and become itself obsolete.

1.2.2.4 Innovation–technology–dissemination of technology/innovation

Drucker (1985) defines innovation as an action that renders a new wealth-generating capacity to resources. Thus, according to Drucker, innovation creates economic resources. The concept of the economic resource as an element, however, is devoid of meaning unless a specific use is designated for said element. On the other hand, technology, as a term, refers to the following elements:

The hardware, that is, the objects produced
The techniques and processes (such as the processes related to materials production)
Full systems for the production of materials (including individuals engaged)

At the same time, technology is utilized by people as the "basic standard" (Kline, 1991) as a means in order to increase its own force, in the sense of its capacity to help us attain objectives that would otherwise seem beyond our grasp, or at attaining them faster, cheaper and more effectively.

According to this approach, technology is a social-technical system, as it includes both technical elements as well as a social organization, economic particulars and legal and statutory parameters, among others. In this light, the full understanding of innovation in technological systems presupposes the understanding of many of their constituents and of the kind of correlations that develop between them.

Socio-technical systems – and technology, in particular – exhibit great complexity, while they, simultaneously, also involve not only a great number of individuals and materials but also multiple interactions between people and people and people and materials. This makes forecasting with respect to the entire system difficult. Despite all this, some estimates may be put forward with respect to their parts. Learning and improving entire socio-technical systems can be attained through the experience from inside the system and through the feedback that is developed. It is for this reason that feedback in the context of such system must remain open, respond expediently and be clear and precise.

An innovation may improve the performance of a socio-technical system, through interactions taking place across five fields:

The production process
Social rearrangements in the production system
Economic or legal issues
Marketing (socio-technical systems for distribution or use)
The system as a whole

A broader definition of innovation: innovation is every change to the socio-technical production, distribution or usage systems, that offers improvements to cost, quality or the service of customers and employees.

1.2.2.4.1 INNOVATION MODELS

The linear model, which denotes a serial temporal presentation of phenomena. Such a model is fairly simplified, based on several assumptions, while it does not take appropriate account of elements which may or may not be important for innovation.

The chain-linked model (Kline, 1985) is deemed appropriate for the process of innovation for two reasons. The first reason is that it includes all processes of this procedure which are deemed significant – it does not omit, that is, any important process. The second reason regards the fact that the model implies its proper function, provided it has been correctly applied.

When people innovates, they utilize the entire reservoir of technical knowledge, together with the scientific knowledge accumulated over time. This stockpile of technical knowledge includes, on one hand, scientific principles but also includes other elements, such as mechanical analyses for categories of problems, the science itself, codes, techniques, know-how and so on. The mind and body of technologically specialized people is also a great reservoir of technological knowledge.

In the chain-linked models of innovation, knowledge is differentiated from research. This is done for two reasons: The first is that knowledge regards a state of operating and can be accumulated over time. Research, on the other hand, is a process and has, therefore, a beginning and an end – thus it is temporary. The second reason relates to how much knowledge acts as the stimulus to begin the process of design, while research takes the baton when knowledge fails to offer design solutions, due to the higher cost of research, the greater requirements in time and its more problematic production – compared to the case of the simple deployment of existing knowledge.

1.2.2.4.2 INNOVATION ACCORDING TO STEELE

Steele (1989) designates innovation as the creation and introduction (of any kind) of change that ensues as the result of a deliberate action, focused on a specific issue. The author also suggests that such changes must create value for the customers and improve the conditions for the viability of an enterprise.

Depending on their magnitude, such changes may lead to small changes or big discoveries; thus, covering a great spectrum of innovations. What differs between different kinds of innovations is the level of risk, the level of uncertainty and the level of needs in terms of resources that complement each category.

1.2.2.4.3 KEY ELEMENTS REGARDING INNOVATION

Uncertainty is the first key element of innovation. Uncertainty may derive from the lack of information, from technical-financial issues for which there is no available solution but can also result from an existing weakness in assessing the consequences of a decision or action.

The second key element of innovation is its close dependence on the progress exhibited by science and scientific knowledge.

A third element is the trend emerging as the result of the necessity for additional scientific research. This can be seen either through the increase of the level of technology employed in the new methods for the manufacture of products or in the efforts to promote new products or/and technologies themselves.

A fourth element relates to the nature and conditions for research, where vertically organized laboratories with bureaucratized research prevail.

A fifth element regards the limitations posed by the temporal interval that intervenes from the moment a scientific discovery is made until the moment such is applied on a product which is characterized as ready to be launched in the market.

A sixth element which emerges is the observation that we come across innovations less frequently in self-inclusive sectors and more in the areas of "contact" between different sectors, a view expressed also by Leontief (1993). Three features are contributing toward this: cross-sectorial information exchange, the increased complexity of innovations and the increased interdependence of innovations.

A seventh characteristic is the fact that a great percentage of the efforts made toward innovation results in failure.

The last element is the observation and changes to technology cannot be described as flexible responses to market conditions: this change is directed based on the most evolved form of an existing technology, while the nature of each technology determined the conditions under which products and methods are incorporated in the shifting economic conditions and the technological change is a cumulative activity.

1.2.2.4.4 PARTICULARITIES OF INNOVATION

Difficulties in predicting the effects of an innovation

The emergence of an innovation may be complemented by a series of effects on factors relating to the economy, as well as technology. The effects of such an emergence are difficult to predict, even in the case where this innovation is called to cater for the needs for which it was materialized.

There are, of course, other more complex cases for the application of an innovation, where the task of forecasting its effects becomes even more complex. There are cases where this innovation is available for more uses inside the same sector. There are also cases where the innovation may be applied to a different sector than the one for which it was originally planned. There is also the case where there is not designated goal for the application of the emerging innovation, and, thus, it is applied in an activity different from the one the body promoting the innovation had in mind.

Asymmetry of the innovative activity

Schumpeter (1939) expressed the view that inside the economic space, there are specific activities producing innovations and other activities which do not produce them but can be rendered as recipients of innovation – although their acceptance rates may not be the same. This view has gained momentum in the relevant literature (Kaminski, DeBresson and Hu, 1997; Xu, DeBresson and Hu, 1997; Vernardakis, 1993).

The importance of selecting the time

The selection of time is that element that can guarantee success – or failure – for an innovation. On one hand, the side of offer depends on time in such a manner so that the technologies which will accentuate the innovation to have been sufficiently developed and be accessible from the bodies who pursue to innovate. On the other hand, there is demand, for which the choice of time is also very important, since one of the conditions for the acceptance of an innovation is for this side to acknowledge the capacity such innovation offers to cater for needs. This, in turn, presupposes the maturity of appropriate social-economic conditions.

These two must be simultaneously satisfied, in order for the existence of innovation to be meaningful and to carry value and, of course, to lead to success.

Time is important for innovation as the rate by which innovations are created increases. Simultaneously, it must be observed that time also assumes a different dimension for innovation, as innovation is characterized by its own life cycle: At some point in the time continuum the innovation shall emerge, while it may even compete – or substitute – an already-dominant innovation or some that will emerge at the same time. The desideratum is for the innovation to be established and, provided it can do so, to reach the stage of maturity, where, it may, in turn, face the challenges stemming from an emerging innovation, which will either fail or, ultimately, displace it.

There are two points that merit attention here: To begin with, the duration of the life cycle of an innovation cannot, generally, be known from the start (with the possible exception of semiconductors). Moreover, in the case where a dominant innovation is being targeted by an emerging one, then the first will defend itself by realizing improvements, perhaps even great ones and even it is "deep" in its maturity stage.

Having said this, there are also exceptions, where a return to an older innovation was witnessed, thus rejecting a more recent one.

Innovation and environment

Environmental factors play a significant role with respect to the development of innovations.

The dominant religion in a region may promote or hinder the efforts toward innovation. The geographic locality and location can also influence such a development. All parameters relating to the environment can affect, to a lesser or greater extent, the intensity by which innovation is "produced".

Cultural features are also very important. This occurs on the grounds that for an innovation to have a reason to exist and to be perceived as important, it must be perceived as useful. Its recipient must perceive that this innovation offers him or her value, as Bassala (1988) observes.

Interaction of innovations

Innovations in general seldom appear in isolation. They are usually combined with the need to find an innovation that will function complementary to some original one.

Of course, the type of relationship developed among technologies, as well as the nature of the interaction between them, is difficult to probe, even for the specialists of the field. An initial difficulty lies with the fact that the interconnections appearing between different technologies are many and present differences. There are cases where one particular innovation is forced to wait for the availability of some specific inflow or necessary ingredient. The need itself for such an inflow may be sufficient to lead to the emergence of an innovation which may, in course, find unforeseen applications. Finally, there is also the case where an innovation causes an increase of productivity in an activity, and, via and by means of such an increase, the same phenomenon is observed in other activities. This fact, of course, differentiates activities based on their gravity. Technological progress in the context of specific activities may have a greater effect on the corresponding progress of other activities, while in other cases such progress in some activity may not correspondingly affect another one.

Technological change and its effects

According to the modern theory for economic development, technological change constitutes one of the three main factors determining the increase in productivity – the other two being the accumulation of natural and human capital (Vernardakis et al., 1995). Infrastructures, economies of scale, the structure of the market, changes to demographic characteristics and the quality of capital and labor inflows are secondary factors. The transfer and mimicking of other technologies and know-how, the conditions and level of competition and international trade are also, according to researchers, factors which may affect the increase of productivity.

Despite the fact that it is acknowledged that such factors contribute to the increase of productivity, the manner and level, however, of their contribution is deemed difficult to evaluate, on account of complex and multifaceted interactions appearing between them but also due to their small magnitude, as has been pointed out by Englander and Gurney (1994).

Given the preceding, the reason for which technological change is emphasized as the most important factor becomes apparent. In all its manifestations, innovation contributes to an increase in productivity, regardless if it regards new products, new production methods or changes to the organization. For this reason, technological change, as a tool for acquiring a competitive advantage, is ceaselessly developing, reinforcing the level of technology included in products while at the same time rendering the need for research and development greater and an imperative.

This phenomenon contributed to the realization of the exceptional importance of knowledge, the value of the human factor as an element producing but also carrying knowledge and, more recently, of the importance that the incorporation of technology to the human factor assumes. Technology and humans constitute, with respect to the accumulation of knowledge, two sides that are as different as they are closely related to one another.

The emphasis on technological progress itself brought about two other consequences. It created, on one hand, a classification of products based on the level of technology they incorporate, while, on the other hand, it changed the rules and function of competition itself. The production of innovations is itself the criterion for competition, when one refers to High Technology and rapid technological progress products.

Should one approach technological changes from a macroeconomic perspective, these characterize not only the major business circles that relate to the international economic system but also each country individually (Vernardakis et al., 1995). Each country assumes a different speed, depending on its culture vis-à-vis technological changes and the challenges that come along with them.

Technological changes have contributed to the establishment of new sectors, the decay of other, older ones, as well as the merger of different sectors and the fragmentation of others. The need that emerges for enterprises is to shape a culture that will render the business a carrier for the accumulation of knowledge and not simply an organization pursuing the sterile accumulation of capital.

Technological developments have influenced the structure and organization of businesses. They shape the relations between businesses and other bodies, the methodologies they follow for production and the choices that complement them, and, in general, the selection and shaping of their objectives and strategies themselves.

Innovation and technological change are inherent in the wider social-economic system. This is evident also on account of the fact that as environmental conditions change, their features are perceived in different ways. Technological change, as a process, can lead the transformation of an economy. It is a destabilizing force, while at the same time being a force imposing order, both with respect to the orientation of the change as well as with respect to the dynamic adjustment process that takes place. Simultaneously, the social and institutional environment may reinforce or hinder this process of technological change through the conditions it imposes.

Elements of the research and development process and their effects on the process of innovation

According to Kay (1988) the features of the process for research and development are the following.

Research and development are not specific to a product (creating technological synergies or spectrum economies) but rather to the enterprise, creating external economies and ownership problems. If there is no sufficiently defined product, the enterprise may end up allocating R&D costs to multiple products. If, on the other hand, the company itself is not clearly defined, this may be an indication of a low comparative advantage with respect to the R&D activity.

Time delays frequently emerge in research. By itself this, of course, is nothing noteworthy, but can, however, under certain conditions lead to or assist in the creation of problems, such as loss of proprietary knowledge, encumbrance of costs and increase of uncertainty.

Uncertainty may be manifested in three different forms:

- Concerns with respect to the taking of future decisions
- As technological uncertainty
- As uncertainty regarding market success.

Finally, expensiveness is an element that differs from sector to sector.

The consequences of these characteristics tend to change as the research and development process moves toward its completion. Consequences from the three first features decrease as one moves toward the final stages of R&D, while consequences ensuing from expensiveness tend to increase.

The first important effect of the characteristics above relates to uncertainty, which directly affects financing for R&D, since it is the enterprise itself that is called to cover it and not the market.

A second effect relates to the fact that possible delays, uncertainty and the non-specific nature of research and development influence more the manner by which resources are allocated, especially when the R&D process is at its initial stages. Delays and the ensuing uncertainty may, in turn, discourage possible interested investors.

Third, cost itself, uncertainty and possible delays can operate as obstacles with respect to the interest that smaller or more specialized enterprises can show for the development of specific strategies (aggressive or not). On the other hand, the non-specific nature of R&D – as well as possible benefits resulting from following the pioneer – may encourage more toward the direction of adopting a defensive strategy.

Fourth, one ought to be reminded of the observation that being at the forefront of innovation does guarantee success, since innovation pioneers have to deal with the four characteristics analyzed earlier.

Finally, the fifth characteristic relates to the observation that costs for R&D have significantly increased, which has shaped a fertile soil for joint ventures, especially at the early stages of research.

Process for the adoption/dissemination of innovation

The process for the adoption of an innovation is fairly complex and comprises five different stages:

- Briefing on and realization of the innovation
- Shaping of opinions on the innovation
- Decision making in favor (or not) of the adoption of the innovation
- Realization of the innovation – provided it was thus decided
- Evaluation of the effects ensuing from the application of the innovation

This is a process that takes time to complete. Some or more of these stages may prove more time-consuming, while, at the same time, there are several factors at play across the entire scope of the process. There is also the case where overlays are observed between the stages, something which may give the impression that some of the stages have not taken place (Beal and Rogers, 1960).

Rate of dissemination of innovation and factors affecting it

The characteristics of the innovation/technology that is being disseminated, which largely explain the rate for the adoption of an innovation (Kearns, 1992), include the following:

- The comparative advantage offered by the innovation: the rate by which it appears to supersede the one it is anticipated to replace. These include the economic benefit, the low cost, the lessening of inconvenience, social status, saving in time and effort, the directness and immediacy of rewards.

- The compatibility it presents: the apparent degree of consistency between the innovation and existing values (Walsh and Linton, 2000; Bower and Christiansen, 1995), past experiences (Carter, 1994) and the needs of its potential recipients.
- Its complexity: This regards to how easy or hard it appears to be with respect to understanding and using it.
- The potential to test it: This is the degree by which a potential recipient is provided with the possibility to test the innovation before they decide to adopt it.
- The ability to monitor the effects from adopting it: This is the degree by which the recipient of an innovation is provided with the capacity to ascertain the effects it may bring.
- The number of businesses that constitute potential recipients of the innovation
- The manner by which the potential recipients make decisions. A decision may be regarded as optional if it relates to individuals who are decision makers, or as collective if it regards small or larger groups of people with commensurate authority. The receptiveness of an enterprise as to the implementation of changes affects the rate of dissemination of an innovation inside the company. The level of this receptiveness depends on the general features of this enterprise (Mahler and Rogers, 1999), the structural features of this enterprise (Meyer and Goes, 1998) and the connections between the enterprise and its environment.
- The channels via which information on innovation is exchanged between innovation producers and potential innovation recipients. The may be the mass or interpersonal media. Their importance differs depending not only on the stage of the dissemination process (Beal and Rogers, 1960) but also on the recipients themselves (Rogers and Shoemaker, 1971).
- The nature of the environment (Vernardakis, Stephanidis and Akoumianakis, 1995) of the social system.
- Attempts by intervening factors in order for the innovation to be adopted.

Dissemination of innovation/technology

The dissemination of technology and technological innovation assists – on one hand – the exploitation of the benefits afforded by the innovative process, across the entire spectrum of the economy, while it simultaneously contributes to the reinforcement and progress of productivity.

On the other hand, the process of the dissemination of innovation is used as a carrier of useful data and information that relate to both the performance as well as the more general effect that the application of the innovative process as well as the innovation itself may carry.

The following are the principal characteristics of the process of the dissemination of innovation:

- The number of those carriers who are anticipated to constitute potential recipients of these innovations and, together with this, the philosophy that these carriers apply during their own decision-making process

- The information that relates to this particular innovation and the manner by which such information is exchanged between those carriers that develop it and those carriers that accept or adopt it

"Epidemic" models

"Epidemic" models were developed and utilized in order to describe the process for the dissemination of innovation, by employing the analogy that describes the spread of a disease on the level of an epidemic.

According to this phenomenon, that analogy offers the following description on the process of the dissemination of innovation: As a technological innovation begins to spread, the number of carriers adopting it increases at a high rate until it reaches that level where the number of those carriers who have not adopted it becomes so small that the rate of dissemination for this technological innovation decreases significantly.

At the initial stages of the process, the informing available to enterprises is minimal, while in parallel the risk assumed for adopting the (new) innovation is high. During the process for the dissemination of the innovation and as more enterprises accept the innovation, they become privy to more information on this particular innovation, simultaneously decreasing the risk of adopting it. The rate by which the innovation permeates during this stage increases – with this happening limitlessly. This means that the remaining possible recipients of the innovation become less. Finally, the rate of permeation rapidly decreases, gradually leading to the completion of the process.

In general, various studies resting on the epidemic model have given the conclusions that follow. The curves describing the permeation assumed a sigmoid appearance – were shaped like an *S*. An accounting curve could describe the phenomenon of the spread of a technological innovation more completely.

Without becoming engaged in a detailed mathematical description and looking at the diagram, we could observe the following: The rate for the spread of a technological innovation can be rendered by using an accounting intertemporal curve, a curve that exhibits features that approximate the "S" shape. Christensen (1992) characterized the conception of such a curve as a useful framework for one to describe the phenomenon of the replacement of old technologies by newer ones – on the level of industry. Simultaneously, models that utilize this type of curve allow the analysis of the evolution in the performance of any technology (Nieto et al., 1998).

Meldrum (1995) suggests that the sigmoid technology curve depicts the relation between the performances of a technology and the amount of effort required in order to effect improvements to these performances. As Foster (1986) supported the utilization of this curve may lead to the emergence of significant issues for the case of High Tech Marketing, while it simultaneously may reinforce the marketing interfaces inside a business.

Along the S curve what can be seen is that during the initial stages of the development of a new product relatively large effort must be devoted to product

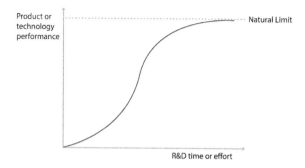

Figure 1.8 S-type curve

small or marginal improvements to performance. As a technology becomes better understood and more widely employed for the manufacture of products, improvements to performance will be attained with less effort on development. At this point, relatively small investments will begin bringing major performance improvements, until the technology reaches its limit (as expected) – that limit is depicted as an imaginary axis to which the curve asymptotically tends. As this occurs, it will be increasingly more difficult to achieve further improvements to performance. At this stage, the technology has matured – if we refer to this phenomenon in the life of the technology terms, although the same may not hold for its market life.

The vertical axis regards the dimension of the product's or process's dimensions, while the horizontal axis related to the time of the magnitude of effort made. The selection of the unit depends on the researcher's objective (O'Brien, 1962). Thus, if the researcher intends to measure the relevant efficiency or potential productivity of the work for each new product development team, then he or she will prefer to place the engineering effort on the horizontal axis (Foster, 1986), whereas if he or she pursues to assess the impact of the maturity of a technology on sales or the competitive ranking of a business, then it is preferable to select time (Becker and Speltz, 1983; Roussel, 1983; Thomas, 1984).

This model rests on a normal distribution of the adopters' categories – a typical bell curve. Its representation on a cumulative form renders the result one observes as an "S"-form curve. From the viewpoint of strategic marketing, the growth phase of the product's life cycle was identified via this curve (Brown, 1992).

There are two elements that are of special interest on this curve: the first regards the point in time where the level of diffusion appears to be significantly increased, while the second relates to the slope of the diffusion curve during the phase where it exhibits such increase.

A second point on the curve regards the delimitation of that area, where the curve's slope, described earlier, begins to perceptively decrease.

Three distinguished phases can be observed during the diffusion of a technology in an industry, as such is represented by an S curve.

During the first phase, one can observe great uncertainty for the result of the development process. Simultaneously, the risk for the realization of the investment is great, the number of the enterprises utilizing the new technology is low and the diffusion process is slow. This is the phase during which the learning process begins and the rate of innovation in technological performance increases at a low rate.

Upon the passage of time, the usefulness of the new technology becomes apparent, and it is successfully consolidated. The process of its diffusion is attained and the wider and more complete understanding of the features and uses of the technology brings improvements in the technological performance indices.

As the percentage of enterprises who have not yet adopted the new technology is less than that of the enterprises that did, or those who have delayed the adoption of the new technology do not pursue to be oriented toward a newer one, the rate of diffusion is dramatically decreased, while in time the technology – as was cited earlier – approaches the limit of its performance and, in parallel, loses its ability to be productive.

There has been criticism against this model, but said criticism cannot negate its value as a tool. Researchers such as Lee and Nakicenovic (1988), Cox (1967), Swan and Rink (1982) and Tellis and Crawford (1981) have criticized the usefulness of S curves as a forecasting tool, since there are inherent weaknesses in this model.

A weak point of the epidemic model approach is the hypothesis that the businesses – potential recipients are generally homogeneous and differ only with respect to the level they are deemed as progressive. Thus, the fact that every business can develop its own, different rationale on the adoption of an innovation, as well as to assess in a different way the capacity with respect to its own profitability is not acknowledged. As Christensen (1992) points out, important differences can be observed between businesses with respect to the level of performance where a technology appears to mature. Thus, another point relates to how the selection of the adoption time for the same technology may differ for different enterprises. Another weak point regards the hypothesis that the environment of the businesses – recipients of an innovation is static, as is the number of such enterprises itself. Both hypotheses do not rest on realistic foundations. Having said this, the course of every product cannot be illustrated using an S curve.

In order to close this gap, other models have been proposed, such as that by Davies (1979). Davies takes account of the differences exhibited between enterprises and concludes by proposing different diffusion curves for different product categories. Another model was developed by Metcalfe (1981), who pursued to cover various gaps relating to the issue of innovation offer, where the epidemic model seems to fail. He concludes that the appearance of a technology creates an adjustment chasm and that the development of demand for this technology is proportionate to this chasm.

What must simultaneously be taken into account is that it is rare for a technology to be diffused without competing against other technologies. This affects both the level as well as the rate of its diffusion.

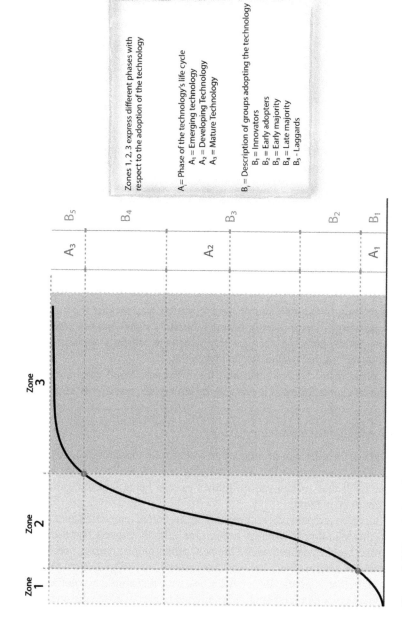

Zones 1, 2, 3 express different phases with
respect to the adoption of the technology

A_i = Phase of the technology's life cycle
    A_1 = Emerging technology
    A_2 = Developing Technology
    A_3 = Mature Technology

B_i = Description of groups adopting the technology
    B_1 = Innovators
    B_2 = Early adopters
    B_3 = Early majority
    B_4 = Late majority
    B_5 - Laggards

Figure 1.9 Description of a technology's life cycle including the groups adopting the technology, using an S curve (adapted on Brown, 1992)

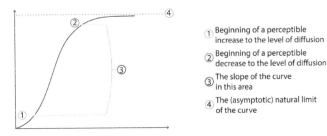

Figure 1.10 Points of interest on the S curve

Pursuant to the rationale receding, one must take account of the fact that together with the emerging innovation, others (not necessarily competing ones) are also diffused. This can create, in course, operating interdependencies that must be taken into account for any further research or productive endeavor.

Factors affecting the rate of diffusion for an innovation

The factors affecting the rate of diffusion for an innovation are distinguished to those relating to the recipient of the innovation and those regarding the innovation itself.

Factors relating to the recipient of the innovation may include the size of the recipient company, a factor usually deemed the most significant one; the rate of development for the industrial sector within which the company operates; and the nature and quality of that businesses' management.

On the other hand, factors regarding the innovation itself may include the expected benefit (on a financial level) and the anticipated cost for its adoption.

Cross-sector diffusion of innovation

The process for the diffusion of innovation from sector to sector assumes a more complex nature compared to the corresponding process realized inside a sector. The course itself that an innovation follows as it is being introduced has been observed not to be random.

The sectors who are potential recipients of an emerging innovation are expected to react to this stimulus at different times. One initially expects that the sectors who will react would be those where the new proposal guarantees, more or less, the attainment of certain objectives – not necessarily cost-related. From this point onward, a path that is predictable will follow, with the adoption criteria for the emerging innovation along it being differentiated to purely economic one, as one moves toward its end point.

DeBresson (1991) depicted precisely what path an emerging innovation is expected to follow during its cross-sector diffusion.

The reason this behavior is observed is, on the initial level, the needs for there to be a direct relation between two activities, which assumes the form of an offer–demand relation, in order for an innovation to be diffused from one activity to another. It is frequent, therefore, for "neighboring" activities to facilitate the diffusion of an innovation via themselves.

This, of course, does not by itself suffice for an innovation to be adopted by a neighboring activity. A reason for this is that in the case of a push application for an innovation, this innovation may overlap with neighboring activities and create interconnections with other ones. A second reason lies with the fact and any activity develops different motives for the adoption or not of an innovation. According to DeBresson (1991), the differences that arise are related to the activities that have been cited earlier.

Forecast of the rate of technological change

The rate of change for a technology describes the rate by which the generalized performance variable for this technology is improved. Such a parameter is an indication of the usefulness of such an improvement in the context defined by a wide array of applications. For a business to know the rate of change for technologies is very important when the process for the development of a new product commences but also, and more generally, in the context of business planning.

It constitutes a special need, therefore, for a business to be able to forecast the rates at which such changes to technologies can take place. Three different approaches are applied:

Projection of fast and present trends to the future,
analysis of the factors structuring and shaping such trends and
investigation of possible changes to these factors.

These are implemented serially. What is initially pursued is to detect and identify the trends – provided such have been formed. After detecting the trends, it is pursued to further analyze the factors shaping and driving them. Finally, after having detected said factors, their behavior when exposed to change can be investigated.

Technological performance factors

Technologies are systems described and defined via the use of different variables and specifications. What is important is to detect the performance of the technology which simultaneously determined the usefulness of technological change for the recipient.

In order to do this, the parameter of technological performance must be designated. This regards the effectiveness of a conversion, a change in the technology, as perceived by its recipient. Its designation and selection in order to forecast the evolution of a technological system are two of the ways to correlate the value of such an evolution with the technology's recipient.

The graphic representation of the evolution of the parameter relating to techno-logical performance reveals an S-type curve. This curve is utilized as the basis in order to perform a projection forecast with respect to the technology.

With respect to the evolution of the technology, three generalized periods have been identified, which may be observed on the technology curve itself:

An initial period of the new invention
An intermediate period of technological improvement
A final period of technological maturity

Technologies rest on natural phenomena. Every specific sigmoid technology curve assumes an (upper) natural limit with respect to the level of its evolution and which may be due to a specific natural phenomenon. The nature of this phenom-enon also designates the area of the technical performance for such a technology.

One can observe the evolution of a technology with respect to time along the length of the sigmoid curve, when such a technology rests on a specific natural phenomenon. When, however, a different natural process is employed, one will observe a different evolution, which will be illustrated using a new a different sigmoid curve, to which it will "jump" from the original one.

The first observation regards what is called increasing progress and relates to improvement carried out on a technology employed by this specific physical pro-cess. The second observation regards the so-called interrupted progress, during which one observes a jump from an initial sigmoid curve to a new one, as the evolutions and improvements done to a technology are attributed to a new and different from the original physical process.

The sigmoid curve of the technology does not constitute some model that can describe the process of technological change, since it cannot explain the rate of change for the technology's progress. It constitutes an analogy that has been his-torically observed and verified and which can describe the progress of a technol-ogy and can be utilized in order for one to resort in assessing the rate of change for the technology – without, however, been able to be utilized to forecast the manner by which such change can manifest.

It is, thus, an analogy describing the intertemporal evolution of the basic perfor-mance variable for the technology.

When a structural change by means of a technological substitution (emphasis on the physical phenomenon) is realized, then it is expected that the graph for the aforementioned performance parameter will shift to a new sigmoid curve for this particular technological innovation.

One may observe that such substitution cannot be described by a new, overall sigmoid curve. Simultaneously the discontinuity areas in the final diagram are not covered by some kind of sum of the original curves. Besides, each curve represents and refers to a specific phenomenon – a basis that distinguishes a tech-nology. When this phenomenon changes, the curves also change and the physical limits to the evolution of the technology are reshaped.

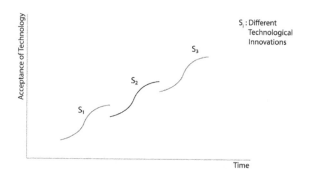

Figure 1.11 Description of the technological substitution model

Adjustment of the s curves of a technology to the technical data relating to the rate of evolution of a technology

This adjustment of the S curves is attained by the following procedure:

- The key technical performance parameter is detected with respect to the particular technology.
- Historical data relating to the technical performance of the specific technology are collected, beginning from the stage of its innovative application. Its evolution over time is presented in a diagram.
- The inherent, in the physical processes, factors are detected, factors that limit the evolution of the particular technology.
- The level of the physical limit for the performance parameter is assessed and the axis that the upper branch of the S curve will approximate is drawn.
- The times at which the two bending points on the curve are observed are assessed – the first in the area of change from the exponential to the linear and the second in the area of change from the linear to the area constrained by the asymptotic axis.
- A condition, of course, is that researchers have not only understood the physical process complementing the particular technology but also are imaginative enough so that they are oriented in the right way.
- Should discontinuities appear, this should be regarded as an indication to search for alternative ways to handle the physical process relating to the technology.

1.3 The "chasm"

Moore (1991) employs the term *chasm* to describe the distance and difficulty faced by High Technology until it attains an opportune and profitable market. It separates consumers to visionaries and pragmatists and places them in opposite

banks of the chasm. Despite the fact that visionaries (or innovators or early adopters) are the first to adopt a new technology (paying, of course, the corresponding
monetary price), the critical number of consumers which will signify the overcoming of the chasm comprises pragmatists. It is they who form the critical mass
signifying the establishment – the beginning – of a profitable, for the company,
environment. He also observes that the passage from one consuming end to the
other is treacherous at best.

The chasm represents the distance – the gap – existing between two different
markets for technology products. The first market is the early market, comprising
early adopters and those who are distinguished by their quickness in assessing the
nature and benefits of a newly developed product. The other side is the market
comprising of the "rest of us", the category, that is, of buyers who wish, on one
hand, to enjoy the benefits of the new technology but, on the other hand, do not
wish to experience the fatigue-inducing events entailed by its early adoption. The
transition from one market to the other is anything but smooth. The factor which
creates such a chaotic distance between these two markets is essentially the differentiation that inherently exists as a characteristic of the two different buyer
groups. It relates to the degree of nuisance that each group is prepared to tolerate,
its disposition toward assuming the entailed risks, as well as the collateral consequences, as pointed out by Siegel (1998).

To give an example, this nuisance factor can, for software users, be translated
into incompatibilities with the rest of the operating system. That which creates
the "chasm" is the different level of tolerance for such issues. Early adopters (or
innovators) place more weight on the material and psychological benefits gained,
even at the corresponding price of the nuisance entailed by their choice. On the
contrary, the cost–benefit function in the overwhelming majority of consumers
(or the critical mass – pragmatists) deems that the cost for adopting the new technology is great and, before adopting it, pose as a prerequisite a different array of
benefits for the product, entailed and following from the new technology.

The consequences of the existence of such a chasm are many and of such an
intensity that they may document the reasons for which ultimately a very large
number of High Tech companies never manage to successfully cross this critical
distance.

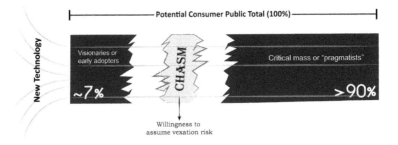

Figure 1.12 The "chasm"

Even in the case where someone can initially succeed with the early adopter approach, managing, that is, to be a victorious first in the market, the effort required for this is huge, and the transformation required of its profile radical, in order for him or her to cross to the other side. Crossing requires the transformation of known marketing habits, by adopting new ones which would seem completely alien at first. They essentially include training the consumer adopting the product at an early stage, by using a "user-friendly" language.

The combination of the fact that many High Tech companies find it extremely difficult to leave the "beaten path", and their failure to foresee if, when and to what extent the critical mass will adopt a product – but also at what rate this will happen – substantiate the chasm and render the estimate of the market's size an extremely difficult and contested affair. Geoffrey A. Moore (1991) observes that if one assumes the higher ground to the problem then he or she will realize that it is but a subset of a wider issue: the manner by which a market behaves as it undergoes change. Both with respect to customers-consumers as well as for manufacturing companies, who are both subjected to the trials and tribulations not only of absorbing and consolidation but also of the use of the new ensuing ingredients. Moore recommends as the vehicle for a successful transition, and crossing of the finishing line or at least minimizing the distance of the chasm, the replacement of the philosophy on selling the product by the philosophy of establishing a relation between the company and its customers. This relation he feels may function as a brake that will thwart the collateral consequences of the chasm. The establishment of a "marketing relation" is essentially a reformulation of the transition from the sales era to marketing era, which may be condensed in the customer-centric philosophy of considering consumer needs and not servicing the needs of the sale.

In this light, it is considered to be a given that the "chasm" and its consequences for High Technology companies are, on one hand, an expression of the markets' reaction to change, save if only and specifically for the case of High Technology products, where the environment is characterized by the intensity of the consequences, and liquidity, is depicted in its purest form. The fact that the factors composing it function as catalysts and its effects in the determination of the variables relating to the market size, but also the time the critical mass is attached to, render it as an uncertainty factor for enterprises, adding yet another distinctive characteristic to the environment in which High Tech companies must survive.

1.4 The significance of High Technology

What emerges as been rendered by the science of economics to the establishment of the framework for High Technology is its contribution to the economic knowhow. In his article "The New Business Cycle", published in *Business Week*, Mandel (1997) attempts to clarify another dimension of High Technology and, thus, to define it from a different perspective, that of its results on the economy. According to Mandel (1997), High Technology plays a huge role in the economy, a role so serious as to cast doubt on the use of the traditional cyclic indices employed, such as the purchase of homes, car sales or even inflation. He argues that it is the first time – and due to High Technology – that we witnessed the coexistence of high economic development (and the consequent low unemployment) and low inflation. Namely, he describes the exact opposite side of stagnation. In other words, he considers that economic growth via High Technology brought about a simultaneous decrease in price levels. His argumentation rests on the increase of productivity originating from the stabilization of economic activities and the improvement of communications, due to large investments in High Technology.

Moreover, it ascribes the increase of the efficiency of business functions to electronic commerce. Although it acknowledges that market demand for "High Tech employees" increased, together with their salaries, it feels that the inflationary pressure from this fact was offset by the fall of computer prices. In addition, it considers that the known boom–burst cycles will cease to appear since the demand for personal computer will bring about a fall in their cost due to the singular cost structure of High Technology products. High Technology products exemplify a high development production of the first unit cost, while the cost of the next units decreases and, therefore, the average cost tends to decrease with the increase of the units sold. To reinforce the argument concerning the end of the cycles, and of the effect of increased demand in cost (and, as an extension, of the other factors that depend on cost) he indicatively cites that in 1996 American consumers spent $282 billion in informatics technologies, namely, 49% more than they spent on housing. Finally, he concludes the framework for the indirect determination of High Technology by means of its results by citing that every newly employed individual at Microsoft creates six to seven new jobs in Washington.

2   Business culture and High Tech enterprises

2.1 Strategic concerns and approaches

2.1.1 Conversion of Core Capabilities to core rigidities in High Tech enterprises

Due to volatile and turbulent changes occurring in the environment for High Tech companies, both on the market as well as the technology level, interest is focused on new products. A conflict thus emerges, as D. Leonard-Barton (1992) suggests, between innovation and the fixed state of benefits for the enterprise, between the two poles, that is, who conflict because of the creation of new core benefits, on one hand, and the maintenance of existing ones, on the other. New products are converted into a visible arena of conflicts between the undisputed need to main-tain the competitive core advantages. In this field, according to the definition of *paradox* offered by Quinn and Cameron (1988), one comes across the following paradox: The core abilities simultaneously favor and hold back the development of innovations.

An enterprise's capabilities are considered unique (core), only when they are able to strategically differentiate the enterprise. The concept of core capability is not new to the science of marketing. Authors such as Snow and Hrebiniak (1980), Hitt and Ireland (1985), and Hayes, Wheelright and Clark (1988) have termed them as unique skills, or core skills/organizational skills. Pavitt considers such skills "special to an enterprise", while Hofer and Schendel (1978) consider them as sources for development and Itami and Roehl (1987) as an invisible asset.

Two conflicting views on the role and the relationship between innovation and Core Capabilities can be detected in the literature. The vital concepts for the sur-vival of a High Tech company appear in parallel to both compete and complement one another.

Hayes (1985) and Quinn (1980) consider the relationship between innovation and Core Capabilities from the viewpoint of complementarity, since to competi-tively succeed depends more, according to them, on gradual innovations created from the exploitation of carefully build, unique Core Capabilities.

On the other hand, and according to Lieberman and Montgomery (1988), the organizational (unique) capabilities are possibly the reason leading enterprises to incumbent inertia when they come across environmental changes.

Tushman and Anderson's (1986) approach is that radical innovations are responsible either for the destruction or the improvement of the sector's capacities and capabilities. Henderson and Clark (199) believe that even very small innovations are able to inflame many years of knowledge acquired by the organization. Finally, Schempeter (1942) very accurately observes that any kind of innovation necessarily includes some degree of creative destruction.

Given that unique capabilities – at any stage in a business's lifetime – evolve and the existence of their simultaneous operation as catalysts or, conversely, brakes for the development of innovative new (high tech) products, a more elaborate reference to their nature and their ingredients is in order but also one focusing on the mechanisms that convert them – in the presence of the development of changes and innovations – to an obstruction.

It is true that most authors consider that they have adequately covered the dimensions of Core Capabilities by using aggressive designations such as "unique", "special", "difficult to mimic", "superior to the competition" and explanations as to how core competences can be cultivated or not. Teece, Pisano and Shuen (1990) offer one of the clearest definitions: (They are) a set of differentiated capabilities, supplementary capital and processes which provide a basis for competitive capacities and a preservable advantage to a particular enterprise.

Dorothy Barton (1992) defines as a core capability the set of knowledge that differentiates the enterprise and provides a competitive advantage to it. She believes that it comprises four constituents:

> Knowledge and skills possessed by the employees: This dimension is accepted also by Teece, Pisano and Shuen (1990), who feel that it is manifestly associated with new product development.

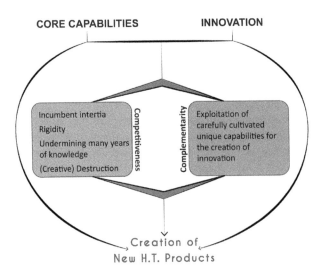

Figure 2.1 The twofold association of innovation and Core Capabilities

Knowledge and skills incorporated in techniques and technical systems: The
result of many years of gathering, codification and structuring knowledge
accumulated in the employees' intellect

Management systems: The third dimension represents the formal and informal
ways to create, but also to manage, knowledge.

The fourth dimension is diffused in the three aforementioned ones. It is the
value ascribed, by the enterprise, to the contents and structure of knowledge.

In order to understand the interrelation and interdependence of product development and Core Capabilities and to accentuate not only both sides of such influence
but also, and principally, to illuminate the "passage", the change from a positively
affecting process to a negative one, especially in the case of High Tech enterprises, it is deemed purposeful to analyze each dimension.

Knowledge and skills

One of the most significant elements in a core capability is full supremacy in
technical and professional skills and the corresponding substratum of knowledge
that is the lydite stone for every important product. For people to be able to be
included in the professional elite of a High Tech enterprise, they must show noteworthy skills and frequently to outdo their potential, to make, that is, possible
what is "infeasible".

Besides, however, excellence with respect to very capable personnel, this
dimension also includes another feature that largely follows from the aforementioned "elite" that composes personnel profiles. The pool of knowledge of an
enterprise is distinguished by a quality directly proportional to the products by the
personnel's elite. It is maintained and reinvigorated by this and the skills that have
been tested in time and are successful.

The problem – the incompatibility that is between the creation of a new (high
tech) innovative product and the already existing Core Capabilities – begins from
the following simple ascertainment: As large as an enterprise may be, its resources
are, by definition, limited. This entails that should it wish to place more gravity –
and resources – to the prominent personnel that represents its competitive advantage, it will inevitably degrade the role, development and participation capacity of
the other operating – but not representative of the workforce elite – departments.
As a chain reaction this entails the risk of creating a gap between environmental
requirements and existing Core Capabilities. The role of the marketing department –
among other things – is to listen to consumers' needs and then, as a connecting
link, to convert such needs to inflows for the other operating departments (principally the R&D department), which will spearhead the process for creating a
product to cater for such needs.

Traditionally in High Tech enterprises the superior workforce comprises engineers –
technologists. Given the resources the marketing department is, by necessity, downgraded; thus, the process of the unhindered and effective contact with the environment is interrupted. Poor listening entails errors or a lacking transfer of the

necessary information flow (the fifth productive factor as many claim it to be). The core advantage tends to be renewed and developed toward the same direction (that of technical superiority), and this is undisputed and widely known among marketing executives, who, as Heyes, Wheelright and Clark (1988) observe, consider positions in High Tech companies not to be attractive, because of their, by definition, downgraded role. One-dimensional empowerment, as the fixed tactic of the core capability of such enterprises, is ultimately converted to an obstacle that hinders the creation of new products. It is a form of turning a blind eye, difficult to acknowledge and to accept, due to the fact that it has connected its existence, as a quality characteristic, with the company's predominance. In order for things to stay as they are (predominance), changes are necessary (upgrading of marketing executives).

Work tools

The same logic is applied also to the "work tools" used by the personnel. Systems, processes and tools, in general, are creations which incorporate, to some extent, the attached knowledge and skills of the personnel in a form that is accessible more easily and expediently. They also compose a piece of the core advantage, since because of their creation and enrichment-upgrading development by a highly specialized personnel, they offer a competitive advantage.

But the capabilities and processes contained in these tools can become obsolete. New product designers can never know what other systems may affect their new products and where incompatibilities may arise. And it is precisely there where the fine point differentiating their conversion from benefits to obstacles lies.

Management systems

Management systems may become part of a unique capability provided they adopt unusual mixes of skills or if they promote beneficial behaviors which cannot be observed in competing enterprises. Incentive systems that encourage innovative activities are necessary and critical features for many Core Capabilities.

But management systems are rendered dry and fixed, averting people with high skills to implement them toward goals which are frequently degraded. Perceptions relating to relatively low priority and importance weaken not only the role but also the importance ascribed by the executive him- or herself when he or she works at a "second-class" operating department.

Values

The value ascribed to the contents and the creation of knowledge and which is constantly reinforced by the leaders of the enterprise while also being incorporated in the managerial practices affects products under development from many other viewpoints. According to Barton (1992), two subdimensions are especially critical: the degree of empowerment for the workforce and the status ascribed to the employees in each operational group.

Empowerment is essentially the result of faith in the employees' skills, in the sense that they can materially contribute toward the attainment of the objective on each occasion, and, therefore, the extension of an individual's freedom of moving without being under the direct supervision of some sort of higher authority.

A possible obstacle is that the limits of activities and freedom are not always clearly defined. When empowered employees exert "heroic" efforts for the company they usually expect payment, recognition and extension of their freedom to act as rewards. But when something goes wrong (either due to the fact that they have transgressed the limits for freedom the enterprise affords or if the product, despite a technical success, failed in other ways or if their self-sacrifice ends up bringing small attention and recognition) they are disappointed, feel betrayed and frequently leave the enterprise.

The second subdimension, namely, the ascription of high status to those employees considered to represent the moving force and the manifestation of Core Capabilities, is responsible for the attraction, keeping and offering incentives to talented individuals who appreciate the knowledge base that creates the unique capability. They are attracted not only by the challenges created in High Tech environments but also by the high status entailed by holding a position in a cutting-edge technological company. Every company shows a prejudice toward that base where its history is rooted.

The success or failure of new product is ascribed principally to those whom, because of their great insightfulness constantly empower the status of their own operation.

It is clear that (new) products receive an enormous held from Core Capabilities. Indeed, these unique skills constantly generate new products and processes, since a major part of the creative capability is focused on discovering new opportunities for the application of accumulated knowledge.

But when new product development required the contribution of skills which are traditionally rendered smaller gravity and respect, the history and point of reference of the enterprise may have inhibitory effects. Even in the case of the existence of a multitude of subcultures, the more senior and historically important ones are enjoying the most kudos. The lower status of nondominant operations is expressed as continuously increasing, as a cyclical feedback process, which limits the capacity to contribute toward the development of new products and, consequently, operating integration – unification, which, as Pavitt (1991) observes, plays a catalytic role for innovation. These vicious circles, as they have been terms by psychiatric science, simulate the examples of self-fulfilling prophecies, as has been observed by Weick (1979), and are manifested, according to Barton, in four ways:

1   Who goes to whom? Usually executives of a lower standing visit the workplace of those with a higher one. Not only does this show an acceptance of their fixed status, thus also reinforcing it, but limits the learning ability of senior executives with respect to the works being carried out in "lower" operating departments.

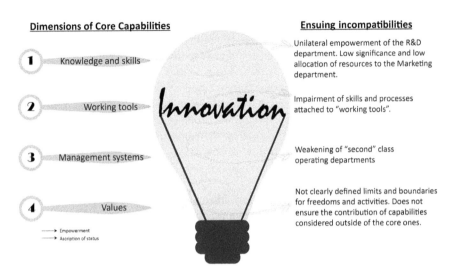

Figure 2.2 Incompatibilities between Core Capabilities and innovation

2   Self-fulfilling prophecies. Expectations relating to the role and status of individuals may lead to their self-realization. As it has been documented by many unconscious interpersonal expectations management experiments, prejudices may lead to the Pygmalion effect: namely, A's expectations from B may affect B's real performance, either positively or negatively.
3   The reliability of source arguments is directly affected by the status of the source.
4   Differences in specialized vocabulary – terminology employed by each group.

To summarize, one may observe that while Core Capabilities constitute an essential ingredient for success, they may easily be converted to factors deterring the development of new products. When market conditions are subject to changes, the evaluation of the unique capacities is rendered important. Routines, procedures, preferences on the sources of information and the, at any time, fixed viewpoint of the market – these are all factor associated with the foundations of unique capacities – can become obstacles for the realistic approach to a new opportunity and, thus, must be constantly reassessed and reevaluated.

2.1.2   *Proposed strategic approaches for avoiding the conversion of core benefits to basic incapabilities in High Tech enterprises*

Cannibalism

Jakkie Mohr (2005) proposes creative destruction as one of the tools that will assist a High Tech company avoid falling prey to the obstacle entailed by the transformation of unique capacities.

Another term that is frequently employed instead of creative destruction is *cannibalism*. As Mason and Milne (1994) point out, marketing executives traditionally employ this term, which frequently refers to the cannibalism of sales, namely, the decrease in sales of a product on account of the sales of a new product by the same company. In fact, in most cases cannibalism is considered by marketing executives as a state to be avoided at all costs. Copulsky (1976), for example, discusses how enterprises can avoid the mistake of cannibalism during product development. Kerin, Roger, Harvey and Rothe (1978) observe that cannibalism "may be an unwelcome consequence of the development of a new product". To the contrary, Chandy and Tellis (1998) consider that cannibalism is a legitimate tool that may promote radical product innovation and, consequently, contribute to the long-term viability and success of an enterprise. The belief is that cannibalism is a multidimensional structure and may manifest itself in two forms: One is the capitalism of capital, while the other is the cannibalism of organizational routines. Henderson and Clark (1990) define as capital the tangible characteristics, such as the production line or the equipment participating in it, and intangible ones, such as knowledge and specialization in an enterprise or even access to the distribution channels. The success of a new technology developed by an enterprise can become self-destructive for capital investment in previous technologies by the same company.

The cannibalism of the investment of an enterprise in organizational routines which are defined by Nelson and Winter (1982) as the established processes employed by the enterprise for the performance of its daily functions – activities may originate from their incompatibility with a new technology.

Chandy and Tellis (1998) analyze investments between capital and routine ones, since they consider that these are the principal constituents of an investment by a company and are, thus, the critical variables for understanding the unwillingness for cannibalism or the resistance against creative destruction that companies frequently manifest.

According to Deshpandé and Webster (1989), willingness for cannibalism is that concept which refers to the limit where a company is adjusted to decrease the real or potential value of its investments. It is a behavioral attitude by the main actors –decision makers inside a company, the roots of which can be traced to the culture, value and beliefs of the company. It constitutes a critical factor on account of the fact that market leaders frequently adopt a wary attitude distinguished by an unwillingness to embrace or and promote radical innovation in their market. This unwillingness (or, alternatively, the lack of willingness for cannibalism) is due to the fat that they already have a solidified basis of specialized investments via which they can cover and cater for such markets. Chandy and Tellis (1998) consider that willingness for cannibalism of the same (by definition) products is a magnitude that bridges and stands midway between full unwillingness, originating from the reasons cited earlier, and the presence of (a) internal markets, (b) "champion" products and (c) a future focus on markets, namely, factors which compensate for the destruction caused by cannibalism for the company and provide the framework of offsetting benefits for a given decision to creatively self-destroy. Overall, for a business, therefore, to proceed with cannibalism it must compare the benefits that are developed (and push toward creative destruction) for the future focus on the market and internal company markets and are always under the strong influence of "champion products, with the cost entailed by such destruction on its investments, namely, on its capitals and its routines.

The role cannibalism plays is of great importance for High Tech enterprises, because of its direct interdependence with and potential influence on innovation. Willingness to cannibalize is, indeed, considered by scholars such as Chandy and Tellis (1998) as a mobilizing force for the creation of innovation. This can be better understood by studying the behavior of S-type technology curves. When a new technology, T_2, is at its embryonic stage there are two available options: either to further promote the current technology or to transition to new technology, T_2. Leonard (1992) observed that a business resting on the use of current technology holds large specialized investments the value of which is closely related to the current technology. Maintaining the current technology allows the company utilizing it to capitalize on these specialized investments. Converting to the new technology requires new investments by the company in that new technology, and thus, it is plausible for it to necessitate that the company renders its investments on the currently used technology obsolete and useless. A company unwilling to cannibalize will go on using current technology T_1. Its efforts may result to some changes to the market and will, possibly, give the appearance of success. However, they would still be the death throes of a downfallen and continuously on-the-decline technology. By keeping on investing in technology T_1, technology T_2 is brushed aside, and those catalysts contributing to the establishment of a friendly environment for the development of radically innovative products will not be formed. Adherence to an old technology may, as Foster (1986) and Utterback (1994) observe, be the cause of a company's decline. On the other hand, a company willing to destroy its already-existing technology and one that encourages its personnel to familiarize themselves with and work on new technology diffuses significant resources toward the direction of radical innovation. Such a protective environment on the side of the company has more chances to lead to innovation and signifies the company's intention to be the market leader with respect to such innovation.

Market leaders are usually unwilling to cannibalize their specialized investments until it is very late. This is understandable, up to a point, since such types of investments (specialized), by definition, lose their value if they are not applied and do not "collaborate" with a given/specific technology. Enterprises distinguished by their leading role in the High Tech market by definition hold many specialized investments, the results of, usually, long-term efforts by top and senior management, who have connected their own course with that of the company by means of the success of the technology that embodies the reward for their long and strenuous efforts. Thus, there is a forceful professional and personal link which may lead to irrational, or suboptimal to say the least, decisions.

At least three different fields have studied this behavior, trying to interpret and analyze it. Brockner and Rubin (1985) have studied why decision makers continue to use ways of action from the past, even when this has been proved to be not optimal, while Boulding, Morgan and Staelin (1997) observe that such behavior is the key issue relating to new product management. Economists and sociologists probe the reasons for which businesses exhibit such an inflexibility with respect to the way they act, in order to effectively respond to the mandates shaped by the changes to which their environment is subject.

The history of innovations, however, shows that a new innovation, for example, T_2, is frequently not launched by those managing technology T_1 but by some other party and in some cases, as Clayton (1997) and Foster (1986) observe, by someone outside the sector. Those managing technology T_1 tend to confront T_2 by further investing in T_1.

Kerin, Roger, Harvey and Rothe (1978) feel that cannibalism splits into two: the expected (or planned) and the unexpected, the result of the bad management of the product development process.

The theoretical roots of cannibalism can be traced to the cross-like elasticity of demand theory, which proposes that the percentage change to the price for product A is affected by the percentage change in the price of product B. Depending on this relation of influence, products are distinguished as independent, complementary or substitute. In the case of the substitute product (as cannibalism is alternatively referred to from the viewpoint of a Microeconomic theory) a decrease in the price for product A tends to decrease the quantity in demand for product B, taking account, of course, of the ceteris paribus proviso. In the case of marketing the sentence "with all other factors fixed" (ceteris paribus) rarely holds true. Thus, from the viewpoint of marketing, the theory of cross-like elasticity, appropriately expanded, will include, besides price, the product's physical characteristics, advantages, alternative promotional channels and so on. Economic theory proposes that income from cannibalism is essentially redistributed income, from the viewpoint that part of it originated from the income that would have been generated by the substitute product (of the same company). In this light, economists feel that the loss of earnings from a cannibalized product must be considered part of the cost of the new product. Here the proverb "having your cake and eating it" surely applies.

The same scholars, however, consider cannibalism and, indeed, the preventive type as a legitimate and viable solution, a solution that is called for the viability of an enterprise, since it is the alternative to changing, on the side of customers, to products by different companies instead of changing to different products from the same company.

Especially in High Tech environments, the need to cannibalize or/and cannibalism frequently appear due to the fact that High Tech products lead for a finite and very brief period as cutting-edge technology, until they are replaced by better products of a newer technology. This translates to a nonexistence or failure to exist for a longer than a short duration, scale economies, experience curves and a simultaneous rapid impairment – destruction of the success registered on each occasion.

Consequently, it is alternatively proposed for High Tech companies to impair on their own the cutting-edge technology on each occasion by developing the basis for the next technology to play this role and to simultaneously adopt a brute realism which will render them capable to themselves decrease the value of their previous (specialized) investments or, otherwise, to apply cannibalism.

Concisely and taking account also of the viewpoint of cannibalism from the perspective of an economic approach, the differential advantage for creative destruction may be represented as follows:

> Whether company X applies cannibalism or not, the present high (cutting-edge) technology/product will be obsolete in time t + ... Instead of letting its competitors "steal" the market share (e.g., by turning a blind eye or insisting on investing on the present technology), the company "cannibalizes" its products itself by a (prior) cannibalization of the present technology so as to attain the preservation of its (leading) position throughout time. The differential advantage is that in case the company does not cannibalize, it will lose the entire market share, while if it cannibalizes it will gain (some) part of what would have in any case been lost, when the competition would steal the market share, by developing the next cutting-edge technology itself.

Making the assumption that the market share tends to decrease with the passage of time (and, consequently, as the product moves through the last stages of its life cycle), curves ΦΘ and MΠ, which represent the market shares for the products (and the technology attached to them), decrease (negative slope). Curve MΠ represents a newer product (with cutting-edge technology). In the case where the product represented with respect to its sales by curve MΠ is launched by the same company, then cannibalism will be represented as the area enclosed by points ΓMΘ. If product Ψ is introduced by some other company, also from the High Tech sector, then the additional loss is that enclosed by points M′ΓΘΠ, while the total loss now amounts to M′MΠ. Of course, a rudimentary logic and the

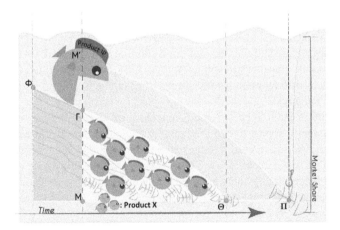

Figure 2.3 The differential benefit of "cannibalism"

theory of optimization recommend the "virtual" sacrifice of the area enclosed by ΓΜΘ (since share ΓΜΘ would have been lost anyway) in order to claim Μ'Γ'ΘΠ, against any other alternative. In other words, here cannibalism appears as a one-directional legitimate and appropriate action.

Nault and Vandenbosch (1996) consider the willingness to cannibalize as a factor so strong that it may propel and become the vehicle for the managerial and administrative support of radical innovation.

Corporate imagination

Another tool, which may be developed and strategically deployed, so that the extremely fast conversion of core benefits to significant obstacles stalling the progress of High Tech enterprises can be avoided lies with the concept of corporate imagination, a term introduced by Shanklin and Ryans (1982) or, alternatively, creativity. The fact that many enterprises use the creation of innovative products as their base and consider the percentage of participation of innovation to their revenue as an index measuring success gives a sense of the importance of the continuous renewal of the knowledge depository.

Corporate imagination presupposes the skill to shape a vision for the future that will include markets that do not already exist and which will break the norms of present markets, as Mohr (2009) has pointed out.

Hamel and Prahalad (1991), feel that the competitive game is transferred from the advantages offered by the reduction of production costs, to the field of fundamentally new markets and that the businesses that will prevail would be those in a position to define and build these markets. They see organizational-creative imagination as a necessary prerequisite tool and observe that a company will strive to create a new competitive field only if the horizon of opportunities it discerns extends beyond the boundaries of its present markets. The opportunity horizon of the business represents its collective imagination with respect to the ways by which a significant new advantage may become exploited and utilized so as to create a new field for competition or to reshape the already-existing one. The most important step toward this direction is the logical process via which enterprises may release their organizational imagination and, in a chain-reaction manner, become able to recognize and probe new fields for competition and consolidate their control and dominance with respect to the emerging opportunities offered by the market.

The shortsightedness by which corporations consider emerging opportunities compared to the protection they afford to the exploitation of present markets acts as an obstacle to this process. Despite the fact that it is understandable for there to be concerns arising from and in relation to the effects that the utilization and turning off the flow of interest on emerging opportunities will affect profits today, if it is allowed to dominate the concerns and become the focal point, then it is possible that it will avert any interest for future opportunities in a univocal manner.

As Hamel and Prahalad (1991) point out, organizational creativity comprises four main ingredients.

Figure 2.4 Manifestations of corporate imagination

Change of price–performance hypotheses

Understanding how emerging technologies can cater for the satisfaction of customer needs that are not yet satisfied or their satisfaction in a more efficient way
is, as Hamel and Prahalad (1991) suggest, of vital importance for the discovery of
a new competitive field.

The strategic approach dictating marginal changes to the already-existing products is, up to a point, understandable, in the sense that it will facilitate the already-
existing customers using such products. It is, however, clear that these regard
marginal improvement to already-existing technologies, which, in turn, will
improve already-existing data. Given the magnitude of resources of any potential
enterprise and the fact that they are not infinite, the investment of time, money
and effort in new products is, instead, recommended, products that will probably
rest on new data – products, that is, which are supported by completely different
performance hypotheses.

This argument is further supported by S curves, according to which marginal
changes to products via marginal changes to already-existing technologies, have a
limited and very brief life, and the increase of utility that they can offer customers
is at a lower rate than that of the new technology. Moore's Law, of course, which
essentially corroborates the fact that "marginal" improvements to technology lead
to the value of the given performance of a technology being halved every roughly
18 months, has been affirmed for quite some time. But it appears that this law has
already marginally approached its natural limit, and it was precisely this that led
Japan's Ministry of International Commerce and Industry to invest US$30 million

in neural networks and quantum physics, in order to be able to shift the existing paradigm in the performance-price model valid until today. Executives frequently consider the price–performance relation to be linear, a fact that limits their capacity for radical innovation. The reversal of this hypothesis usually leads to the discovery of a hidden competitive field. Companies refusing to doubt the present price–performance relation frequently suppose that the existing product is the only starting point and basis for the procedure relating to the development of new products.

Although the phenomenon where new technologies are launched by "parachuting" companies, companies which come from sectors other than the threatened one is not rare, a fact that demonstrates the inflexibility and shortsightedness of marketing that holds back the envisioning and creation of new technologies by High Tech enterprises. It is imperative that High Tech carriers realize the fact that the marginal cost of improvements to existing technologies tends to be increasing the more such a technology comes closer to the natural end of its life. Thus, the need to develop a new technology becomes imperative.

The willful blindness shown is characteristic. The rigidity or resistance to change frequently hides behind cost decrease (via a more effective and efficient productive process); however, with respect to already-obsolete products, it is reinforced by the devaluation of the introduction of the new technology on account of the small size of the carrier launching it, as Shanklin and Ryans (1982) point out.

Escape from tyranny

Tyranny is defined to be the shortsighted view of the tendency of many established businesses to focus specifically on the production of specialized solutions for customer needs utilizing present technology. Such a view, ab initio, excludes the possibility that the same needs be treated in radically different ways.

The tyranny of the served market is one of the key reasons for the creation of a vital space and suitable environment for parachuting companies. It is the reason for which new innovations are introduced by companies from outside the sector. Frequently such newcomers change the rules of the game by being the first to transition to the new technology that makes its first steps, after having already accepted the new hypotheses on the price–performance ratio for the new technology. Corporate imagination presupposes that the company's horizon expands enough for it to recognize opportunities beyond and between the limits of the areas in which it competes.

Array of benefits

Prahalad and Hamel (1991) suggest that this trap be avoided, a trap that moves in the same logical framework as marketing's shortsightedness. Against considering a business as a portfolio of products, they recommend viewing it as an array of core benefits, a way capable to dramatically change and expand the business opportunities horizons. If executives are not capable to see beyond the specific boundaries of the current market they serve, then they will pass by opportunities which depend on the combination of skills by different departments in their enterprise. They, thus, propose to expand the transparent boundaries between their company's products.

Another manifestation of corporate imagination can be detected in the guiding and encouragement of consumer to articulate the needs they may have not even realized. Technical superiority is useless if it does not coexist and go hand in hand with a deep understanding of the consumer so as to cater to some of his or her needs. The skill of being a market leader by resting on envisioning the future presupposes a strong skill to see through events and not to be consumed by processes and rules. In order to render this "before-the-customer" approach, it is deemed purposeful to create operating multidisciplinary teams and processes that would allow the briefing of customers on emerging technological capacities.

Hamel and Prahalad (1991) consider that businesses may be classified in one of the following three groups: those asking their clients what they want and repeatedly end up as their followers, those who succeed – even temporarily – to force customers toward directions they may not wish to follow and, finally, those who facilitate and guide their customers where they wish, even if the latter have not consciously realized it. For this third approach to be possible, conventional marketing research does not suffice but must be assisted and complemented by a deep knowledge and understanding of needs which follow from expectations and the customers' lifestyles.

Many major companies have familiarized themselves with the use of given approaches to marketing tools for the analysis of the markets they serve, so as to be able to find the optimal combination of features for their new products. But such approaches relate, in most cases, with the limits for the data pertaining to the markets where these companies presently compete. The use of new research techniques, less traditional but very useful for High Tech environments, is mandated by organizational creativity. Leonard and Rayport (1997), in their paper "Spark Innovation through Empathic Design", propose that despite the fact that the objective may be to be close to the customer and listen to his or her needs, the customer very often cannot articulate his or her needs. This inability to express the need, and therefore to legitimately guide the development of new products, is frequently attributable to the fact that the description of new products is limited by their experiences and ability to envision new innovations. In order for companies to overcome this obstacle, they resort to a series of techniques which constitute empathetic design.

Anthropology lends these techniques to marketing and they relate to obtaining information through monitoring consumers' behavior in the particular environment. These techniques can uncover needs and problems with which consumers feel so content that they do not to deem them as problems – even more to express them as such, as needs requiring a solution. The authors, however, do not recommend the abolition of the traditional marketing research techniques but, rather, to complement them with these techniques.

With respect to research methods, Prahalad and Hamel (1991) feel that innovations capable of reshaping the market and the boundaries of the industry, while at the same time being able to create a new competitive field, are created on the fertile soil that exists when the conventional view of servicing customers and products resting on a "matrix" of needs and operating characteristics is replaced. For this reason, an act of corporate imagination would be to break down a product to its operating features and to properly rearrange these features in a manner that would compose the discovery of a new product (innovation), which would satisfy needs that were not adequately catered for previously. Besides the fact that the conceptualization and realization of markets in terms of needs and functionality are rarely implemented by very few companies, the number of those companies possessing the creative imagination to translate those needs and convert them to new product concepts is very small.

Expeditionary marketing

The creation of markets and their penetration before competitors includes risk. On many occasions the establishment of the desired market never happens. Even, however, in the case where such a market emerges, the rate will be slower than expected. Companies that enter emerging markets first have an incomplete skill to understand conditions fast and accurately make the right decisions. The manner by which companies minimize the risks related to the mapping of the virgin territories of new markets is via a process termed expeditionary marketing. Expeditionary marketing is essentially a sequence of consecutive approaches to unknown markets. It aims to designate not only the precise direction toward which targeting ought to be made (namely, the specific combination of operating product features that contain value for customers) but also the distance from the targeted market (the techniques and other obstacles that must be overcome in order to attain that combination of price and performance which would allow the opening of a new competitive field).

A product is considered successful when it combines the exact proportions of functionality, price and performance which would allow it to deeply and expediently penetrate the targeted market.

Despite the existence of many policies aimed to the increase of the launching rate for successful products, market research carried out around a new product proposal is frequently embarrassingly inaccurate. Among its other issues, it also runs the risk of overestimating or underestimating the emerging opportunity with usually catastrophic results. There are two ways to minimize the risk entailed by the creation of new markets.

One is to follow, and not pioneer, entering the new market but wait until one feels that its product offer will be superior of that from the pioneering one, being subsequent, and thus released from the issues faced by the herald's proposal. But here a company runs the risk that its opponent and forerunner, with respect to launching the product, to be able to quickly overcome its issues and to consolidate its position, enjoying the advantages from being the first to enter the market.

Patience, thus, is neither the most opportune way to lessen the risks entailed when launching a new product to the market, nor is it devoid of problems and concerns. Since the objective is to gather understanding as fast as possible, a series of low-cost and fast-rate incursions into the market – expeditionary marketing – may bring the objective within the sights of the company faster.

What is requested, therefore, is the rate by which a business can acquire a deep knowledge of the formations of the features of price and performance so as to be able to unlock the market, on one hand, and to recompile and reshape its product offer, on the other. In other words, the solution to the practical problem posed is to maximize the number of frequent, low-expense incursions in the new market.

Expeditionary marketing increases the rate of successful products traded by a business not be increasing the rate of success but by increasing the number of market opportunities, of niches and of product combinations probed, thereby increasing the rate of acquiring new knowledge on the market.

2.2 Culture of innovation in High Tech enterprises

Jakkie Moore (1991) proposes the strategy of recognizing the nature of innovation as a means for the preservation of innovative culture. At the same time corporations confront the loss of innovation, they have been entangled in bureaucratic procedures that filter the new product development process based on formal plans and processes. This procedure, despite its analytical nature and rationale, share little and is minimally compatible with the nature of innovation itself, which is nonlinear and unexpected, as James (1985) observes.

Instead of using a step-by-step process for the filtering of new product ideas, innovation can be managed more efficiently as a business process. The idea of the creation of an internal environment which favors innovation and entrepreneurial spirit has taken on many different names: Burglerman (1983) calls it "Autonomous strategic behavior"; Hutt, Reingen and Roncetto (1988) suggested "Emerging processes", while Pinckot proposed "Intrapreaneuring".

The features that Jakkie Moore (1991) suggested a corporation must exhibit in order to preach a climate favoring innovation are the following:

The need that a business identifies in a market, which originates from the organizational idea of strategy;

the roles and competences of key actors are not adequately defined in the beginning, but become clear as strategies evolve;

the filtering process for ideas is carried out via informal carrier, which has access to the capacities of the technicians and marketing executives, not by means of formal managerial processes;

communication between the corporation's personnel tends to be carried out via less "prescribed" organizational decision-making channels and more via unofficial channels;

the commitment to the idea depends on the assistance afforded to it by product champions.

According to Maidique (1980), the executives creating, defining or adopting an idea for innovation and who are willing to assume major risks in order to complete it are called product champions and play an important role in the creation of innovation. They are frequently referred to as mavericks or crusaders, and it is they who break the rules and transform companies, assume the risks and, generally, turn everything upside down in the organization. Because of their commitment they work incessantly and will conspire behind the scenes to tap on resources that would allow the materialization of their ideas. They are, in other words, those who by means of their powerful motives and aggressive arrogation, their technical skills and knowledge of the market can overcome the obstacle of the natural reluctance to cannibalize that governs enterprises and drive, as Rajesh and Tellis (1998) point out, the process of radical innovation. Business culture promotes their influence, and senior management actively supports them.

Additionally, there are other characteristics that abet the establishment of a culture of innovation in a corporation. The motives and time offered and the dissemination of the desire to innovate are tools offered by major High Tech corporations. Several organizations share the financial risk entailed in an innovation, by the simultaneous concession of a percentage right on the potential profits it will bring. Ideas which fail do not carry penalties and punishment, since even failure is part of the corporate spirit and often the basis on which a major success for the organization rests.

Since the establishment of such a climate is usually difficult within the context of a major organization, authors such as Behnam and Walleigh (1997) recommend the isolation of a team working on an innovative idea and its placement in a different physical location. The idea behind this tactic is that when organizations develop an innovation they do so "despite the organization" and not "on account of it".

It is, of course, obvious that such an approach, despite its possible advantages, would become a target for criticism. Should a company wish to be and remain innovative, it ought to establish the mechanisms that would allow the birth and development of innovation within the daily physical operational processes of the business. The fruition of innovative culture must take place without special protective mechanisms.

Besides, as Gary and Prahalad (1991) note, the leverage of Core Capabilities in new spaces is not consistent with the simultaneous protection offered to new endeavors by corporate culture.

This is why Hamel (1997) refers to such teams using the term *orphans* and suggests that they isolate creative dialogue and make the emergence of new ideas in the corporation's hierarchy more difficult.

According to Jakkie Mohr (1991), the idea of isolating the process for new product development from the established and installed processes of the organization is a dilemma. Ideally the conditions for the development of innovation of the processes of the organization themselves would have been established. On the other hand, if the corporation is difficult to move, such an approach could be a temporary solution until conditions change.

2.3 Composition of strategic-culture approaches

The bold diagram in Figure 2.5 represents the relation claimed by Mohr to exist between core competencies and time. Both P_1 and P_2 curves begin with a positive slope which after climaxing (at max P_1 and max P_2 correspondingly), becomes negative. This illustrates that the framework of core competences (as described and analyzed by Mohr) is transformed over the passage of time and in turbulent markets to core rigidities. Curves P_1, P_2 thus describe the inherently existing qualities of core competences in High Tech markets.

More specifically,

1   from point O (line separating core competences/rigidities and up to point A, P_1 exhibits a positive slope. This happens since the product has an impact on the market share comprising early adopters or innovators. The small, positive slope is interpreted as resulting from the fact that the competing core competences and the matching between the need the technology wishes to cover, the degree by which it wishes to cover it and, in general, the factors constituting the ingredients of the three factors of uncertainties have not been fully clarified.

2   from point A to point B, the curve does not appear to be continuous. This occurs so that the chasm may be represented. The chasm is the pinnacle of uncertainty groups which characterize High Tech markets and is, essentially, the distance separating the winning of early customers (or visionaries or early adopters) from consumers who are pragmatists and who essentially constitute the critical number for the share that is necessary for the adoption of the product technology. The step from winning the early adopters to winning the critical mass is essentially the factor which will judge the likelihood of success for the technology. The existence of three such kinds of uncertainty is the reason for the discontinuity of the curve, since a failure to transcend (or to effectively soothe) these will translate to a negative slope, namely, a course opposite of the desired result. Note that the prerequisite is not only to transition from early adopters to pragmatist consumers, but that the rate of transition is also very important, since it, too, constitutes a variable included in uncertainties. Consequently, one is interested for the distance from A to B to be the shortest possible (the three groups of uncertainties are distance variables) and the transfer to be the shortest possible (Core Capabilities are transition variables).

3   point B to max P_1, core competences have multiplicative, positive results provided the chasm has been overcome. The slope of P_1 is more positive due to the "spiral" (increasing rate of increase for benefits) created by the adoption of the technology – the core competences framework and the positively correlating magnitudes.

4   points I and K in the positive part (B-Max P_1) of P_1 represent expeditionary marketing. The introduction of marginal improvements and the assessment of the public's reaction together with a parallel evaluation of the recommended

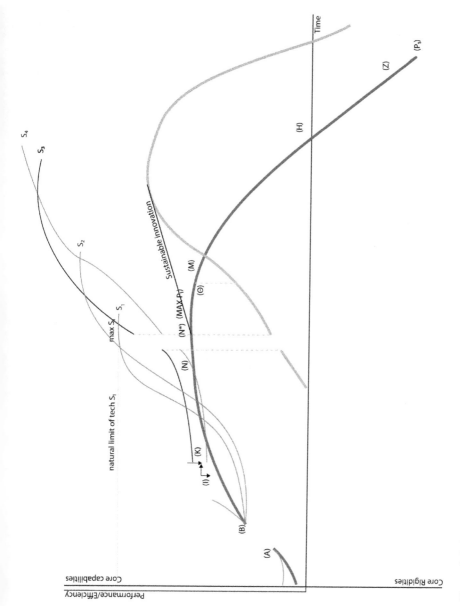

Figure 2.5 Composition of strategic–culture approaches

improvements/changes based on the feedback, combined with the fertile soil provided by the framework of Core Capabilities, assists to the convergence of the perfect strategic fit of technology need that satisfies – a way of satisfying. Additionally, it also contributes toward the more efficient utilization of the core.

5   Max point–decline. Decline follows climax. Here one observes the result of the shortsighted view of the satisfaction of needs or the tyranny of the served market dictating that existing present needs be satisfied by the same – existing technology. The negative inclination of the slope is absolutely interwoven and proportional to the slope of the S_1 technology curve. In the case where the max point of P_1 corresponds to the max (natural technology limit) of S_1, then the negative slope of P_1 after the max point will be steeper, since the core advantages will be depleted at an increasingly faster rate because of the technological impairment (and the fast rate thereof) of S_1. If the max point on P_1 corresponds to an upward moving part of curve S_1, namely, S_1' then again the Core Capabilities will tend to decrease (since technology S_2 takes its baby steps), but the fall will be slower, since technology S_1 has not reached its physical limit but simply converges to it.

6   points H to Z. The entire core competences have transformed to core rigidities. The core competences of continuously shifting dynamic and unstable environments, such as that of High Technology (and with a short product life cycle) can easily – with the passage of time – transform to an inhibitory factor for further innovative development. The core competences (which reflect to a large extend or/and comprise preference to existing – known technologies – routines – practices, the norms, values, culture and status) have created and consolidated a framework – a specific viewpoint for considering things which tends to treat through the same prism the new ones and other events. The "old" (and successful) recipe for success tries using the same mediums to perceive and interpret signals – ideas – events and convert them to materialized – useful – accepted innovation. Upon the passage of time and in the presence of an extremely dynamic environment, core competences are transubstantiated into core rigidities, they become, that is, a factor for voluntary disregard of even willful blindness. And needless to say, they correspond to negative performances.

7   points N and Θ. N is located on an upward part of curve P, while Θ on an downward one. They represent potential points of transition both to the new technology S_2, as well as to curve P_2. If N is projected on some point on P_2 before the chasm of P_2, then (and in the presence of the new framework for core competencies), the company begins the course afresh and always has to confront the chasm of P_2, while it has at the same time destroyed its core competences, while P_1 was still increasing (positive slope). On the other hand, however, it can be said that being the first company to launch the new technology, it will also reap the advantages of being the market herald (if, of course, it overcomes the chasm of P_2). If N is projected on a point on P_2, after the chasm, it enjoys the still–positively turning effects of the core competences on P_1 while not assuming the risk of the chasm (although it also is not

forged by it) and forfeiting the advantage of being the market's first mover. Regarding this advantage, it is manifestly more pertinent for High Tech markets, not only due to the short life cycle of the products, fast impairment and reliability issues, among others, but also due to the fact that as a follower, it may learn and readjust technology, utilizing the feedback generated by the competition and their actions. In other words, regardless of whether the market forerunner succeeds or fails, to implement expeditionary marketing's dogma without the risk of failure but also with smaller positive effects than if it would have attempted it itself.

With respect to Θ, we observe that based on its projection on P_2, the company will possibly become of the "me-too" type and that the transition to a new framework for core competences will be intra-corporately be easier since conditions will have matured (P_1 on the decline).

Finally it must be noted that transitioning from any point on P_1 to P_2 requires and presupposes the renunciation or even destruction of the existing (in P_1) core competences to an extend proportional to the distance of the point on P_1 from the horizontal axis. Of course, the existence of a golden section is not precluded, namely, the continuation of the course along the entire length of P_1 (or up to the point where there are positive economic results or clear reasons recommending this) and the simultaneous (with the contribution of resources) reconstitution of core competences and a course on P_2. Such a "portfolio" of core competences minimizes risk and ensures (as much as "ensures" can be valid in this context) sustainable leadership and development.

8   point M is the point of intersection between P_1 and P_2. It shows that the new technology has been introduced and has to a large extend replaced the old one. To the right of point M, the difference between the old and new framework for core competences tends to increase because of the simultaneous existence of a negative slope on P_1 and a positive one on P_2.

9   with respect to P_2, the preceding analysis and a respective comparison with a P_3 can be made. But its max point is higher than that of P_1 since (even given the positive magnitude of the effects of core competences) new technology S_2 has a higher performance than S_1; thus, based on the multiplicative relation between them (spiral), the performance of core competences (new ones) is respectively increased.

Finally, S curves represent the known technology curves, while the parallel lines on the time axis show the natural technological limit, namely, the point beyond which it would be impossible to improve the technology, even marginally. There is also a correspondence of the chasm with the discontinuity in the S curves, because of the fat that technology can also be abandoned due to factors which (largely) constitute technological uncertainty.

3   Integration

3.1 The role of marketing in High Tech enterprises and the importance of integration

3.1.1 The role of marketing in High Tech enterprises

> Marketing research: "When marketing visits the workplace of engineers to see what they are up to".
> Marketing: "What one devises, when he cannot sell his products".

As strange as it may sound, the quotes above are "jokes" made by engineers at the expense of the marketing department (Workman, 1993). Perhaps the principal role assigned to the marketing department is the role of the joining link and channel of communication between the company and its customer base. It is, in other words, the representation of the customer's voice inside the company. This voice is of vital importance, especially for High Tech companies, and it should not only be heard loud and clear but also be directly aligned to and collaborating with the knowledge borne by the R&D department. High tech enterprises must excel in two sectors: first, with respect to their ability to constantly innovate and, second, with respect to their ability to successfully transform such innovations to products which contribute to the satisfaction of customers' needs and preferences. If the role of marketing is to listen to customers' voices and their needs, but also to render the satisfaction thereof possible, a powerful marketing department entails a greater capacity for listening and wider pool of ideas to satisfy customers. Thus, a greater scope of application and combination of innovations so as for them to find useful applications. Song and Parry (1997) consider that High Tech enterprises must effectively combine the R&D and marketing departments if they wish to be successful. A great number of research papers accentuate the critical role of the effective and efficient contact between these two departments (indicatively Griffin, Abbie and Hauser [1996]; Gupta, Raj, and Wilemon [1986a; 1986b]; and Dutta, Shantanu, Narasimhan, and Rajiv [1999]).

3.1.2 Integration/obstacles to the integration of the marketing and R&D departments: a first approach

Integration of the marketing department with the R&D department

At its simplest, the concept of an organization can be described as the total of individuals possessing various skills and knowledge and governed by values, attitudes and beliefs and who can work either individually or collectively in order to fulfill the roles assigned to them. This, logically, presupposes the formation of a management hierarchy that holds the power and responsibility for attaining the objectives and goals. In order for this to be effectively implemented in a High Tech environment, management plans for not only the optimal size of its operational units but also the coordination requirements for the specialized, but at the same time interdependent, departments. Observations of the kind that "the marketing department rarely reports what types of products are needed, and when it does, it wants them ready by yesterday" or that "customers beg for the improvement of the edition of product x, but no one is working towards it" are so frequent as to be considered even trite. When things go well it is easier for someone to ignore the symptoms from the alienation of the departments, since all are engaged in the present and neglect to see the future, which seems to be at a distance. When the horizons are shortened and the accumulative results of turbulences become felt, then the weaknesses of the company's system block, or severely limit, the process of innovation, while they do so at the exact moment this is most needed.

From all the common grounds originating from the operating congress of the departments during the process of innovation, that called to match the product with a market is the most sensitive one. This "congress" or otherwise integration of the marketing and the R&D departments is considered to be of determinative importance, since the successful performance of common activities is rendered to be a very critical factor ensuring the short- to medium-term product offers.

Souder and Chahrabarti (1978) define integration as the symbiotic interrelation of two or more entities, which concludes to the production of clear benefits for them, that exceed the sum of the pure benefits produced by each entity in isolation. Lawrence and Lorsch (1967a), on the other hand, define integration as the process for acquiring a unification of the efforts by various subdepartments, aimed toward the attainment of the organizational objective. What appears to be common in both definitions is the emphasis placed on the result of integration, the additional benefit.

The approach to the contact between the R&D and marketing departments differs significantly between different businesses in different sectors. The ideal case, perhaps, would be for an uninterrupted and continuous contact, not subject to limitations and a clearly defined communication which would take place through steadily developed communication channels. After he describes the ideal degree of communication and the factors composing it, Millman (1982) observes that in reality, very few products and markets permit of such a degree of stability to be developed on the level of relations. Reality is closer to being in a constant state of changes with respect to products and markets, as are organizations themselves, as well as the individuals operating within them. In an effort to contribute to the knowledge of the obstacles posed because of the problematic communication between the marketing and R&D departments during the process for the development of innovative products, Millman makes the assumption that it is a joint responsibility of the marketing and R&D departments to become the guardians of the preservation of their good relations and to make efforts toward ensuring that all conflicts are resolved before they turn to a fixed characteristic of the way the company operates.

It is well known that a company is characterized by two dimensions of its operations; on account of them it may be classified as a closed system but, and at the same time, as an open one. With respect to the second characteristic, a company is considered to be an open system since it, by necessity, comes to contact with its external environment, to whose influences it is subjected. Despite the fact that the external environment comprises of factors which extended beyond the control of the organization, their composition, however, is a variable which must be constantly under the control of the company's officers, be interpreted by the company and feed the company with information and/or feedback. Most organizations claim to be aware of the environmental influences on them, but few are adequately prepared so as to effectively respond to their challenges and mandates. The overwhelming majority probably reacts to emerging customer needs instead of trying to predict them. And if it is some truth to the definition offered for Business Management, which designates as its objective the effective and efficient performance of the business's functions via its human resources, then it is also true that the organizations prepared to change, and that can offer sufficient incentives so as to align to this direction the entirety of the individuals composing the enterprise, will have a clear competitive advantage. Millman's list, focusing on British enterprises, is, to an extent, valid globally. It observes that marketing's lack of orientation and inefficient communication are the two key obstacles responsible for the noncompletion of an innovative product or the lack of its commercial exploitation and not the lack of innovative ideas or technical skills. Overemphasizing the R&D department without a simultaneous integration of marketing's philosophy from early on is the key ingredient responsible for wrong product launching times. Moreover, the extensive attention and focus on the technical features of the product offer instead of an integrated offer of these features as part of an integrated product idea solution responding to market needs are a second reason.

Besides, the multilevel nature of the innovative process has been widely misunderstood, since it results to drawing dividing lines, which, in a chainlike manner, are converted to obstacles during the development from the birth of an idea to a product and the launching of that product in the market. In order to speed up the launching process, executives frequently succumb to the temptation to cancel one or more stages of the development process, as Fotiadis and Haramis (2002) observed in the context of software development. This reflects a short-term horizon which occasionally – if not always – undermines commitment on the general level.

ACARD (1978) underlined that organizational problems, specialization and a lack of communication act decisively against innovation, as does brushing aside market views, arising either from the distancing of the R&D and marketing departments or because of the expectation that the new products will create new markets.

The US National Science Foundation (1973) directly criticized organizational practices, views and methods, while Mansfield (1969) used econometric analysis on technological innovation and observed that personality features, interests and education, among other characteristics in senior and executive management, play an important role for establishing the rate by which an organization will introduce innovation.

But it appears that there is no single optimal and ideal planning or easy way to attain integration. Certain companies seek their radical transformation by means of a small-scale restructuring and easing of the limitations established by the existence of intradepartmental borders. Unofficial communication – under these conditions – must be revitalized, and coordinating skills ought to be considered as an integral part of operating capacities.

Obstacles to integration

The "twin" obstacles of culture and professionalization are frequently cited in the literature discussing innovation. Shibutani (1995) observes that differences in the form of departments ensue from different contacts and association. Maintaining the social distance via the additional separation of operating departments or their disagreements or even the different bibliography, the survey led to the formation of different cultures. There are several cases where the fundamentals of marketing are so alien, where the lack of trust and fear of losing power and authority are so great, that they can cancel any effort to influence the R&D department. Clarke (1974) insightfully points out that marketing represents a different way of thinking – a different starting point, less accurate in its details with respect to predictions but more qualitative than that of the R&D department. It can incorporate and include both exotic notions, such as social behavior and attitudes, as well as making use of different terminology and constantly complicating the entire picture of technical (technological) thinking.

Many scholars and observers have suggested that the individuals staffing the R&D department are, to a large degree, preoccupied with expanding their knowledge and opportunities to carry out creative work. In many cases this acts as a counterbalance to any material or social benefits management may wish to offer as a reward. Raudsepp's surveys (1965) underline that when compensatory emoluments are absent or lacking, involvement or insistence on salary and other similar work factors gain increasing attention. The extreme adherence to work has undoubtedly led to a degree of introversion and reinforcement of the researcher's faith and trust to his or her direct research group and his or her profession and not the company that has hired him or her. Twiss (1974) further supports this view, by claiming that a technologist considers him- or herself to be principally a professional and not a businessperson. The technologist's education and natural inclinations allow him or her to associate with similar professionals from other companies while limiting his or her association and contact with other executives from the same company.

One of the problems, thus, emerging between the two departments is that, on one hand, in order for them to effectively handle the needs of the modern multi-dimensional and multivariate business environment and, indeed, the difficulties that distinguish High Tech environments, they must be allows to maintain their individual identity while, on the other hand and simultaneously, they must be encouraged to work together, abolishing the intellectual boundaries of specialization or difference in culture, in order to efficiently move toward the attainment of the common objective. It is, essentially, a hunt to find the golden section between integration and separation.

As the orientation of companies increasingly approaches the acceptance of marketing's philosophy, the common prospects of marketing and R&D departments must be expanded while there must also be an overlap of their activities, up to a point. Millman recommends that the two groups must approach one another, via the establishment of joint service common objectives for the groups.

Throughout the course of the innovative process there are many parameters that may hinder and threat both the commitment of the groups as well as the commercial launching of the products. This is, to a degree, expected, as companies making significant investments in the R&D department now try to place itself closer to the market, having denounced its pure and sealed technological orientation. Although it is not necessary for this transition to be smooth, if it is not, however, it will signify that more attention must be paid to information flow and the management of these common grounds of activity.

Managerial decisions are made in a context of imperfect knowledge of technology, markets and human behavior. While some executives perceive that obstacles to innovation are also and equally imperfectly understood.

In modern markets, most companies must implant the collaboration between the marketing and R&D departments. In the primary forms of economic organization, knowledge was centrally held by the business unit, which was identified with an individual who combined the knowledge of what was needs with how he or she could develop it. The feedback from the market was direct, fact and convincing. This may happen even today, provided the size of business units is small enough to permit it.

Unavoidably, the evolution of companies frequently demands the separation of roles and the establishment of marketing and R&D departments, with specialized functions, which, by necessity, create a distance between these departments. This distance increases as the specialization of the departments is developed. The ensuing decrease in the communication, even the contact between the departments causes a decrease (at least proportionally) of their capacities to combine their specialized skills and, in a chain reaction, cause a reduction in the ability of the company to launch successful products.

Both the marketing and the R&D department provide inflows for many company activities, some of which are very critical for the survival success of the enterprise. Figure 3.1 attempts to depict the competences-activities of the departments in a way that includes both the more apparently defined joint competences-objectives as well as the points of reference for their autonomous activities that are more departmentally controlled. In the latter, the dominant role belongs to the department in question, with the other one acting as an ancillary with a consulting – in theory – role, which is only fragmentary activated (at irregular intervals) and only when the organization faces a crisis.

It is easy to understand and especially, but not exclusively, in a High Tech environment, the creation of new products cannot be considered to be either static or the independent variable of the activities–skills–knowledge–actions of the one or the other department. Both departments' responsibilities to contribute (and clearly to provide a combining skill) evolve as new technologies become feasible, consumers' tastes and preferences shift and the competition launches new products, as well as limitations posed by the environment or governments also change. As Child (1972) and Hage (1980) observe, there is a constant flow of resources, materials, information and technical specialization across the borders of the two operating departments so that product development be rendered possible.

The need for the effective management of these flows between the marketing and R&D departments has been acknowledged as important in the 1970s, and thus, researchers like Child (1972), Mintzberg (1979) and Khandwlla (1972) began working on it. The management of the contact point was considered critical during the 1980s and continued to be significant for the successful course of the company since then. Businesses experienced emphatically intense competitive pressures pushing them to deduce new product development times, to attain a greater rate of success in launching new products and to achieve all this with a smaller waste of resources. Many organizations adopted structures with fewer levels of hierarchy, intra-collaborating teams and inter-associating managerial processes.

Booz, Allen and Hamilton (1968), as well as Lawrence and Lorsch (1969), point out the many obstacles for the attainment of collaboration–communication between marketing and R&D. As a result, empirical research, such as that carried out by Moenaert and Souder (1990a), has established that disharmony is the rule rather than the exception in the relations between marketing and R&D departments.

Obstacles due to personality differences

Researchers such as Garroad and Garroad (1982) and Lucas and Bush (1988) have found that there are inherent personality differences between the personnel of the two departments. There is evidence that such differences are due to a natural interpersonal distance between the marketing and R&D departments.

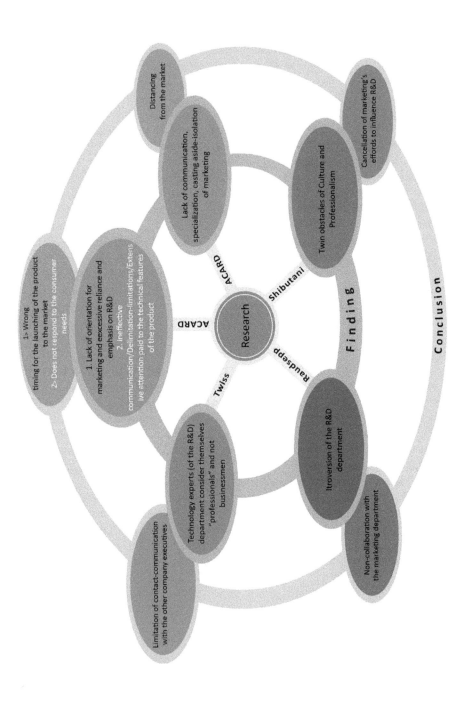

Figure 3.1 Researchers – findings and their consequences

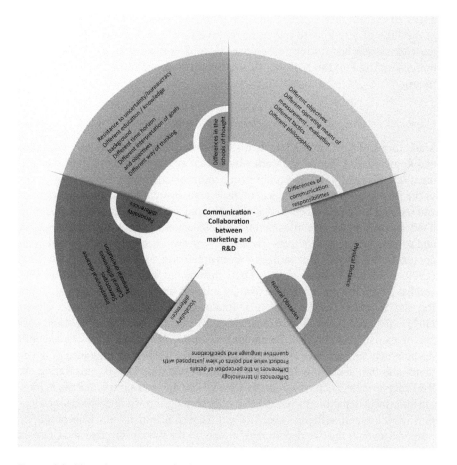

Figure 3.2 Obstacles to communication–collaboration between marketing and R&D

The heads of the marketing and R&D departments were found to converge with respect to several of their habits while differences were detected on the level of their time orientation.

Furthermore, this difference was observed irrespective of whether the marketing and R&D departments were integrated within the company or not. Despite this, cultural differences have been one of the most frequently identified obstacles to the collaboration of the two departments. This implies that the real obstacle may be an obscuring of perception because of stereotypes and not differences of personalities. When there are such obstacles they may also raise higher walls between the teams, even if such stereotypes have not been documented and are not grounded in reality. If one or the other team believes in them, this, in itself, can be an obstacle to mutual understanding.

Due to the fact that many of the obstacles attributed to personality differences or stereotypes can become the mightiest obstacles to communication in the face of attempts to lessen or remove them, as noted by Block (1977), their existence has turned researchers to look for mechanisms that improve understanding and the building of trust and communication between the two functions.

Obstacles attributed to different schools of thought

Marketing and R&D executives frequently differ with respect to their education and knowledge background. Marketing executives usually come from management schools, while R&D executives are engineers. The educational background of the first focuses on solving general problems, by combining data and intuition and seeking to attain success in business. An engineering background, on the other hand, focuses on the scientific method of making assumptions and checking them and solving technical problems. These "worldviews" are further reinforced in the context of the operating departments in an enterprise, as it is noted by Dougherty (1990, 1992) and Douglas (1987). These differences were first published in 1967 and have been documented since then by scholars and researchers such as Gupta, Raj and Wilemon (1986a; 1986b), Zeithalm and Zaithalm (1984) and Galbrath (1977). The worldview of marketing executives tends toward the short-term horizon of a small-scale project. Technologists, on the other hand, focus on scientific development and are true to their scientific nature while their tolerance of uncertainty and bureaucracy is lower. Although not manifest in every marketing and R&D department, such observations are a visible fact and signify that the marketing and R&D departments run the risk of becoming limited and self-defined and, thus, develop self-sufficient societies within which to exist. As Duncan (1972) observes, even if the two departments are inside the same enterprise and share the same organizational objectives, the prism through which each department interprets these objectives differs.

Moreover, distinct and different ways of thinking entail possible difficulties in the understanding by the other department of the goals, solutions and mutual concessions or trade-offs that each department makes. In order for collaboration to be possible, there must be an understanding of the way the other department thinks.

Obstacles due to vocabulary

As the two distinct schools of thought evolve so are the verbal obstacles between them. The marketing department has and employs its own terminology, as does R&D. Marketing professionals speak in terms of product value and perceivable positions. The R&D ones speak in the quantitative language of specifications and performance. When there is no efficient communication, consumer needs and the engineering solutions to satisfy them become disconnected, despite each group thinking that they are talking about the same thing. Even small divergences in vocabulary frequently signify very different solutions and frequently are the difference between a successful product and a failure, as Griffin and Hauser (1993) observe.

The two groups differ even on the level of detail. If each group does not understand consumer needs on that level of detail necessary for it to perform its duty, then the process of communication will result in disappointment.

Obstacles due to communication responsibilities

Organizational obstacles are created due to different priorities with respect to goals and responsibilities, as Cooper (1990), Dougherty (1992) and Singh, Reve and Stern (1983) observe, different means for measurement that do not abet integration (market share vs number of patents, as noted by Khandwalla [1972]), and differences with respect to the perceived "legitimacy" of product development that Dougherty and Heller (1994) have suggested. And while these factors are clearly controlled by senior management, the organizational change to eradicate such obstacles can pose obstacles itself. Midlevel executives who have reached that point in their careers based on the previously held criteria must now learn the different rules of the game in order to continue their ascent in the company's ranks. Since they have been "integrated" while also succeeding via the old system, many are hesitant to make the change to the new organizational tactics and philosophies. This confusion can cause a resistance to any "aliens" to the department and thus dampen the collaboration between the marketing and R&D departments.

Physical obstacles

Allen (1986) has observed that the possibility that two people will communicate at least once a week dramatically decreases if the physical distance between their offices is more than 10 meters (by 10%). When marketing and R&D are located in different cities there is clearly less interpersonal communication, even using modern technology. Distance reduces chance encounters, the transfer of information or the clearing of issues, even if such take place around the coffeemaker.

Great distances render face to face contact between the two teams extremely difficult and lead to delays in decision making. The isolation entrenches the different ways of thinking, while encouraging the evolution of a specialized and distinct vocabulary, facilitates short-circuits and, ultimately, accentuates perceptions on personality differences.

Griffin and Houser (1992), combining the finding ensuing from the obstacles cited earlier, and with the assumption that the communication between the marketing and R&D departments is a key factor for new product development and the increase of sales, assume that such obstacles must either be eradicated or decreased in order for the company to achieve long-term profitability.

The conclusions of research by Garroad and Garroad (1982) and Moenaert and Souder (1992) support that, ultimately, the degree of integration between marketing and R&D needed depends on the environment the company is active and product development takes place.

3.2 Presentation – analysis of integration models

3.2.1 Integration as a factor of perceived environmental uncertainty and the strategy on innovation

According to Souder and Moenaert (1992), every innovative process inherently includes four kinds of uncertainty. These are technological uncertainty, which refers to the optimum choice of technology to be adopted for use; the uncertainty relating to consumer needs; the uncertainty driven by competitive product offers with the same target audience; and, ensuing from these three discussed earlier, the uncertainty with respect to the allocation of resources, in order to reduce the first three. More specifically, they claim that resource uncertainty is composed of human, financial and technical resources that ought to be committed/allocated in the best possible way. Human resources uncertainty relates to the selection of the type of personnel that will staff the R&D or/and marketing department, its skills and the uncertainties relating to the appropriate engineering and processing capacities or even the uncertainty as to whether the innovative process will muster appropriate support from the higher levels of management.

The financial uncertainty relates to securing the funds that will be deployed for the development of the innovation, while technical uncertainty regards the needs in infrastructure necessary to develop the innovation. The uncertainties composed and which relate to the resources of subsets of those just cited can also constitute factors delaying critical decision making while, in a chain reaction, leading to ignoring and not exploiting opportunities, especially when the innovation game is played in an arena that is a turbulent and volatile environment with intense competition and rapidly obsolescent technologies. It must be stressed, as Jauch and Kraft (1986) acknowledge, that while the three kinds of uncertainty (technological, competition and consumer) are considered to originate from outside the company, resource uncertainty originates from within.

Consumer and technological uncertainty can be considered to be the two most significant sources of uncertainty principally because they positively affect the other two kinds of uncertainty. A positive correlation exists also between resource and competition uncertainty, with the first being dependent on the second. Scholars have suggested that the more an organization decreases the gap between necessary and existing informing, the more, that is, the uncertainty relating to technology, competition, resources and consumers is minimized, the better the likelihood for the financial success of the new innovative product.

The decrease of the uncertainty with respect to the preceding factors can be measured in two dimensions, the qualitative and the quantitative. The quantitative dimension measures the volume of informing, while the qualitative measures the accuracy, compatibility and, therefore, utility of information depending on its pursued objective. High-quantity and low-quality reduction of uncertainty entails that the organization holds basic knowledge across a wide spectrum of issues, while the converse means deep knowledge of isolated topics. The goal is, of course, the deep and wide enrichment of the information available to the organization. As the gap between the desired and necessary and the attained level

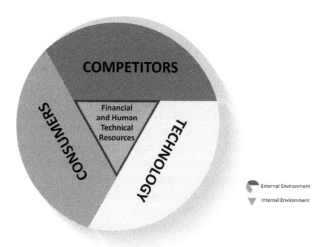

Figure 3.3 Uncertainties and the environments that activate them

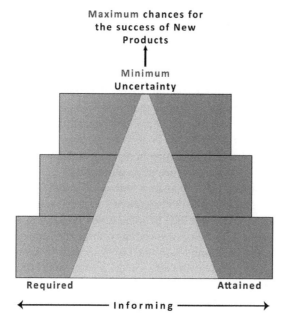

Figure 3.4 The critical role of informing as a factor for the success of innovative (High Tech) products

of informing is bridged, the more successful the innovative effort will become, as was observed by Tushman and Nadler (1978).

The basic theme of most models Saren (1984) calls "hybrid" and which have been proposed by, among others, Crawford (1983), Miaoulis and LaPlaca (1982),

Hisrich and Peters (1978) relates to the transformation of ideas to marketable products. These models include levels of activities as well as decision gates (hence their characterization as hybrids). The activities included in these models can be considered as distinct information-processing activities, while decision gates reflect the formal choices made by enterprises with respect to the activities which affect the flow of information between activities.

Souder (1987) suggests that innovation groups can be considered as work groups, the members of which perform specialized and operationally designated roles. Major empirical studies performed by Cooper (1979a; 1979b); Maidique and Zirger (1984); Rothwell, Freeman, Horlsey, Jervis, Robertson and Townsend (1974); Souder (1987); and Souder and Chahrabarti (1979) have demonstrated that the integration of operationally specialized functions and, in particular, the functions of the marketing and R&D departments, is a necessary condition without which there cannot be success for innovation.

It becomes increasingly clear that the concepts of the specialization (differentiation) of the departments and integration are more complementary than competing. Indeed, in order to succeed in an innovation, the existence of both differentiation and integration are necessary, which is also supported by Lawrence and Lorsch (1967a, 1967b), Schneider (1987) and Souder (1987). Differentiation is essentially the division of the organizational system to subsystems. It is necessary since the ability of the organization to optimize the individual's goals that need to be attained is the result of specialization. On the other hand, integration, being a symbiotic relation, is deemed to be the necessary bridge between the specialized parts, which work toward the direction of the innovative product.

In other words, the term *integration* regards the strategic pairing of the operationally specialized departments while their individual orientation is maintained. Its objective is not to dismantle the operational specialization of either the R&D or the marketing department. In the context of its objectives is to stir up eagerness for collaboration and coordination in making strategic decisions and actions which are essential for the emergence of an innovation.

According to Souder (1987), human resources allocated to a particular project are called to play specific roles with reference to these activities (where a role is the anticipated behavior ascribed to some given position in an organization). Thus, for the purpose of decreasing uncertainty, these roles are connected to a list of information with which individuals must work in order to decrease uncertainty. Thus, all the people who have officially – in the context of the organization – been called to complete a project constitute a work group.

Technological innovation is an amalgam and result of information-processing activities by almost all operational departments. Consequently, the roles that these departments are called to play are, too, operationally designated and the innovation work group is composed of operationally specialized subdepartments. According to Kotler (1984), the role of the marketing department includes analysis, planning, application and control of programs that have been designed to create, build and maintain useful relations and exchanges with the targeted markets so as to attain the organizational objectives. The role of the R&D department includes

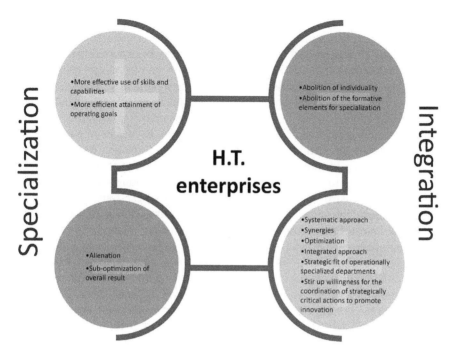

Figure 3.5 Specialization and integration

the development of scientific-technological know-how and its applications so as to attain the organizational objectives. Thus, the marketing department's staff is responsible for most of the information relating to users' needs and the provision of a major part of the information relating to competitors and resources. The corresponding and anticipated obligations of the R&D department include the provision information on available technologies as well as those used by the competition. One may observe that this is a natural consequence of the operational differentiation, which determines the type of information held and processed by the members of the organization and by organizational subdepartments. Resting on the roles of the marketing and R&D departments one may safely draw the conclusion that they constitute the main factors of technological innovation. According to Schneider (1987), as well as to Lawrence and Lorsch (1967a), it is differentiation that creates the need for integration. This can be understood since market information is unknown to the R&D department while, at the same time, the marketing department has no access to technological data. Thus, the marketing and R&D departments become the providers of known information to those departments that, on account of their operating roles, do not have access to, and, correspondingly, the recipients of information from those departments having access, on account of their duties, such information, thus alternating between these two roles, the roles of the provider and the recipient of critical and necessary information. Therefore, in the course of the innovative process arises the phenomenon of a retrospective interdependence, which is manifested precisely because these types of information and the flow thereof subsist throughout the process of innovation (Thompson, 1967). In this light it can only be expected for integration to play a determinative role in the performance of innovation, as Cheng (1983) points out. Ames (1968) sums things up by suggesting that, ultimately, the high degree of customer orientation expected from industries brings integration and operational interdependence between the R&D and marketing departments to the foreground, as critical variables for such enterprises. By means of communicating information the members of the group disclose information and disseminate knowledge to the other members. Individuals, of course, do not share information only with the members of the people that form the operating subgroup to which they belong but also with other operating subgroups. The transfer of information is rendered the vehicle that caters so that the individuals participating in the organization can have access to the already-acquired information.

An innovation group can be considered also as a self-sufficient communication network, where each participating individual can be considered as a knowledge pool. Should further information be required for the proper fulfillment of the role of an individual in this group, then he or she will logically go to some other member of the same group in order to get said information while minimizing the effort to acquire it. Correspondingly, if an individual of the group considers that he or she holds knowledge – information that is useful to some other member – it is very plausible to assume that he or she will decide to share such information and knowledge.

A two-stage model has been the focus of theories on the organizational adoption of innovation: The first stage is the starting point, the launching stage if you like, while the second relates to implementation. During the first stage all information that is necessary to evaluate the innovation are collected, and the decision to develop said innovation is, subsequently, made while the second stage sees the performance of those activities which are necessary in order for the innovation to become an operating reality (Rogers, 1983).

This two-stage process can be also expanded to relate to the process for the development of a technologically innovative product by the company. The value of this framework of the two-stage process for the study of integration between the marketing and R&D departments in the context of the process for innovative products development has been suggested by Souder and Moenaert (1990a; 1990b). They define the starting stage as the stage for the planning and design of an innovative product and the application stage as the stage of its development. During the planning and design stage, the organization aims to differentiate the idea of the product to be developed and decide whether the company will invest resources in this idea. If it will, then the organization moves to the second stage, which includes the interpretation of the product idea to the product. The activities that take place at this stage aim to the development of both the product as well as the subsequent marketing strategy that will be employed.

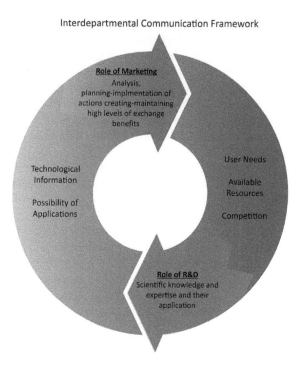

Interdepartmental Communication Framework

Figure 3.6 Marketing–R&D communication channel

A survey by Victor and Blackburn (1987) suggests two variables that that uncertainty depends on

> [v]ariability which refers to the number of special cases one comes against during the fulfilment of an objective and analysability which refers to the degree by which the processes determining the sequence of steps that must be made for the fulfilment of an objective are known. If now, technological innovation is considered in the light of reducing uncertainty, then variability refers to the volume and rate at which uncertainty arises. analysability reflects the degree by which there are processes to detect and reduce uncertainty. Since technological innovative products can be considered as a process for reducing uncertainty, then it logically follows that the degree of variability and analysability will change during the life cycle of the project. And since the basic characteristic of a technological innovation is change, then both analysability and variability are subject to changes. Thus, from the perspective of reducing uncertainty, the key challenge to be addressed is, then, to acknowledge, to the maximum permissible degree, the relative potential uncertainty (namely, to decrease variability) and to identify the tools for reducing it (namely to increase analysability).

Perrow (1967) created a matrix with analyzability and variability as its dimensions and with levels of intensity for each dimension, creating four possible combinations of high/low variability/analyzability.

Reducing variability and increasing analyzability during the course of the life of a project are key conditions for successful technological innovation. The goal is to transition from a relatively low analyzability and relatively high variability to the opposite on both variables. The wider the horizon of knowledge and informing for the company, the smaller the number of ensuing unknown constituents. In parallel, the organization needs to discover or choose the tools and processes to reduce uncertainty.

By means of the communication and conveyance of information between the R&D and marketing departments during the design stage there will be a significant contribution in reducing variability also assisting in the identification of the appropriate tools and processes.

Silver, Cohen and Rainwater (1988) suggest that the contribution of knowledge is greater at the early stages of an innovation. These are usually characterized by high perceived variability and low analyzability. As a greater volume of informing unfolds, variability decreases while analyzability increases. The challenge here is to decrease variability and increase analyzability at the design stage. This will minimize the emergence of unpleasant surprises at the development stage. Moreover, it clarifies what should take place at the development stage.

Resting on the previous discussion, Souder and Moenaert (1990a, b) suggest that the success of innovative technological products is characterized by the maximum reduction of variability and the maximum increase of analyzability during the planning stage.

According to the preceding proposition, the most efficient teams would achieve both conditions. Should such attitude be characterized as efficient risk reduction, then surely its attainment would have not been possible without communication between the marketing and R&D departments.

According to Hauptman (1986) there are two types of information. One can be considered as the type of "innovative information", namely, the kind of information that would be useful for the solution of problems and regards information relating to experimental, analytical and explanatory efforts carried out for the development of the product. The second type is "coordinative" information, what March and Simon (1998) consider as the system that activates interdependent activities and refers to that information which regards works and schedules assigned to the members of the team as well as information relating to its expected result. Hauptman's research was carried out in the software development department of ICL and suggests that "information needs depend on the type of work performed".

Communication oriented toward coordination can be more key than the communication of innovative information for reasons more structured and resting on a fixed and mature technology. These are the objectives found at the lower end of the scope of the R&D department and which are represented by technical services and possible software development. They do not require a great scope of technical specialization for the optimum performance.

Hauptman's typology of information is judged to be very useful by Souder and Moenaert. According to what was discussed earlier, the transfer of coordinating information becomes more important during the development stage. If, for example, the marketing and R&D departments have agreed on an agenda of information at the planning and design stage, then the development stage can be devoted to the exclusive application of the selected tools and processes in order to reduce the identified uncertainty. But this is rarely the case, since new uncertainties emerge and the relations between the two departments need to be redefined based on the new data in order to be optimally coordinated. However, since there was an effective reduction of uncertainties during the planning and design stage and, provided variability was reduced to its minimum and analyzability increased to its maximum, then Souder and Moenaert (1990) expect the need for the intradepartmental transfer of innovative information to go back to its normal level.

One must also point out the fact that the communication of an excessive amount of innovative information contains the risk to create counter-economies (or, alternatively, negative economies), since it acts as the starting signal to restart the process and the, logically entailed by its, redefinition of new products/markets/technologies combinations. This is a good reason for what Souder calls the "too-good friends syndrome" in the contact of the marketing and R&D departments to be negatively associated with the success of innovation. Namely, the net result of the constant exchange of innovative information between the two departments and the absence of constant challenges with respect to judgment by both departments with respect to the other will be negative.

Thus, in summary one can claim that it is not the conveyance of information, in itself, that will lead to the further decrease of uncertainty, since each stage has its own requirements on informing. While Souder and Moenaert (1990) assume that the operational decrease of uncertainty at the planning and design stage is more closely associated with the exchange of innovative information between the two departments, the role of the influence of the exchange of coordinating information is upgraded at the development stage. And while there is no ceiling on the exchange of coordinating information, there is both a floor and a ceiling for innovative ones: An excessive rate of transfer will delay important decision making and act dilatorily to the taking of action, while, on the other hand, too low a rate can become an obstacle to perceiving changes in the market, the technological environment, the competitive one or even the resource environment.

Based on the preceding claims, and their corresponding documentation, Souder and Moenaert (1990) formulate the three following assertions:

- The effective reduction of uncertainty at the planning and design stage is positively associated with the exchange of innovative information, and to a lesser degree with the conveyance of coordinating information between the marketing and R&D departments.

- If the decrease of uncertainty at the planning and design stage was efficient, then the decrease of uncertainty is positively associated with the exchange of coordinating information between the departments and in an inverse *U* shape with the exchange of innovative information. While if the decrease of uncertainty was not optimal during the planning and design stage, then the decrease of uncertainty will be positively associated both with coordinating and innovative information exchanged between the two departments.
- Whatever the decrease of uncertainty at the planning and design stage, there is a starting point for the exchange of innovative information at the development stage. Beyond this staring point, the results of the exchange of innovative information with respect to the reduction of uncertainty become negative.

In the case where the organization is engaged in a framework for the development of radical innovations, with new and unknown technologies and/or is moving toward unknown markets, then the degree of variability increases and analyzability, correspondingly, decreases, even in the case where an efficient strategy for reducing uncertainty has been adopted. A learning process must subsequently be developed in order to enrich the existing body of knowledge. Consequently, the desired changes in the magnitudes of variability and analyzability will come about more slowly, leading to the following conclusion:

- The smaller the degree of familiarity of the company with the technology or/and the market, the longer the interval needed to reduce variability and increase analyzability will be.

The complementarity of operating principles is a key concept for data processing activities. The transfer of information between the marketing and R&D departments must serve convergence for reducing uncertainty, namely, the degree by which the members of the group developing the innovation share the same objective goal and act complementary to the activities aimed to reduce uncertainty.

Convergence can be broken down into two subsets: convergence within the departments (interdepartmental) and intradepartmental convergence. In order to perform its maximum, convergence must be attained in both dimensions. According to Souder (1987), the diffusion of data and information on the project frequently leads to creative synergies: Each department offers its own pieces to the puzzle of innovation. The allocation of knowledge, data and perceptions is the basis for establishing the roles of each group and determining the areas in which each can best perform. The transfer of information nourishes mutual understanding on the roles of others and, consequently, assists the determination of what is expected by each one.

Rogers and Kincaid (1981) observe that convergence is a dynamic process. The attainment of convergence is a critical factor at both stages of the innovation. The convergence of objectives and assumption of complementary activities will guide the operational reduction of uncertainty, while both intra- and interdepartmental convergence will lead, according to Souder and Chakrabarti (1980), to the improvement of decision making and better implementation of innovative programs.

According to Souder and Moenaert it is expected and inter-/intradepartmental convergence at the planning–design stage to be dependent primarily on the exchange of innovative information. The members participating in the project team at this stage must synchronize and fine-tune each other's knowledge. If the reduction of uncertainty was satisfactory at the planning–design stage, then inter-/intradepartmental convergence will be established via the exchange of coordination information, where the members of the project team are called, at the development stage, to synchronize their activities. When one moves to the development stage the need to exchange innovative information is clearly reduced, and may even become counterproductive. The preceding results to the following:

- The decrease of uncertainty by the marketing and R&D departments and success during the planning and design and the development stage are positively associated with the degree of inter- and intradepartmental convergence.
- Inter- and intradepartmental convergence between the marketing and R&D departments in order to decrease uncertainty is positively associated with the transfer of knowledge at the planning and design stage and the transfer of coordinating informing during the stage of the development of innovation.

The diversity of integration mechanisms in the literature can be grouped into three categories: The determination of tasks (1) refers to the designation and scheduling of tasks that must be completed by the team. Different roles and activities are designed, planned and coordinated from the beginning. The transfer points are accurately designated and operating roles become clear. Consequently, the determination of tasks is, as Katz and Kahn (1966) point out, a useful tool to make the roles performed in a system of roles formal. The roles established provide to the participants in the organization that general framework which can be utilized for the establishment and consolidation of planned coordination. The inherently tumultuous environment of technological change can undermine the success of the objectives pertaining to the determination of tasks, as Galbraith (1973) and Moenaert and Souder (1990a) have observed. Organizational structural planning (2) includes those activities that must be performed for the adjustment or change of the organization's structure. It is, perhaps, the most widely accepted mechanism.

Structural approaches can be generally included in two categories: those that expand the boundaries and those that abolish them altogether. In the case of expanded boundaries, operational differentiation is maintained. The abolition of the boundaries presupposes and includes redefining the boundaries for the subsystems based on the results. In other words, and as Galbraith (1973) and March and Simon (1958) observe, autonomous tasks are created. Of all the coordinating structures presented and successfully tested, such as, for example, job rotation, the establishment of multifunctional groups, the designation of intradepartmental representatives and others, Young's duos, namely, the combination of a researcher and a marketer, who work simultaneously, autonomously and jointly, is a particularly effective mechanism. Souder and Moenaert (1990) claim that a nomological approach that takes account of the environments prevailing in the market and technology, the relative cost for each method and the level of particularity of both customers and development teams is the most efficient way to organize technological innovation, a point also raised by Gibson, Ivancevich and Donnelly (1985), while, as Rogers and Agarwala Rogers (1976) observe, climate orientation is the method that aims to promote the awareness of the coordination and integration between various functions.

The "arrangement" of the organizational climate (3) is perhaps the most effective mechanism. Factors such as extroversion, harmony and trust support the integration of the R&D and marketing departments and activities promoting such conditions, consequently, effectively promote the purpose of integration. The key responsibility for the creation of such a climate lies with senior management and the heads of the marketing and R&D departments.

Another variable that must be checked if one is to attain the objective of influencing the performance of the project's teams is the intradepartmental flow of information. At the planning and design stage, the organization must maximize the flow of innovative information, while during development, it must pursue to maximize the exchange of coordinating information and limit the flow of innovative. All three mechanisms cited earlier assist integration. The questions that arise, given the interactions between the types of information, the stages and the success of the innovation, are whether the effectiveness of integration mechanisms is feasible at the development stage and what type of information is most needed for it.

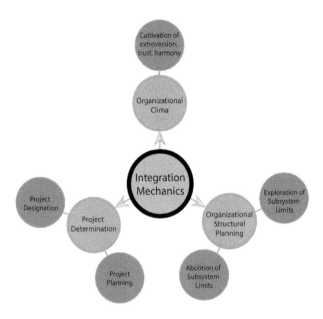

Figure 3.7 Integration mechanics

With respect to the formality of the relations, views are widely contrasting. Several researchers, such as Moenaert and Souder (1990a) feel that the existence of formal structure in relations is positively associated with intradepartmental communication, and the use of information (a position advanced by Deshpande and Zaltman [1987]; John and Martin [1984]; Gupta and Wilemon [1988]; and Moenaert and Souder [1990b]) while others suggest the existence of a negative relation between formality and innovation [Hage and Aiken, 1967]) and intrade-partmental innovation (Hage, Aiken and Barrett, 1971). Souder and Moenaert (1990) feel that the contradictory findings by surveys are the result of differences in the analytical viewpoint adopted on each occasion and possibly tend toward the adoption of a golden section, designated as the balance between the codification and the autonomy of work, a position also accepted by Baker, Winkofsky, Langmeyer and Sweeney (1980). At the design stage, the relation between formality and the success of design activities would be graphically represented as an inverted *U*; namely, the lower level of formality pushes the staff engaged in the project to interact while a great degree of formality could prove counterproductive, slowing down and dampening desired behavior. If uncertainty has been decreased, then the critical factor during the development stage would be the availability of coordinating information. If the reduction of uncertainty was satisfactory during the design stage, then innovative information ought to be limited. A greater analyzability would entail that the project's team can rest on structured knowledge and logical analysis in order to gain more knowledge. On the contrary, the team must rest on processes stemming from its inventiveness so that it may acquire more knowledge. The preceding leads to the formulation of the following proposition:

• Success at the design stage is connected with the degree of formality in an inverted-U relation. If the reduction of uncertainty was satisfactorily efficient during the design stage, then formal structures contribute more toward the successful outcome of the development stage than less formal relations. But if uncertainty was not satisfactorily decreased during design, then a medium-sized formality in structures would be the contributing the most at the development stage.

The preceding proposition is in no way intended to degrade the utility of the existence of informal structures and communication channels or the development of informal interpersonal relations. Souder and Moenaert (1990) claim that the use of interpersonal and informal channels will contribute more at the design, rather than the development, stage. Informal interpersonal communication channels tend to respond better when the needs for information are placed in an environment characterized by high uncertainty. This supports the view that an informal centralist structure will be useful at the design stage. On the contrary, the development of an informal face-to-face contact may create "local" convergence.

Souder and Moenaert (1990) observe that behavior diverging from the assigned roles contributes more toward success at the design stage than at the development one.

As individuals diverge from the sealed confines of their assigned roles, a behavior reinforced by the low formality of structures or, correspondingly, by the decentralized structure of the organization, existing structures become more flexible and free and allow access to other operational activities, thus permitting awareness and understanding of the existence of other, different roles. It is obvious that this caters for the exchange of innovative information. Souder and Moenaert (1990) complete their theoretical framework by formulating the following propositions:

- Decentralization contributes more to the success of the design phase than of the development one. Provided the decrease of uncertainty was successful at the design stage, then law decentralization assists success more during development than decentralization. In the opposite case, a medium state of decentralization is the desired one.
- The force (cohesion) of the communication link between the operating heads contributes more to success at the development stage than at the design one.
- The allocation of competent personnel contributes more to success at the design stage than at the development one.
- The intradepartmental flow of human resources will contribute more to success at the design than at the development stage.
- The prevailing climate (harmony, trust, extroversion) is more important at the design stage than at the development one.

The view adopted considers that a decrease in the four types of uncertainties is positively related with the success of innovation. The goals and works of marketing and R&D are subject to two variables, variability and analyzability. Innovation can be divided into two stages, the (planning–) design stage and the development stage. At the design stage, the conveyance of innovative information reduces variability and increases analyzability. Intradepartmental information exchange creates a convergence between the two groups, that is, pushes toward this mutual goal, which positively relates to the decrease of uncertainty and the successful outcome of the project. The result of integration is more positive, since it produces synergies, than is the aggregate of the individual efforts by the departments, while it also includes the continuous decrease of variability and increase of analyzability. Intradepartmental communication also improves convergence on the level of roles. Demands on information are differentiated depending on the stage of project development. Thus, at the design stage the project is more dependent on the exchange of innovative information, while the development stage requires more coordinating information. Should variability have been effectively decreased at the design stage while analyzability has been sufficiently increased, then the exchange of coordinating information will contribute to the decrease of uncertainty and will maintain and/or improve the convergence of the departments. If variability has not been adequately decreased and/or analyzability has not been sufficiently increased at the design stage, then the development stage will depend on the exchange of both innovative as well as coordinating information. However, an excessive flow of innovative information at this stage is counterproductive.

The flow of both forms of information can be structured in the most efficient manner via the determination of the project, organizational planning and climate orientation.

The primary role of the design stage ought to be stressed. The great importance of the integration of the marketing and R&D departments from early on and the clarity in defining the problem are obvious. The framework suggests that group activity must focus on identifying uncertainty and finding the tools to reduce it.

During the development stage, a more formal and centralized structure is recommended.

The critical role of the design stage is stressed. The discerning difference between success and failure is deemed to be the magnitude of the fundamental analysis of development activities before the development stage and the uncovering of surprises and new ingredients, that are expected to characterize an innovation, at the design stage. Consequently, information flows must be maximized across all levels at the design stage of an innovative product.

Despite the fact that formality can become an obstacle to innovative behavior, the existence, however, of even a very small degree of it is deemed to be necessary. This means that the management of innovation requires an implementation of the codification of work which favors adaptability on the level of the subproject.

An appropriate strategy would be to set and place goals, in the form of the joint development of a technological strategic plan inside the organization and to use an organizationally adjusted plan for the development of new products.

The implementation of this strategy increases intradepartmental communication while simultaneously leaving a lot of room for innovative behavior. Furthermore, it is considered that such types, for the formalization of structures, do not block informal communication and interpersonal relations, nor do they deter out of role behavior. They provide a platform for the different parts to meet and promote the exchange of ideas and information.

Finally, during the development stage, an approach demanding the existence of a connecting communication link between the heads of the departments makes possible the sufficient yet not excessive or inadequate exchange of coordinating information between the two departments.

In the earlier discussion on uncertainties and the role they play in the process of the development of innovation for a new technological product, one more variable can be added: the nature of the force that offers the impetus and starting signal for innovation and the identity of the individual who initiates the process certainly constitute determinative factors for both the innovative process and its success. Rubenstein, Chakrabarti, O' Keefe, Souder and Young (1976), observe that the driving force and the identity of the individual that sets the innovation in motion jointly determine the success of the innovation. This implies that there is a powerful connecting ring providing potential access to some of the forms of uncertainty and this particular uncertainty is largely deadened.

With respect to the identity of the individual or team that initiates, even spearheads, the process of innovation, it has been found that ideas, the conception and the formation, of which began in the marketing department, result, in most cases, to successful products than those borne in the R&D department or "ordered" by senior management. Indeed, according to Souder (1983), the reason this happens is because it is obvious that an idea for a product born in the thought-framework of the marketing department has been shaped and influenced, to a major extent, either from listening to consumer needs or as an effective response to the challenges posed by competitors and their product offers.

If, on the other hand, the idea is initiated inside the R&D department, then it might possibly be a reaction to a technological opportunity which, however, is not directly or indirectly or obviously connected to some needs that have been expressed by consumers. If the idea originates from senior executive management and given that three kinds of uncertainty originate from the external environment, the situation gets worse.

A key conclusion from the thoughts above is that technological products structured and developed based on the knowledge of market needs or as a response to competition inherently have better chances at succeeding than do the products that capitalize on a technological opportunity. Of course, one should never underestimate the importance of technological opportunities and knowledge. The high degree of positive association between technological trailblazing and ability for technical but also commercial success has been documented by the research by Souder (1987). Technological supremacy allows the gathering of more and qualitatively better informing and knowledge and putting it to better use.

The four kinds of uncertainty that constitute the set referred to as innovation uncertainty determine the needs in information processing for the innovation to be successful while, at the same time, they are being determined both for their magnitude and type by the identity of the initiator and the impetus that started the innovation.

On the other hand, the abilities to process information are determined by the structure adopted for the project, the distribution of resources, the organizational climate, the degree of intradepartmental integration and the support of senior executive management.

These processing needs interact with processing abilities, and what ensues from this dialectical relation is a decrease of uncertainty. A small difference between necessary and acquired information means better decision making and better implementation of the decisions made, from a qualitative viewpoint. But both the quality of decision making and the quality of their implementation simultaneously affect the reduction of uncertainty.

From a dynamic viewpoint, however, the model is not exhausted in the one-dimensional relation of the positive effect on the increase of the likelihood of success for the innovative product from the (interacting) relation of the reduction of uncertainty and the improvement of decision making and implementation. Businesses, like living, biological organisms, possess the ability to learn, as is characteristically noted by Kolb (1971) and Morgan (1986). Organizational learning as a process includes the acquisition, communication and interpretation of knowledge relating to the organization and its use for decision making. Shrivastava's article "A Typology of Organizational Learning Systems" (1983) has established that a business also learns in the course of technological innovation, noting that before a product is characterized as a failure, account ought to be taken of its contribution toward the development of the organization, the establishment of a market or/and the boost it gave to technology. New products are heavily influenced by the performance and history of their predecessors and, in turn, affect the success of failure of their successors. The experience and expertise of the working team that were acquired during the life cycle of a previous innovation are transferred to what follows from each innovation, the new innovative products. Intragroup learning usually occurs via informal communication channels, namely, informal talks, the movement of employees around departments and friendships, as Meyers and Wilemon (1989) note. As the organization comes into more contact with the innovation, uncertainties decrease, the organization becomes enriched by documented experience, and its knowledge pool is filled. Continuous observation causes errors to be detected while it refines the parameters for decisions and, therefore, improves the quality of the decisions and their implementation. Should one therefore wish to dynamically view the framework, then the flow of the feedback from the result of an innovation to the one succeeding it must also be included.

Since the nature of the innovative process is constituted by information, it follows that the result of integration will create synergies in terms of information. The transfer of information becomes the vehicle allowing the integration of the mixed members. Access to information from outside the department will assist the members of the team to navigate their own efforts. This type of informing allows its recipient to superimpose the perspective of his own role and positively affects the adequacy of both the marketing and R&D departments. This way, issues can be identified/underlined which had not been previously addressed or need more clarification. Thus, the flow of information between the marketing and R&D departments also bears on the quality and quantity of information. These two features are "in role"; namely, they relate to the group playing the particular role. But beside and beyond this, the transfer of information also influences the convergence of information produced by the marketing and R&D departments, which is characterized as compatibility of information.

Making sound decisions does not simply rest on how well one or the other operating department has performed their duties well, but also on to what extent did the exchange of information trigger the checking mechanisms for their relevance.

The reduction of uncertainty for each function must act complementary to the other, and this is perhaps the most important virtue of intradepartmental/intrafunctional information exchange. Concisely, the transfer of information between the marketing and R&D departments creates a mutual understanding of the roles, assists the clarification of what is expected by everybody and helps guide and direct operational functions. Additionally, the side benefits include the qualitative result of reducing uncertainty and of matching solutions coming from both sides.

The preceding discussion can be condensed to the following conclusions:

1   The adequacy by which the marketing (R&D) department performs its activities and consequently the reduction of uncertainty of its side is positively

related to the amount and quality of information that the marketing (R&D) department has received from the R&D (marketing) department in the course of the project's development.

2   The higher the degree of the mutual understanding of roles by the marketing and the R&D departments, the greater the convergence to the mutual reduction of uncertainty by each of the two functions will be. Mutual understanding is positively related to the quantity and quality of the information exchanged by the two departments over the project's life cycle.

Additionally, Moenaert and Souder (1990) also believe the following:

3   The transfer of information from the marketing to the R&D department is a positive function of (a) the quality of the sources used by marketing to derive its information, (b) the magnitude of the reduction of uncertainty that marketing has succeeded in bringing about and (c) the quantity and quality of the information provided by the R&D department to marketing. The same correspondingly hold for the provision of information by the R&D department to marketing.

4   The transfer of information from the marketing to the R&D department is negatively related to the amount and level of resources deployed by each department. The same holds, correspondingly, also for the amount and level of resources utilized by each department. The same holds also for the R&D department.

With regard the third part of the third proposition, the authors formulate it based on the principle of reciprocity, while as to its second part, it is expected that something exists before it may be transferred. Regarding quality and the qualitative and professional approach to issues researched by the marketing department, it is obvious that it will have a positive effect on the corresponding magnitudes of the information it will transfer to the R&D department.

The fourth proposition simply observes that a great human resources investment in the corresponding departments means a greater number of individuals forming the interdepartmental network and therefore a greater weight placed in the immediate operating environment to which each individual belongs.

The fifth proposition is as follows:

5   The transfer of information from the marketing to the R&D department will become maximized at some intermediate level of behavior outside the role for marketing, while this also correspondingly holds with respect to the R&D department and is justified as follows:

The behavior outside the role, namely the transcendence of the operating boundaries of the department where someone belongs, occurs under several circumstances, amongst which the research to acquire information from another operating department, when it is not adequately provided by it. In operating organizational structures most hesitate to transcend the boundaries of their role, for reasons such as

a they will be judged based on the operating criteria of their own department;
b they may offend the other department;
c they show a lack of specialization;
d they are borne with the alternative time cost;
e they fear failure;
f they stir up suspicion.

However, behaviors outside the roles can also intrinsically ensue as variables of either an essentially inadequate informing or a lack of a specific agenda.

Thus, while, on one hand, the appearance of such roles is intrinsically connected to a weakness, in the absence of which (namely, in the presence of high quality/ large quantity of information that is intradepartmentally transferred) it would not have been manifested; on the other hand, it is also connected to a positive feature: The more the experience acquired from other operating departments increases, the better the needs of that department for informing are understood and the more comfortable the individual behaving "out of role" becomes with sharing information from his or her own department in order to facilitate his or her own needs as the recipient of information from the other department (principle of reciprocity). Additionally, the phenomenon of operational shortsightedness is also avoided.

The sixth proposition is causally documented in the three types of organizational structure cited earlier and their characteristics:

6 The more elaborate the definition of a work and/or the more self-inclusive the structure or/and the more harmonious the climate between marketing and R&D departments is, the higher the quality and quantity of information exchanged.

Finally,

7 the flow of information between the two departments will increase if someone with experience or training from the R&D department is placed in the marketing department.

This is an artificial two-step approach for the dissemination of the information process.

3.2.2 Model – the framework for the necessary and attained integration and for the contribution of integration to the success of innovative products

Gupta, Raj and Wilemon (1986a) insist that the intradepartmental collaboration of operating departments plays an important role in the process of the development of new products, but it is integration that plays the leading one, the systemic integration of the marketing and R&D departments, especially in the context of the development of innovative products.

Resting on the positions expressed by Wind and Robertson (1983) and Hutt and Speh (1984) that the relation and interdependence of marketing and the other operating departments have been given little attention, they find it surprising, given the tremendous importance placed by the Marketing Concept to interrelation, considering it to be among the core values of its philosophy, and attempt to establish a framework. This framework is intended to clarify and address the following issues:

1   How much integration is needed? Perhaps certain companies (industries) demand a higher rate of integration? Which are those factors which affect the rate of integration that is needed between the R&D and marketing departments?
2   How much integration can be attained and which are the critical factors that affect its attainment? How can management influence these critical variables in order to attain the desired level of integration?
3   What is the relation of influence that is dominant between innovation, success and integration? To what extent do the attained levels of integration between R&D and marketing contribute to the success of innovative products?

With respect, therefore, to the perceived need for integration, one can observe that it is a variable dependent on the new product strategy followed by the company, but also on the environmental risk/environmental uncertainty as they are perceived by the company. The association is positive; namely, an increase of the level of uncertainty and the adoption of more aggressive strategies will entail an increase of the levels of awareness for the need to integrate, as Freeman (1974) observes.

With respect to the attained levels of integration, these depend directly on organizational variables, such as the structure and systems for rewards, the attitude to risk by senior executive management, how emphatically sees senior executive management the need for the integration of the marketing and R&D department and on differences in culture and the social texture of the marketing and R&D departments.

The distance between perceived or fair or wanted integration and the realized one affects the rate of success for a new innovative product.

Research by Lawrence and Lorsch (1969) and Galbraith and Nathans (1978) stresses that uncertainty originating from the environment and combined with organizational strategies is responsible for the determination of the need to collaborate and control. Hage (1980) feels that the issue at large is how the environment itself affects the organization and how the organization itself can shape the environment. Combining the views by Child (1972) and Lawrence and Lorsch (1969), Hage concludes that sometimes there is room for strategic choice and decision, while at others limitations are posed by the environment. Zeithalm and Zeithalm (1984) move along the same lines and propose a similar environmental strategy.

With respect to the key factors determining the rate of integration necessary, it is evident that they depend on the requirements posed by organizational strategy and the commands dictated by environmental uncertainty.

Freeman (1974) and Parker (1978) propose six groupings for enterprises, depending on the type of innovative strategy they adopt and deploy. Businesses with an offensive strategy aim for market leadership via technological and purchasing leadership. They place enormous weight on being the first to launch new products or technologies to the market or to create new markets altogether. Businesses following a defensive strategy, while hesitant at being the first to launch a technology or innovative products to the market, at the same time do not want to be left behind the competition. Rarely, therefore, will they play the role of the pioneer, but they will frequently follow as second, with products slightly modified to be better and with smaller production cost needs. This happens since by being "second", they get to learn and exploit mistakes made by the "first", because of the luxury afforded by the time frame. The imitative strategy dictates that one should follow the leader. The imitative strategy involves following the leader. The activities of the R&D department are focused on scientific-technical services. Companies which are subcontractors, branches or, in some other way, dependent on other companies follow the dependent strategy. Companies adhering to the traditional strategy see no reason pushing them to innovation, while the opportunistic strategy is adopted by companies that demand little to even no services by the R&D department for their operations and simply invest in marketing and sales in order to exploit emerging market opportunities.

Another typology for the classification and understanding of the organizational strategy observed was proposed by Miles and Snow (1978). They employ a two-fold criterion for differentiating between strategies: on one hand, there is categorization depending on the enterprise's objectives while, on the other, there is its degree of familiarity with new products, markets and technologies, as Cooper (1983b) and Crawford (1980) observe. It is only logical for a business actively engaged in markets for completely new and unknown products and technology to need more informing (and more efficient one at that) on the market and the technology, in order to reduce the risk of the product's failure. To gain this knowledge, as a chain-reaction process, it may now need to activate the web of collaboration and the integration and coordination of the intersecting efforts by the marketing and R&D department. Needs to process-treat data are drastically reduced as one moves to the stepwise – with respect to requirements as such were developed based on the criteria employed by the authors – typology of prospectors, analyzers, defenders and reactors, with the direction of reduction from prospectors to reactors. Gupta and Wilemon (1986a, b) employ the hypothesis that needs for integration – close collaboration–unification of efforts and joint, integrated efforts are decreasing as one moves from prospectors to reactors.

Environmental uncertainty is the second constituent that influences the degree of required integration. This refers to the ability of the enterprise to anticipate changes in its competitors' strategies, in customers' requirements for new products, in technology, in the emergence of new competitive forces in the market and in the new limitations relating to the product's design and performance. The effects of environmental uncertainty have been surveyed both in light of the organizational needs for the management of information as well as from the viewpoint of needs to differentiate and integrate various operating subsets. The contingency theory on organizational structure, as elaborated by Galbraith and Nathanson (1978), has emphatically stressed the importance of environmental uncertainty for the structure of the organization which must correspond to the different levels of requirements for information processing, a point also raised by Downey, Hellriegial, and Slocum (1975) and Duncan (1972). A multitude of contingent factors have been included by Mintzberg (1979), who claimed that besides the age of the organization, its size and state of ownership, the most important factors relate to its environment and regard magnitudes of stability, complexity, differentiation and hostility. These environmentally associated uncertainties reinforce the need for data processing and, therefore, the need for the coordination, cooperation and control between organizational subgroups, a point made by numerous scholars and researchers such as Achrol, Torger Stern (1983), Galbraith (1977), Galbraith and Nathanson (1978) and Khandwalla (1972). The surveys, now considered classics, by Burns and Stalker (1961), Woodward (1965), Lawrence and Lorsch (1969) and Khandwalla (1972) accentuate the fact that the greater the environmental uncertainty, the greater the degree of specialization or differentiation inside the company. It is precisely this differentiation that permits and justifies the compartmentalization of uncertainty pursuant to departments. However, an expansive and extended establishment of departments will result in issues of coordination and synchronization. Thus, a high environmental uncertainty will possible lead to the creation for the need to better manage information and to greater intra-corporate coordination between the departments.

The preceding discussion leads to the formulation of the proposition that the larger the perceived environmental risk, the greater the need for the coordination–collaboration between the marketing and R&D departments.

The second axis of the framework model proposed by Gupta and Wilemon (1988) deals with how much coordination–integration between the marketing and R&D departments can be attained. According to the authors, the real integration that is ultimately attained in the context of an enterprise is a function of the following three factors:

a   organizational structure,
b   the attitude by senior executive management toward the integration of the marketing and R&D departments and of the actions senior management is prepared to take to realize it and
c   social and cultural differences between the marketing and R&D departments which become manifest in the course of the development of new products.

The role of organizational structure is rendered as an important variable in the realized integration, since structure is that element that establishes the capacity for data processing, both on the level of the various (operating) subsets as well as, and consequently, on the level of the organization as a whole. According to Dalton (1980) and Rubenstein, Chakrabarti, O'Keefe, Souder and Young (1976), references in the literature that aim to find the relation between structure and performance are controversial and confusing. Structure is certainly a critical factor that can become a hindrance or catalyst specifically for integration and can, by extension, correspondingly influence innovative activities. Zaltman, Duncan and Holbek (1973) observe that conflicting requirements cannot coexist in the organization's structure, depending on the stage it is in with respect to the process of innovation. The need to structure different frameworks depending on whether one is at the beginning stages or the application stages for the innovation is also underlined. Gupta and Wilemon then refer to a composition of research findings, also citing the positions of organizational behaviorists within its framework. The organizational structure becomes "tangible" in terms of the following:

a   Complexity: Complexity is a function of the number of specialized personnel and its professionalization inside the organization, as was pointed out by Hage and Aiken (1970). Consequently, corporations that succeed in innovation – and given the increased likelihood of a high number of highly specialized personnel – is logical to experience higher levels of complexity. A generally accepted hypothesis is that as complexity increases, so does the level of difficulty in attaining integration between operating subunits in the context of the organization.

b   Formality: Formality is defined as the emphasis given inside an organization on conformance to rules and procedures during the performance of one's duties and work. According to Kanugo (1979), formal frameworks and compartmentalizations can cause alienation and trends of non-mingling between the specialized professionals. Besides, Kahn, Wolfe, Quinn, Snoek and Rosenthal (1964) found that while formal frameworks are responsible for reducing uncertainties, it is, however, possible for them to be equally responsible for an increase in role conflicts. On the other hand, Organ and Greene (1981) suggest that formality does not necessarily have purely negative effects on the professional personnel of an enterprise. Deshpande (1982), in his survey on the extent of use of information ensuing from marketing research, observes that less formally structured companies have a greater likelihood to better utilize research findings. On the other hand, John and Martin (1984) stress that the reliability and functionality of the outcome of a plan increase as the formal marketing planning frameworks increase. With respect to its effects, formality has a double and contrasting role and implications.

c   Concentration: This relates to the power hierarchy and the degree of participation in decision shaping and making. Concentration increases the higher the level of the hierarchy, inside the organization, that will make the decision and the lower the degree of participation of the other levels in the decision-making process. Zaltman, Duncan and Holbek (1973) stress that strict adherence to the hierarchy of power reduces organizational innovation since it encourages only positive feedback to performance. Decreased participation in the decision-making process can also act as an invisible wall to perceptions and ideas emerging during the development of innovation. On the contrary, a great participation can increase commitment to the completion of the project, as it lends an air of "ownership". A negative relation between concentration and the use and utility of the results of marketing research, but also of the reliability and functionality of the schedules, was established by the empirical surveys carried out by Deshpande (1982) and John and Marting (1984), while Wind (1982) refers to integration problems for centrally oriented structures.

Conflicting reports exist also with respect to the dimension of concentration. Thus, while surveys and research papers by Hage and Aiken (1970), Palumbo (1969), Blau (1973), Daft and Becker (1978) and Hage and Dewar (1973) found a negative correlation between the degree of concentration and the results of innovation, Hage (1980) underlines that in the presence of a change in values, concentration can be positively connected to innovation. Hage observes that the mechanist organizations that are characterized by small rates of change also constitute the land where radical innovation can take place, since it is there that a crisis will most possibly arise, as happens to an organizational structure susceptible to dictatorial practices. Galbraith and Nathanson (1978) offer what amounts to probably a more correct representation of reality, by claiming that there is no one "good" structure, but the structure which would potentially be characterized as optimal is the one that adjusts to the needs and mandates by the environment of goals and objectives.

This is the theory explaining why certain organizational structures are more adept to higher levels of adjusting–annexing–adopting innovation and more productive with respect to research teams, a conclusion drawn also by the National Science Foundation (1983). Sophisticated innovations require an organizational structure where specialists coming from different schools of thought and who have different mentalities can become integrated into the context of groups that operate smoothly. The recommended structure is compatible, if not identical, with the findings on electronics businesses, as Burns and Stalker (1961) demonstrate, as well as for NASA, as Galbraith (1973) observes.

Summarizing, one can suggest the following as the distinguishing features of such structures:

1   Low levels of formality
2   Selective decentralization
3   Mutual adjustment as a coordinating mechanism
4   Diffusion of the decision-making power between managers and nonmanagers

The attitude exhibited by senior executive management is the second variable affecting the level of attained integration. Souder (1977, 1981) and Souder and Chakrabarti (1978) believe that senior management can either promote or hinder the development of a productive communication channel between R&D and marketing. In the more effective cases of integration, Souder and Chakrabarti (1978) found that a joint reward system is in place for the marketing and R&D departments and that the new departments felt the success or failure of the project to be their joint responsibility. Both (operating) groups felt that their collaboration was appreciated by management and that there were many signs pointing to this. Moreover, researchers such as Quinn (1979), Roberts (1978, 1979), Roberts and Fusfeld (1981) and Wind (1982) have suggested that the attitude by senior management with respect to the assumption of risks was found to have a positive influence for the successful outcome of innovation. It is, moreover, implied that the encouragement for developing good relations between the marketing and R&D departments on the side of senior management plays an important role.

The third factor that is determinative for the attained integration is the differences in culture and the social differences between those who lead the marketing and R&D departments. Brown (1983) essentially states the obvious by claiming that in the context of an organization, when two groups share a common place (interface), then there will essentially be two versions on what the future may bring: Their relation will be either compatible or incompatible with respect to the communication between them. Biller and Shanley (1975) feel that there are special problems in the contact of the departments on account of differences in culture and social ones. Shibutani (1971) found that the causes generating such differences are evident even in the "form" and composition of these groups and relate to the study of different writings, the social gap between them and, in general, the different way for socialization and the different social interrelations in place for each group. Gibson (1981) stresses the fact that the set of values of the people manning the R&D department is different from that of individuals composing other groups and, indeed, to a degree where their requirements of management are differentiated as is their behavior under certain conditions. Clarke (1974) notes that marketing represents a different way of thinking, a different set of principles, perhaps less detailed, with respect to accuracy, but more qualitative from the corresponding one by the R&D department. Twiss (1974) observes that technologists consider themselves to be more of a professional than a businessperson. Their inclinations and education render them able to associate more easily and freely with other similar professionals in different companies than with other managers from their own company.

Furthermore, because of the stereotypes established in both departments, communication and collaboration between them face additional obstacles. Stereotypes are being borne out of the distance between them on the axis of goals, ambitions, needs, motives, behavior and attitudes.

The literature does not render clear exactly which of these differences undermines integration. Lawrence and Lorsch (1969) focused on differences in the perception of time, interpersonal relations and goals. Miller and Wager (1971) emphasized professional and bureaucratic differences, while Souder (1977) offers the view the R&D department has of the marketing one (claiming that marketing rests too much on conjecture and hearsay).

Gupta and Wilemon are correct in pointing out that such differences on the level of orientations, beliefs and practices, despite being presented as problematic and acting as obstacles to joint decision making and integration, are, however, useful and necessary when intended to be used in order for each department to complete its individual function.

Gupta and Wilemon consider four factors to be critical for integration and the level of its attainment.

1 Professional/bureaucratic orientation

Miller and Vager (1971) define professional orientation as somebody's desire to evolve within the greater network of professional relations that exists in an organization. They define bureaucratic orientation as the preference and desire for recognizability inside the enterprise and the schedules thereof, instead of recognizability by professional colleagues from outside the enterprise. More individuals staffing the R&D department begin and retain their identification inside their professional group. They are highly committed to their skills and seek social recognition by professional colleagues both from inside as well as from outside the company. On the other hand, marketing executives are purely "bureaucratically" oriented.

2 Tolerance of ambiguity

Budner (1962) defines ambiguity as the tendency toward perceiving unclear situations based on what is desired. According to the same author, an ambiguous state cannot be structured or categorized by some individual because of the lack/inadequacy of a satisfactory amount of data. New product development is considered to be an unclear, ambiguous state. It is precisely for this that the way marketing and R&D adopt to deal with the difficulty arising from uncertainty is a factor positively affecting the level of quality of collaboration between them. Marketers feel more comfortable with intuitions and instincts than do R&D executives, who need somber, objective proof.

3 Time orientation

Lawrence and Lorsch (1969) propose a difference in the prism for perceiving time between the two operational groups, with marketing people adopting a more short-to-medium time frame, while R&D executives have a more long-term one.

4 Preferred types of projects – products

Gupta and Wilemon (1990) note that many researchers discern a difference with respect to the types of new products that the managers of the two departments prefer to be engaged in. Maidique (1984) observes that the personnel of the R&D department strive to attain high technical performance, which it considers as a goal in itself – a fact that in no way guarantees its successful course. Technical staff (R&D) is more interested in radically innovative products, while marketing is allured more by the potential of the product under development to be a commercial success.

Several studies have concluded that the success of an innovation depends on a combination of recognizing what the market wants and the technical skills necessary to develop what it wants. The need for an effective integration of the marketing and R&D departments has been emphatically stressed as a critical factor for success by many researchers, including Gruber (1981); Dunn and Boyd (1975); Young (1973); Crawford (1977); Schon (1967); Carroad and Carroad (1982); Monteleone (1976); Rapport, Schnee, Wager and Hamburger (1971); Mansfield and Wagner (1975); Mansfield (1981); Gerstenfeld and Sumiyoshi (1980); Wind (1981, 1982); and Cooper (1983a). Their findings and conclusions are supported also by the work of other researchers, such as Gruber, Poensgen, and Prakhe (1973); Souder (1977, 1981) and Young (1973), and according to it, one of the most significant factors for failure to launch new products lies with the weakness and failure to integrate the marketing and R&D departments from the early stages of the innovative process. Roughly 68.5% of the products developed under a state of disharmonious relations between marketing and R&D were commercial failures (for a total of 58 products), while the failure rate for products developed under a state of integration reached only 18% (for a total of 53 products).

Besides, the positive relation between the integration of the marketing and R&D departments has been perceived and registered by other scholars, from the fields of general management and economics, such as Gaibraith and Daniel (1978), Lawrence and Lorsch (1969) and Mansfield (1981).

Besides the generally accepted and documented existence of a very positive relation between the integration of the marketing and R&D departments and the success of innovation, Gupta and Wilemon offer one more theoretical piece to the puzzle, claiming that the degree of required integration must conform with the innovation strategy followed by the company and the perceived risk uncertainty by it from environmental factors. In other goals, the maximization of the degree of integration is not set as an end in itself but consider as optimal that integration which would minimize the distance between the ideal and the presently attained integration. Souder (1977) suggests that this approach will minimize the cost of integration both in monetary terms as well as in terms of effort.

By combining theoretical and empirical research in the fields of marketing, organizational behavior, the process of new product development and research management, Gupta and Wilemon (1990) propose the model described earlier, which is framed with 14 propositions-conclusions which condense the extracts from their research:

The need to integrate the marketing and R&D departments will decrease as we move from prospectors to reactors.

The greater the perceived environmental uncertainty is, the greater the need for the integration of the marketing and R&D departments.

The smaller the degree of formal structures in an organization, the greater the degree of integration that will be attained.

The smaller the concentration of power (authority) in an organization, the greater the degree of attained integration.

The greater the degree by which personnel participates in decision making regarding a new product, the greater the degree of attained integration.

The more senior executive management encourages the taking of risks collectively by the heads of the marketing and R&D departments, the greater the degree of integration that has been attained.

The greater the joint perception by managerial executives of the marketing and R&D departments that they will be jointly remunerated for the success of a new product, the greater the degree of integration that will be attained.

The greater and more diffused the official acknowledgment of the existence of the need for the integration of the operating departments of marketing and R&D by senior executive management, the greater the degree of attained integration will be.

The more harmonious the operating characteristics of the marketing and R&D departments are, the greater the attained integration will be.

The greater the homogeneity of the professional "bureaucratic" orientation of the managerial executives of the R&D and marketing departments is, the greater the degree of integration attained will be.

The greater the similarity between the executives of the marketing and R&D departments with respect to their tolerance of uncertainty, the greater the degree of the attained integration will be.

The closer and more similar the orientation of managing executives from marketing and R&D departments with respect to the element of time is, the greater the degree of attained integration will be.

The greater the similarities between marketing and R&D managing executives is relative to their preferences with respect to the types of products they wish to be engaged in, the greater the degree of integration will be.

The greater the gap between the required degree of integration and what has in reality been attained, the more the likelihood for a successful course of innovation is minimized.

3.2.3 Systemic approach of the marketing and R&D departments: demand- and offer-driven High Tech markets

Shanklin and Ryans (1984) move in the same wavelength, namely, in the systemic approach of the marketing and R&D departments and the ensuing from it collaboration for the maximum potential beneficial result for High Tech enterprises. They do not consider the approach of the two departments as simply an alternative that pushes High Tech enterprises to the direction of optimizing the results but, rather, as the only direction available, a one-way street. They feel that in this foggy landscape that has been characterized even as chaotic and taking account of the mandates and requirements posed by this rapidly changing environment, the importance of research and development, despite remaining high, should not, however, be overestimated or considered both adequate and sufficient by itself, a fact that stands as the rule today, principally due to the fact that the main body of High Tech enterprises got its initial might from innovations that were developed by the R&D department. Given the conditions prevailing in the environment of High Tech enterprises today, the authors claim frequently requires the complete restructuring of the marketing department and the establishment of communication–collaboration links for the efforts jointly made with the R&D department.

To justify their position, they begin with the commonly accepted assumption that High Tech enterprises are frequently superior and perform better with respect to their R&D departments. However, they view the superiority in this particular sector to be almost independent of the realization of better financial performance or the realization of profits. Their fixed position is that the combination of the R&D and marketing departments is the appropriate recipe for the planning, analysis and, ultimately, exploitation of the opportunities that are presented in High Tech markets, where the sort and shake-out of competitors occur in much shorter periods and shape the landscape faster. The intense competitive features are to a large extend the reason differentiating the High Tech markets.

In order to provide a deeper understanding of High Tech markets, they divide them based on if they are driven by demand or offer.

In the case where technological progress is what justifies the creation of markets and demand, then the market is offer-oriented. The role of marketing in this case is auxiliary and supportive, while it rests and is largely shaped by entrepreneurship and instinct. In the case of a totally new product, a market must be created (Morita, 1981). High tech enterprises that are technology-oriented are frequently associated with businesses that are frequently cited as being innovation-oriented. The basic objective strategical goal of such enterprises is to succeed in making profitable commercial applications of laboratory findings. The R&D department is the principal instigator of marketing and the direction its efforts must take. In other words, marketing is called to satisfy an optional need in the sense that such need is created and rises to the surface after the discovery of the solution to the purchasing problem (of the satisfaction) of the need. Additionally, innovations realized in such High Tech enterprises can have such a wide-ranging spectrum of applications, but this factor, however, either is delayed and seen too late or is neglected altogether with catastrophic consequences for the commercialization of innovations.

On the other hand, there are those High Tech enterprises that are demand-driven, that shape, that is, their orientation principally guided by existing demand. This second state is the natural evolution of the normal course to maturity in the life cycle of such enterprises. There is a reversal of roles in this instance, since the R&D department is called on to offer the technological responses to purchasing problems consumers have already realized and which marketing has acknowledged and mapped, as it ought to have done.

The taking of this conventional role by marketing includes a greater focus on the 4 Ps, while it is less based on the approach of business "genius" and instinct and more focused on creating and bringing closer the cohesive links for the communication and admirable collaboration with the R&D department. In the second case the results that ensue from the workshops of the R&D department follow as a response to the mandates posed by marketing.

Companies engaged in High Tech fields must effectively respond to the continuous challenge of organizational and philosophical adjustment as High Tech markets mature, namely, evolve from being driven by an offer to those being driven by demand. This transition that appears as the result of an evolutionary course to maturity is not an easy to follow and unhindered procedure. The reorientation of executives who had a successful career in High Tech enterprises driven by an offer is difficult and, in many cases, unattainable. Whether a transition which poses as a prerequisite the anterior realization of the change in the factors that shape the scenery within the context of maturity and necessitate restructuring and reorientation based on the demands of a more customer-centric approach will be successful ultimately depends on whether a core capability will be converted to a core rigidity, as was observed by Barton (1992), and whether the High Tech company will ultimately be entangled in a continuous and continuously expanding and dynamic vicious circle of debarment from its customer base. Namely, the special core capability that gave prominence to the enterprise and created its comparative advantage at its initial stages of existence and development can become a critical factor for its disorientation and a literal obstacle during the period of its maturity.

Wishing to escape the confines created by the strict compartmentalization of High Tech enterprises based on the criterion cited earlier, the authors offer a synthesis that is more susceptible to real market limits and which may be condensed to the fact that ultimately the marketing and R&D departments must not operate or be perceived under the light of the dilemma of one sterile state or the other but, rather, under the auspices of a strategically systemic approach.

Two subcategories are deemed to be included in the demand-driven category. The first includes enterprises whose R&D department promotes improvements deliberately, based on the criterion of the speed by which competing enterprises manage to transform conversions to an already-existing technology to a competitive advantage. The exclusive adoption of this approach can lead to delays in the appearance of radical innovations.

The second subcategory does not limit itself within the binding boundaries of a marginal approach to technological steps, but, as the first High Tech marketer, Thomas Edison, observed, they first make certain that something is needed or is desirable and then move on.

Ideas for the creation of new and innovative ideas must be tested under the proviso and filter of whether they will be accepted by the competitive environment in which they will be introduced. This, thus, school of approach to enterprises is essentially mobilized and begins based on solving purchasing problems on each occasion.

In the case of a technology driven by the market, the key direction is offered by the marketing department to the R&D one. The reaction of the R&D department returns to the marketing department in the form of directives and directions on what is technically technologically attainable. The formal marketing research, typically occurring in consumer markets and industrial buyers, is that which will assist the marketing department to guide the R&D one.

Table 3.1 Contrast of demand-driven and offer-driven High Tech enterprises

High Tech enterprises	Characteristics	Roles	Spectrum of product applications	Conversion of core capabilities to core rigidities	Evolution over time
Driven by offer	– More scientifically/ technically oriented – The creation of the market follows the creation of the product – Use of qualitative methods	R&D instigates marketing to find applications of needs for the scientific innovation	Broader	Insistence on the traditional approach causes the conversion of Core Capabilities to obstacles in a dynamic manner	Transition - - - - → Adjustment
Driven by demand	– More focus on the 4 Ps – More need to communicate with R&D – Product creation follows the mapping of the market	Marketing motivates R&D to seek technical/ scientific solutions to realized consumer problems	Narrower	Customer-centric nature ensures the intertemporal preservation and reinforcement of Core Capabilities through their adjustment	

The opposite occurs in the second case, where the R&D department provides the stimulus and the marketing department is called upon to find applications or to, simply, sell the product. This type of flow process can assist in the establishment of new markets that will be morphed by the application of the laboratory products by the R&D department and will resonate with yet to be realized needs.

In the research carried out by Shanklin and Ryans (1984), they detected an additional feature in the two schools of approach outlined above, with respect to the research methods they utilize. Enterprises driven by technology invest more in qualitative research methods. They don't place that much importance on collecting data which, by using some mathematical analytical tool, can offer a representative reference sample based on statistical data. This can obviously attributed to the lack of useful historical data and the low significance of traditional interviews on the potential applications of a new technology.

The authors, however, feel that in both types of High Tech enterprises, marketing must be aware of the capabilities and activities of the R&D department so as to be cognizant of the design-productive capacities and limitations and to be able to perform a realistic analysis.

The relation between the R&D and marketing departments in the market-(demand-)driven High Tech enterprises principally derives through the active participation of the R&D department mainly in the process of drawing up the market plan and delimiting the objectives. The participation of the R&D department in market planning is the guarantee that marketing will not lose the orientation for the product offered by the R&D department. The counterbalance offered by marketing constitutes the new parameters for research efforts. Via this giving and taking of objective goals, the R&D and marketing departments can jointly decide on the targeted market, on the expectations and on the designation of priorities and their coordination.

Integration must be carefully planned since in High Tech environments the creation of groups is an imperative need. To avoid misunderstandings during the advanced stages of the process, objectives and goals must be included in the marketing plan. In their research, Shanklin and Ryans (1984) found that the involvement of the R&D department in the shaping of strategies and tactics was frequently limited and amounted to a consulting role on technical issues at the most.

The needs for integration between the marketing and R&D department for innovative (on the side of offer) High Tech enterprises differ. This is mainly attributable to the fact that capabilities for application are less evident or so chaotically outnumbering that the company must set priorities to exploit them. Thus, the starting point for integration must initially and largely rest on the answers to questions such as what sector is the company active in, which are the perceived opportunities present in the market and which are the priorities for the development of the market. By clearly answering the preceding questions, the same rules apply as those in the case of market-driven enterprises.

In both cases, however, the High Tech groups must be staffed both by the R&D and the marketing departments, since these are the two key departments for the decision-making process, and, indeed, their participation must, according to the authors, be on an equal basis not only throughout the entire High Tech product development process but also after it. In the same way that the marketing department is engaged at the early stages of product development (before it is launched in the market), the R&D department will participate in marketing's activities during the sale of the products. The findings of the survey include the realization that power games and the status each department enjoys constitute one of the key reasons for the tense and strained relations between the two departments.

3.2.4 Integration of the operating departments of marketing and R&D in High Technology: empirical approaches – conclusions

In their article "The R+D Marketing Interface in High – Technology Firms", Gupta, Raj and Wilemon (1985) survey the reasons (by an empirical research) which are responsible for the fact that while the role and importance of the integration of marketing and R&D is widely accepted, and the failure to attain it is one of the principal causes with a significant contribution in the failure of the launch of a new product, such integration has not been attained for the majority of enterprises. They consider that the pursuit of integration must be a mandate for all enterprises independently of the product they deal. Technology by itself is not capable of creating successful new products. Technological progress must be oriented toward what is presented by the market. Despite, however, the fact that integration is a critical factor across the entire spectrum of innovative enterprises, its role become particularly useful in the case of High Tech enterprises.

According to Zarecor (1975) most High Tech companies have been established on the basis of the formation of a good idea. In order to survive and become profitable, they must continuously derive new ideas from the pool of market and technology analysis. This emphatically activates the need for a productive communication–collaboration between the marketing and R&D departments.

High tech companies being oriented more toward the technological dimension, frequently either irregularly or completely inadequately include the systemic approach and results contributed by the data and viewpoint offered by marketing, a point that is raised by Miaoulis and LaPlaca (1980).

A system for detecting and recording the rapid changes to consumer needs that result from frequent technological changes taking place, is very important for the survival and development of High Tech enterprises, which are effectively framed by an exceptionally volatile – hostile – and high-risk environment, as Maidique, Modesto and Hayes (1984) note.

The lack of communication or the ineffectiveness thereof between the R&D and marketing departments, attributable to the specialized knowledge of R&D personnel, tends to create conditions of disintegration and isolation. This increases the likelihood of creating unsuccessful innovations, as Gruber (1981) observes.

The empirical approach adopted by Gupta, Raj and Wilemon (1986a) aims to accentuate four basic aspects which explain, at least partially, the causes of the reality that is the rare, good relations and unhindered collaboration and communication between the two departments. They shed light, therefore, on the factors that relate to the magnitude of not only the desire of marketing and R&D executives for the unification and incorporation of their efforts but also of their desire to exchange information. Second, they analyze beliefs on the currently attained degree of integration, and, third, they find the degree of dissatisfaction of R&D executives with their marketing counterparts and vice versa. Finally, they present the obstacles raised and which render the effective collaboration between the two departments difficult.

They initially identify 13 factors – activities which regard the formal stages of the process for the development and launching of a new product and which are deemed purposeful to be simultaneously and jointly dealt with the involvement of both departments and, in particular, in the context of their collaboration. These activities include areas which could be considered as being of primary interest and competence of either the R&D or the marketing department.

The research establishes that marketing executives wish for their efforts to be integrated with those of the R&D department more than the R&D executives wish the same with respect to the marketing department across almost all 123 areas researched. This "enthusiasm" on the side of marketing for joint involvement (not exhibited to such an extent by the R&D ones) related to the following areas:

setting goals and priorities for new products;
establishing a schedule for product development;
generating ideas on new products;
selecting ideas on new products;
providing feedback (by consumers) on product performance;
providing information on competitors' moves and their product strategies.

For each one of the aforementioned activities, the percentage of R&D department executives who deemed that marketing's involvement in these steps was significant was considerably lower.

On the other hand, despite the fact that the R&D department feels that the need for changes to the products in accordance with the mandates indicated by marketing exists, as does the need to develop new products pursuant to market needs, it, however, feels that it is the competent department that will have the last word and will reserve both the right and the initiative for the decision to involve the marketing department in the process of the proposed changes and the suggestion of market needs. Fifty-nine percent of R&D executives wish for marketing to make recommendations, compared to 81% of marketing executives.

Similarly, 75% of R&D executives wish for a greater involvement of marketing in the process for the development of new products compared to 88% of marketing executives wishing for a greater degree of participation and involvement of R&D in the process. R&D executives wished to be more involved in the analysis of consumer needs than in marketing ones.

Despite the disagreement on the degree of involvement in activities that were observed between the two operating groups, the two departments agree on the five most important areas where their integration is necessary:

1 Marketing's role to provide to the R&D department (a) consumers' requirements relating to the products, (b) regular feedback with respect to the "performance" of the product and (c) information relating to competitors' moves and strategies
2 The involvement of marketing with R&D in the setting of goals and priorities
3 The involvement of R&D in the new product development process pursuant to market needs

The members of the marketing and R&D departments were then asked on the degree of integration that was actually attained with respect to the areas of activities, in order to render the attainment of integration possible. The findings of the empirical survey were the following:

> The R&D department feels that the marketing department does not adequately share information with it; it also feels that it is not sufficiently or adequately involved in the new product development process.

Marketing executives, on the other hand, feel that they both share information with the R&D department and that they participate in the development process together with their R&D counterparts.

While the findings of the survey on the desired degree of participation show that the R&D department did not wish for its engagement with the marketing department to a great degree, however when marketing provides (and thus is engaged) information relating to the market and customers, the R&D department deems that it does not receive such information. It is as if the R&D department initially does not want something and then complains that it has not received it.

This gap in perceptions assumed was quite large for 6 out of 10 areas where integration was deemed to be critical by both departments. Additionally, the R&D department believes that marketing does not adequately participate in the involvement process with respect to the generation of ideas on new products and in finding commercial applications for the product ideas and technologies put forward by the R&D department. Marketing disagrees on this. The R&D department also believes that it is given insufficient and lacking information relating to customer requirements and expectations for new products, results of market surveys, feedback on the performance of products and information on the strategies adopted by competitors. The marketing department expresses the opposite view also in this case.

With respect to the degree of dissatisfaction it was found that marketing executives are far more disappointed than R&D executives with respect to the following:

1 The marketing department would wish for a more encompassing collaboration and a greater degree of its involvement and participation together with R&D at the initial stages-activities of the process for the development of a new product, namely, a higher degree of integration in the decision on the goals and schedules for new products.

2   The marketing department would wish for the participation of the R&D department in the modification of products to be pursuant to the mandates posed by the marketing department and for the participation of the R&D department in the development of new products to be pursuant to the needs of the market.

In the issues just cited and where the greatest degree of dissatisfaction of the marketing department is concentrated, the R&D department shows low levels of discontent relating to its participation in product modification pursuant to the recommendations by the marketing department.

Correspondingly, the points/activities where the R&D department but not the marketing department exhibits the greatest level of discontent include the following:

> The role of the marketing department in finding commercial applications for the product and technology ideas of the R&D department
>
> The lacking dissemination of information on the side of marketing and to the R&D department regarding consumers' expectations of new products and the moves the competition makes with respect to new products
>
> Both departments appear to be equally dissatisfied with the present level of integration and with respect to the analysis of customers' desires.

In the context of their research Gupta, Raj and Wilemon (1984), looked for the causes that create such difficulty in communication. In a total of 459 questionnaires they processed, using content analysis, it was found that there are five principal obstacles for effective integration.

1 Communication obstacles

Roughly 30% of the answers to the questionnaires noted that the greatest obstacle revolves around the communication of critical issues, such as, for example, customer desires and, ultimately, the inability for the departments to come to an agreement on important issues such as market needs and the drafting of a schedule. It was also underlines that the causes of such obstacles include time pressure, differences in priorities and the poor coordination of information exchange.

2 Lack of sensitivity to others' abilities and point of view

Of the responses offered by the R&D department, 22% suggested that marketing executives did not show the necessary degree of sensitivity and respect to the abilities of the R&D department and the compensatory benefits of trade-offs between cost and features.

Of marketing executives, 20% accused the R&D department of not showing sensitivity and respect to the viewpoint adopted by the marketing department or the pressures that characterize market environment.

3 Lack of support by senior executive management

The key obstacles that originated on the side of management related to its short-term orientation and the pressures for profitability within a short time frame, the purely technological orientation it adopted, the lack of understanding with respect of the orientation of the marketing department's function and the promotion of performance measures blocking the effective integration of marketing and R&D. The lack of clear direction, deficient adherence and provision of motives are also part of the factors employed to signify this lack of support.

4 Difference of culture and personality

Thirteen percent of marketing executives and 7% of R&D executives consider differences in culture and personality between the two department to be an obstacle. The "engineers' ego" and a very "professional" attitude and the interest marketing shows for power games, as well as their reaction to change, were articulated as constituents of this variable.

5 Lack of marketing knowledge

Both the R&D and the marketing department underlines that lack of knowledge on the competition, the market, the customers and product applications constitute obstacles to integration.

It is interesting that both marketing and R&D executives considered almost the same factors to be obstacles for their effective integration, with marketing executives placing more weight on differences of culture and personality to be more responsible, while R&D executives blamed the lack of marketing knowledge. Other factors cited as obstacles include

lack of role clarification;
separation of the two departments;
inefficient organizational structure and planning;
weak marketing department;
inconsistent and conflicting directives from the R&D department;
contradictory and conflicting relations between the two departments, long since in place;
the historical dominance of the R&D department as the driving force for determining product strategy, and lack of human and monetary resources.

The findings may be summarized in the following:

- The existence of a gap in perception between the R&D and the marketing departments with respect to the scope of their involvement and of information exchange during product development. The R&D department does not wish to be as involved with marketing as marketing desires, nor does it wish for marketing to take initiatives. Both departments, however, are disappointed by the current level of integration.

• Despite the fact that R&D and marketing executives expressed conflicting views with respect to the precise ideal degree of integration for every activity, they are, however, coinciding at a remarkable degree with respect to the relative importance of integration across every activity.

The findings of the research appear to have the following consequences:

1   Marketing executives must investigate the reasons for the existence of a gap with respect to the beliefs by the marketing and R&D departments on the provision of information. The lack of reliability, utility, validity or appropriate form for the information provided by the marketing to the R&D department may be to blame for this difference of views. It is no accident that 60% of R&D executives and 56% of marketing executives believe that the informing provided by marketing is lacking in terms of reliability.

2   Because of the small disposition by the R&D department to be involved with marketing and the smaller – compared to marketing's – desire for marketing to be involved with them, a potential obstacle is raised for the effectiveness of integration. Senior executive management must emphatically stress, using clearly expressed actions toward this end, the need for the unhindered collaboration between the two departments.

3   Senior executive management ought to implement joint rewards systems that will encourage collaboration between marketing and R&D. It may also dictate a market-oriented culture and provide the R&D department with processes that will assist the evaluation of market needs while simultaneously offering marketing executives with a way to understand the challenges and limitations of technological development.

4   The corrective actions toward the direction of achieving an effective and efficient integration can begin with those activities where the greater level of dissatisfaction is observed and which gather the greater (common) relative importance.

The theoretical model by Gupta, Raj and Wilemon (1986a) was adopted by Parry and Song (1993) in order to be empirically tested in Japanese High Tech companies. The incentive for the research where 247 Japanese R&D professionals were interviewed was offered by the climate of general assumption of the fact that Japanese High Tech companies are more efficient than the corresponding American ones in converting basic research to commercial products, acknowledged by, among others, Abbeglen, Stalk and Kaisha (1986) and Kotler and Fahey (1982). It was found that the Japanese executives in companies that emphasized on openings to new markets and new product areas perceived of the need for the integration of the R&D and marketing departments as more imperative than did those who worked in companies that pursued and followed more conservative paths to innovation (analyzers). The analyzers, in turn, considered the required integration more necessary than companies placing less importance on innovation (defenders). Parry and Song also discovered that great uncertainty with respect to the demand shown by consumers and high rates of technological change make management believe that more integration between the R&D and marketing departments is needed.

Another analysis of the findings of this research in Japanese companies concluded that the individually stated higher levels of integration were associated with individually higher rated successful product development schedules both for marketers and R&D executives. The most important goals for integration as were recommended by both groups are

development and consolidation of goals, activities and priorities;
analysis of customers' needs;
design-planning of guidelines-users and services;
design of communication strategies;
dissemination–distribution of information on the strategies and reactions of the competition.

According to an article in the *Wall Street Journal* by Murray and Lehner (1990), while Japanese scientists win fewer Nobel Prizes than American scientists, they are better at converting research to products. Articles by Carey (1990) and Dentzer (1990) support this view describing America as the land of many brilliant ideas, the sort of ideas that are revolutionary and win Nobel prizes; however, it falls behind with respect to practical innovations, namely, the translation of inventions to products.

In the literature review performed by Song and Parry, they concluded that the integration of the R&D and marketing departments critically affects the success

Perceived Urgency of the Need to Integrate

Figure 3.8 Perceived urgency of the need to integrate, following the Miles and Snow typology

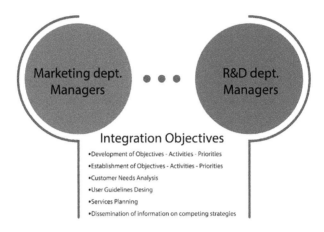

Figure 3.9 The most significant integration objectives as they were suggested by marketing and R&D executives

rates for new innovative products, and many factors have now been recognized that play the role of the catalyst for the propulsion or slowing of integration.

Song and Parry propose a series of assumptions that reflect the theoretical background of knowledge on the integration of marketing and R&D departments in the US and which they project on Japanese High Tech enterprises. To check the validity of their framework, they carried out research in 274 R&D executives from High Tech organizations in Japan.

They follow the logic dictated by the assumptions and the model created by Gupta, Raj and Wilemon (1986a). In other words, they adopt the logic that the environment, with its risks and uncertainties, and the strategy toward innovation adopted by the enterprise will determine, on one hand, the required degree of integration while, on the other, the attained level of innovation in the organization is a function depending on two variables: organizational climate and organizational structure.

The hypotheses Song and Parry tested on Japanese High Tech enterprises is as follows:

1 In Japanese High Tech companies the perceived need for integration is greater in the responses given by R&D executives, who believe that they belong, with respect to the classification of enterprises pursuant to the relative emphasis they give to innovation that was suggested by Miles and Snow, to the category of prospectors than by those who feel that they work for defender companies.

2 The perceived need for integration of the two operating departments (marketing and R&D) is an increasing function of the perceived environmental uncertainty risk.

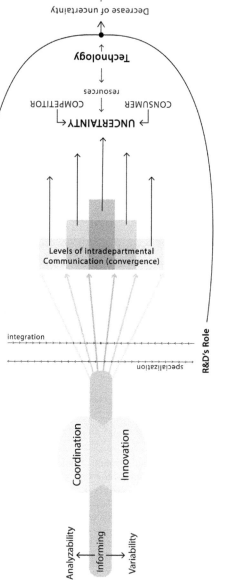

Figure 3.10 Theoretical framework of integration as a function of the perceived uncertainty

3   The perceived level of attained integration is negatively related to the perceived level of "formality" in education.
4   The perceived level of attained integration has a negative effect on the perceive degree for the concentration of decision making power (authority).
5   The perceived level of attained integration is positively related to the degree and magnitude of the participation of employees in the decision-making process on new products.
6   In High Tech organizations in Japan, perceived attained integration is positively related to the level of the quality in the relations between the operating departments of R&D and marketing.
7   The perceived level of integration is a positive function of the percentage of R&D personnel with professional experience.
8   The perceived level of integration is a positive function of the perceived level of support by senior management for the integration of the R&D and marketing departments.
9   The perceived level of integration that has been realized is a positive function of the level to which senior management encourages the assumption of risks.
10 The perceived level of realized integration is a positive function of the perceived level of the use of a joint reward system.

With respect to the first assumption, one observes that it adopts the theoretical approach by Miles and Snow regarding the strategic orientation for innovation and its use as a tool to classify enterprises. Of these strategic types, prospectors place more emphasis on product and market development. Given this emphasis, the R&D departments of prospectors tend to exhibit the greatest need to get information on customers and competitors from the marketing department. Thus, the higher levels of integration will be a guarantee for the conveyance of such information from marketing to R&D. Analyzers adopt a more careful and conservative

Table 3.2 Miles–Snow typology and the perceived need for integration

Types	*Characteristics*	*Hypothetical need for integration*
Prospector	Serves broadly defined, dynamic markets and evolves by means of the systematic development of new products and the identification of new markets.	High
Defender	Serves small fixed market segments and develops few new products. Evolves by increasing its market share with respect to the targeted markets. Tends to ignore developments outside its targeted market.	Low
Analyzer	Exhibits characteristics from both types above. Serves a combination of fixed and dynamic markets. Extensively utilized market monitoring mechanisms to identify products/markets.	Medium

strategy regarding innovation and, thus, need lower levels of integration. Analyzers exhibit characteristics common with both prospectors and defenders, characteristics that serve a mix of fixed and dynamic markets, while they extensively deploy marketing mechanisms to monitor–oversee the market so as to more quickly to a new product or new market which has recently acquired a degree of acceptance, as Miles and Snow (1978) point out. The fact that high levels of environmental uncertainty require great organizational skills for the management and processing of information, as Zahra (1987) and Achrol, Review and Stern (1983) observe, skills that are assisted and improved by high levels of intradepartmental integration, and the fact that businesses frequently develop specialized and differentiated departments as a response to uncertainty, meaning that the need for intradepartmental coordination is again increased, as Khandwalla (1974) and Lawrence and Lorsch (1969) point out, led Parry and Song to formulated their second hypothesis.

The bibliographic review by Parry and Song on Japanese business reality supports at least some relation between the attained levels of integration and the organizational structure and culture (as was supported by Gupta et al). Structure comprises two elements: the formality of relations and the centrality of decision making. Both Ruekert and Walker (1987a), as well as Zaltman, Duncan and Holber (1973), have found that "formality" of relations can, on one hand, decrease the conflict of roles between the departments and thus be a positive element toward the direction of attaining integration, but it can, however, also undermine it, becoming an obstacle to the flow of information between the two departments. The first dimension appears to be supported more vehemently by Ruekert and Walker, who consider formality to be positively related to the perceived effectiveness of the relations. According to Yoshino (1968), Japanese management considers business organization as hierarchically related collective units rather than individual relations. Due to the fact that emphasis is placed on the collective fulfillment of objectives, the responsibilities of individuals are very vaguely defined. This observation is also made by Noda (1975), Ouchi (1981), Tsuji (1975), while Vogel's (1979) and Yoshino's (1968) analysis point to the same direction, as did Hiroshi Takeuchi in his article "The Management Challenge" (1985). Song and Parry rest on Yoshino's view that detailed duties descriptions are not only useless but also not functional and may potentially undermine interpersonal cooperation and thus the authors appear to side with the view expressed by Gupta et al. (1986). Their third assumption is derived from this.

With respect to their fourth hypothesis, the authors observe that Moenaert and Souder (1990) support that centrality hinders mingling and trust, while more attention is paid to informal messages. This observation is consistent with the empirical work carried out by Link and Zmud (1986). Several researchers such as Johnson and Ouchi (1974), Kotler and Fahey (1982) and Vogel (1979) have cited directors from Japan commenting on the lack of centrality in Japanese enterprises. According to Inoue (1985) the decision-making process in Japanese management is directed from the bottom to the top. It is very rare for senior executives to formulate strategic planning or strategy on their own, where decision making appears to be made by senior management and then diffused to the lower levels is in small-size companies. Parry and Song find that not all observers are in agreement as to whether decision making is decentralized and takes place in a participatory manner. Yoshino distances himself from both positions, suggesting that a more accurate description of the Japanese way would be to say that decision-making power is widely dispersed yet not decentralized.

According to Souder's (1981, 1988) argument, the success rates for new products are at their highest when the relations between marketing and R&D are governed by mutual respect, trust and dedication, as well as by perceptions of both competitiveness and interdependence. It is a frequent conception that practices employed by the Japanese adopt transactions typically including respect, commitments and recognition of the mutual dependence. Such images are documented by descriptions of "employment for life", reward systems based on seniority and job rotation practices, as these have been pointed out by Abegglen, Stalk and Kaish (1986), Ouchi (1981) and Vogel (1979). Despite all these, there are indications that there is potentially room for the emergence of disharmony in the relations in Japanese enterprises. Rohlen (1975) reports that in the absence of guiding directives from senior management, the organization of activities between the work groups is difficult. Driven also by the fact that the benefits ensuing from job rotation imply that the perceived level of integration will reflect on the level of work experience, Parry and Song propose hypotheses 6 and 7.

There are several surveys suggesting senior management as a factor with a significant role with respect to the level of attained integration in the US. Besides the research by Gupta, Raj and Wilemon (1987), Maidique and Zirger (1984) also believe that the support by senior management is catalytic. Parry and Song underline the fact that it is difficult to find specific references that will demonstrate the degree of active encouragement provided by the Japanese for the mingling of the two departments, despite the fact that observers have made references revealing the interest the Japanese show to high morale and good intradepartmental relations. But it is clear that practices such as the organization of new product development by means of multifunctional project teams shows that senior executive management in Japan appreciates the integration of the marketing and R&D departments, as Takeuchi and Nonaka (1986) observe. Yoshino (1968) points out that on several occasions senior management failed to clearly formulate the organizational objectives and that such kinds of failures tend to increase conflicts between the two operational teams. The fact that the perceptions of value offered by senior management to the involvement of the marketing and R&D departments, and the work by Gupta who proposes that such fluctuations of perception are connected to the fluctuations of the attained levels of integration between the two departments, lead Parry and Song to formulate their eighth assumption.

The following may be observed with respect to the ninth assumption. The perceptions of the orientation with respect to the attitude toward the assumed risk by senior management in Japanese enterprises, exhibits fluctuations. Gestenfeld and Sumiyoshi (1990) observe that Japanese companies exhibit a tendency to assume risks. Despite the fact that there are several indications for the truth of this statement, such as those provided by Quinn (1985) and Rosenbloom and Cusumano (1978), a comparison of 227 American and 255 Japanese executives revealed that the Japanese showed a smaller capability of accepting new and creative ideas and were less willing to assume risks. Adopting the view of Gupta et al. (1986), Parry and Song (1997) explain the fluctuations ensuing from these conflicting views by attributing and connecting them with fluctuations of the level of integration between the marketing and R&D departments.

The tenth assumption by Parry and Song (1997)rested on research carried out in American High Tech companies, which showed that the use of a joint reward system can improve the level of integration between the marketing and R&D departments.

The results of testing the assumptions of Parry and Song's research are summarily presented in Table 3.3.

Table 3.3 Summary of assumptions and results

Assumptions	Budgeting stage	Planning stage	Birth of the idea stage	Product development stage	After launch stage
The perceived need for the integration of marketing and R&D is					
Greater amongst the respondents from the R&D department who perceive of their company as a prospector and smaller amongst those who perceive it as a defender	Yes	Yes	Yes	Yes	Yes
Positive function of the perceived level of uncertainty with respect to competitive actions	No	No	No	No	No
Positive function of the perceived level of uncertainty with respect demand and technological change	Yes	Yes	Yes	Yes	Yes
The perceived level of attained integration is					
A negative function of the perceived level of formality	No	No	No	No	No
A negative function of the concentration of decision making power	No	No	No	No	No

(*Continued*)

Table 3.3 (Continued)

Assumptions	Budgeting stage	Planning stage	Birth of the idea stage	Product development stage	After launch stage
Directly proportional to the level of participation by employees in decision making regarding the new product	No	No	No	No	No
Directly proportional to the perceived quality of the relations between marketing and R&D	Yes	Yes	Yes	Yes	Yes
Directly proportional to the percentage of R&D department personnel with previous working experience at a company	Yes	Yes	Yes	Yes	Yes
Directly proportional to the perceived level of support by senior management with respect to the integration of marketing with R&D	Yes	No	Yes	Yes	Yes
Directly proportional to the degree it is perceived that senior executive management encourages the taking of risks	No	Yes	Yes	Yes	Yes
Directly proportional to the perceived level of the use of joint rewards system	No	No	No	Yes	No

The conclusions of the analysis have shown the following:

1   The perceptions of Japanese R&D executives with respect to the required level of integration are closely related to their perceptions of the strategy followed by the organization and perceived uncertainty.

2   Perceptions regarding the attained integration of the R&D and marketing departments are not associated with formal structures or the participation of employees in decision making. Also found was evidence supporting the view that higher concentrations of power in decision-making process are related with higher levels of perceived integration.

3   Also found was that the joint rewards systems did not affect the level of perceived integration. Perceptions of attained integration are positively related to perceptions regarding the level of harmonious relations between the marketing and R&D departments on the value attributed by senior executive management to integration, the working background (experience) of R&D personnel and the encouragement by senior management of taking risks.

Of course, one must also stress the fact that the preceding points regard and reflect the views of only R&D executives and not marketing executives.

Moreover, Parry and Song (1997) included in their research the key – from the viewpoint of R&D executives – problems that block the process of integration.

The lack of understanding and respect – appreciation is one of the more frequently cited problems, both for Japanese as well as American High Tech enterprises. To overcome this obstacle, Parry and Song propose (based on their research findings) offering opportunities for intradepartmental exchange of knowledge and mutual visits to clients.

A second frequently appearing problem is the lack of communication between Marketing and R&D. According to Roberts (1979), procedural approaches (joint staffing for projects) and organizational approaches (rotating teams, departments or individuals assigned the objective of integration) improve the flow of information.

Another frequently cited obstacle relates to the goals of the marketing and the R&D departments: while marketing has a short-term view, the R&D department is more oriented toward the attainment of long-term objectives. A large number of R&D executives immediately and directly pointed to the differences in culture as an obstacle for integration. Perhaps these comments show that efforts for "socialization" did not, ultimately, perform as anticipated in certain organizations. It is also possible that the conflicts between the departments were due to the failure by senior management to clarify the mission and objectives of the enterprise.

Also underlined was the fact that both the marketing and R&D departments did not have a clear view regarding the respective activities of the other. It is clear that this uncertainty must be removed care of the senior management and for responsibilities to be clarified without thereby decreasing the level of the flow of information between the departments.

Finally, the syndrome of "not invented here" was cited. To remove this attitude, as Roberts (1972) observes, the marketing and R&D departments must be jointly involved, from early on, in the new product development process so as to jointly develop a sense of commitment and dedication and for the new product to be simultaneously considered by both departments as their common ownership.

Gupta, Raj and Wilemon (1986a) propose a model with 13 propositions showing that the degree of integration a company must pursue depends on the innovation strategy it follows and the perceived environmental uncertainty in which it is active. The unit for their analysis is the company. A higher environmental uncertainty and strategies aimed to cutting-edge technologies increase the company's risk and require an increased level of integration between the marketing and R&D departments.

The authors construct a model – a map – by which they try to connect communication with successful development. Resting on the fact that modern enterprises move to organization schemas with less levels, which means that product development by such enterprises tends to become decentralized and to be treated as product-to-product, they engage on the level of business unit and on the level of product research. This map combines and expands previous models based on the research they have carried out.

Ruekert and Walker (1987) organized a causal map in terms of potential dimensions and in terms of structural processes dimensions and dimensions of results. The potential dimension acknowledges that since the work of the marketing and R&D departments vary, the appropriate degree and type of integration will also vary. The dimensions of structural processes imply actions to which companies must term in order to attain integration. These activities will depend of the circumstances. The dimension of results measures the effects of integration with respect to not only the final results but also the intermediate levels of processes.

Ashok, Gupta and Wilemon (1990), believe that the most prevailing scenario that describes conditions in High Tech markets with respect to the launching of new products is characterized by five factors:

increased domestic and international competition;
continuous development of new technologies which render existing products
    expediently obsolete;
fast changes to consumers' wishes-needs, which further curtails the products'
    life cycle;
increased cost for the development of new products;
increased need to involve external factors in the development of new products
    (for example, clients).

This scenario implies that uncertainties and difficulties in launching new products in High Tech markets are factors continuously tending toward climax.

Fifty-eight percent of respondents felt that technological uncertainty is a basic reason for delays. As a new technology emerges and becomes available for use, the temptation to integrate it in the product under development arises. Of course, this is not the only factor constituting a technological uncertainty variable, other factors include

the compatibility of the new technology with existing products;
the influence on the company's ability to realize gradual changes to its products;
the question whether the incorporation of the new technology will ultimately
    increase demand for the product;
the question whether one can guarantee the quality and reliability of the new
    technology;
the time frame within which the new technology can be acquired or developed.

All these are directly connected with the uncertainty that enters the picture on account of the new technology.

The lack of support on the side of senior executive management constituted another reason for delays for 42% of the respondents – together with the low priority (on the side of Human Resources management), nonrealistic expectations, short-term planning, aversion to risk, a lack of strategic orientation and inability or a disregard for learning from the accumulated experience of past mistakes. The respondents felt that all of these reflect the attitude shown by senior management to innovation and form a cultural framework that adversely affect the viewpoint for considering innovation.

The lack of resources or the inadequacy thereof was offered as a reason by 42% of the respondents. Of course, taking account of optimization theory, part of this problem can be attributed to the lack of support for innovation on the side of senior management. Since the resources of an enterprise, regardless of its size, are ultimately finite, their non-optimal allocation between priorities creates both an artificial as well as a real medium- to long-term sense of inadequacy for those strategic orientations which are not deemed to be "first priority". Many of those citing the inadequacy of resources supported their argument by pointing out the positioning of inexperienced personnel in critical functions and the removal of valuable associates from their posts.

The bad composition of teams, or their complete absence, and the bad intradepartmental communication practices appear one more time as a reason sufficient for delays. Together with a lack of management for product development, lack of control systems, complex structural managerial matrices and ill-defined and frequently conflicting roles, they are grouped under poor product management and were considered reason for delays by 29% of the respondents.

According to the research, the fact of the poor in-depth understanding of the problems; the time lag in its realization, originating from ineffective communication channels; and the low priority given, formed the body for the untimely articulation of the problems, or even the fact that they were not articulated at all.

Cooper (1983b) views the development of a new product as a multilevel, multidisciplinary process that includes

- the feed of ideas;
- their selection;
- the definition of the invention/conception
- the designation of the product's specifications;
- the final design of the product;
- the technical check;
- the assessment of market potential;
- the elaboration of a business plan;
- prototype development;
- the approval by senior management and, finally,
- the launching of the product.

What should also be certainly included and undoubtedly constitutes a critical factor is the management of issues ensuing from the common place of the R&D, production and marketing departments. Both Cooper and Kleinshmidt (1986) and Hise, O' Neal, McNeal and Parasuraman (1989) found that during the development of a new product many of the preceding steps are inadequately performed.

Roberts observes that the management of technological innovation is complex and includes the effective unification of people, organizational processes and plans. If there is a crack in any of them, then the entire process is weakened.

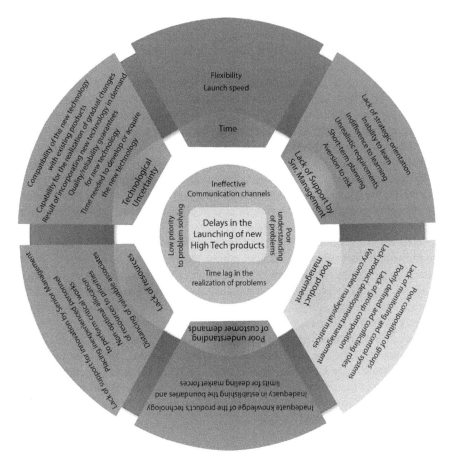

Figure 3.11 Causes for delays in the launching of new High Tech products

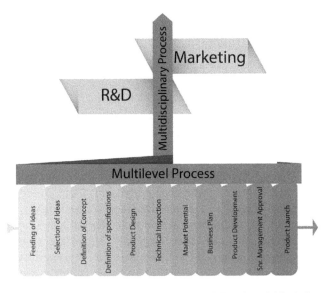

Figure 3.12 New product development process as a multilevel, multidisciplinary process

Roberts believes that an additional dimension that signifies the dynamics of the tumultuous environment is offered by the introduction of the element of time, namely, the simultaneous existence of better new products at, simultaneously, the least possible time. Specifically, with respect to development and launch times for new products, it considers that these form the basis affording a competitive advantage to enterprises engaged in technology. It ought to be noted that Takeuchi and Nonaka (1986) also share this view regarding the catalytic significance of time and note that the rules of the game for new product development constantly change, and most businesses have discovered that it no longer suffices for them to move based on the commonly accepted dogmas of combining high quality with low cost differentiation in order to excel in the modern competitive environment. Speed and flexibility have acquired a prominent role. An article that appeared in the March 1987 issue of *Fortune* magazine follows the same logic, underlining that the risks of a slow new product development are constantly increasing. Companies that delay appear as if they attempt suicide. In another *Fortune* article, titled "How Managers Can Succeed Through Speed" that was published in February 1989, Dumaine notes that those who will prevail in the market in the coming years will be the ones appreciating the benefits of launching new products in the market before their competitors and who are in a position to satisfy their clients' desires faster than the competition. Of course, the idea of compressing the development times for new products is not new, what is new, however, is the realization that time costs a lot of money. McKinsey & Company developed a model which shows that new High Tech products that were not off budget but were launched in the market six months later, were 33% less profitable (in a five-year period). Those that exceeded their budget by 50% but managed to be launched on time, lose only 4% of their profits (Ashok, Gupta, and Wilemon, 1990). In the article "Manufacturers Strive to Slice Time Needed to Develop Products", published in *Wall Street Journal* (1988) it is supported that the competitive advantage enjoyed by those with a short product development cycle is huge, not only can they charge an increased price for their unique products, but they can also incorporate upgraded technology to their goods and respond faster to emerging niche markets and the changes to preferences. Both Davidson (1988) as well as Birnbaum (1988) found that High Tech enterprises with shorted new product development cycles supersede those with longer ones.

Gold (1987) classifies the proposed strategies for expediting the product development process as follows:

Dependence on external sources via markets, strategic alliances or technological conventions.

Dependence to intensified interior R&D department schedules, by means of increasing remuneration for successful performance, via the organization of internal competition and by means of the simultaneous involvement of the R&D department in all the consecutive stages of innovation.

Dependence on innovative strategies by the R&D department such as partially emerging revisions on the acceleration of progress, avoiding seeking perfection and closer integration between R&D and the other departments.

Despite the fact that the strategies proposed by Gold formulate a framework which is a positive step for seeking and understanding the ways by which companies can accelerate the progress of innovation, empirical research is, however, needed to establish which strategies will be more effective and under what conditions and with respect to which products. Another approach is attainable by surveying the defects of current product development systems. Both Takeuchi and Nonaka (1986) as well as Birnbaum (1988), for example, suggest that the new product development process simulates a rugby game rather than a relay race (see Figure 3.13), in the sense that in the rugby game the effort made is individual, but the members of the team depend on one another up to and until the end of the game. On the other hand, a relay race is likened to the tactic followed by many enterprises and is a process where progress is linear and effected by the successive passing of the idea product from one operating department to the next, thus being both inflexible and not efficient. Similarly, Bower and Hout (1988) have discovered that companies with brief life cycles prefer teams from departments or functions and employ time as a critical variable for performance, while insisting that everybody must know information on customers, competitors and the functions of their company.

a. "Rugby game"   b. "Relay Race"

Figure 3.13 Theoretical approaches to the process for the development of new products: "rugby game" or "relay race"?

It was also found that despite the fact that many executives state that they have an established systematic process for new product development, an assessment of what really happens at their companies revealed many inadequacies. A large number of activities – frequently critical ones – are omitted while several key processes are only superficially performed, as Cooper and Kleinschmidt (1986) observe. A similar survey carried out by Hise, O'Neal, McNeal and Parasuraman in 1989 that attempts to connect product success rate with the number of activities in product planning, found that only 34.4% of companies utilizes all critical actions. The research concluded that the carrying out of more product planning activities – compared to carrying out less – was positively related to statistically higher success rates for new products. But what appears to be happening in practice is that companies hastily push their products to the market, ignoring and overlooking very important steps. According to Hise, O'Neal, McNeal and Parasuraman (1979) this leads, in a chain-reaction manner, to poor design, frequent structural faults, lawsuits and expensive callbacks, as well as to potentially higher production costs.

In the research they carried out in 12 major High Tech companies, Gupta and Wilemon (1990) found that among the reasons that urge or even exhort companies to compress their production cycle, one finds the following:

Increased competition
Rapid technological changes
Customers' demand for quick new product development
The attainment of development targets
Pressure from higher levels of management
Desire to lead an emerging market

The same research sought the reasons for which new product development is delayed. Seventy-one percent of the respondents stated that the entire procedure is significantly delayed due to the poor understanding of customers' requirements: inadequate knowledge of the technology of the product and inadequacy in determining–delimiting–treating market forces (suppliers, competitors, other forces). It is precisely this lack of understanding that poses frequent changes to the foreground as a constant in new product development and marketing schedules. Inadequate and lacking intradepartmental relations contributed to the difficulties in determining product and development requirements and frequently froze design specifications. The preceding signify the need for the integration of the marketing and R&D departments and, by extension, of engineers, production, suppliers from the early stages of new product development.

The early involvement of operating departments will assist to attain commitment and the consolidation of product requirements before valuable time and money are spend and before opinions and views on the products are fixed. This will bring a decrease in response times and, simultaneously, a decrease of the frequent and frequently useless and corrosive changes to the specifications, design and production of the products.

In the same research Gupta and Wilemon (1990) attempt to record the most basic problems-issues that ensue in the course of new product development.

Under the characterization "Organizational Style and Management Style" they describe that bureaucracy, inertia, aversion to risk taking and conservatism, as well as the lack of priorities with respect to the efforts for the development of new products constitute one of the problems emerging during the process.

Low-quality marketing research and frequent changes to the product's features, decision making without the prior analysis of consequences and the ineffective use of resources are included in the second variable that composes part of the ensuing problems.

The provision of limited help on innovation and apparent lack of dedication on the side of management by means of the inadequate investments in capital, time and human resources is another reason that hinders the development–completion of innovation.

Small manufacturing capacity – inadequacy of appropriate tools – equipment and facilities, unrealistic deadlines for the completion of production at an unrealistic cost are problems directly related to production lines and constituting the penultimate factor.

Finally, the capstone to the preceding research is the lack of strategic orientation and thinking. Operating departments are frequently exhausted in the resolution of immediate production problems and engaged in organizational routines. This frequently constitutes a shortsighted and certainly not strategically oriented view to which the inability to see "the whole picture" is attributed. The existence of new technologies from collateral sectors that may be employed by the enterprise is frequently not realized. Of course, the lack of strategic orientation is responsible for the instillation of all the preceding in the operating departments. And since the strategy formed naturally flows, in a communicating vessels fashion, also to operating departments, the effects of its absence expand and increase the chasm between where we are and where we want to go, a fact that is adequate and sufficient to interpret the following findings of the research.

The development of new, innovative products is neglected. Because of the little significance attributed to it, operating departments are inadequately equipped with the particulars that would allow unhindered collaboration, are slow to react, do not pay proper attention to important details, fail to promote good ideas in the organization and prefer the pathology of ascribing blame than prevention and assuming responsibilities.

In the context of their empirical survey, Gupta and Wilemon (1990) recorded the suggestions by employees with respect to factors which may accelerate the process for the development of innovative products, a short description and analysis of which follows.

ACTIVE – THE COMMITMENT BY SENIOR EXECUTIVE MANAGEMENT IS EVIDENT

In other words, they propose finding a golden section between short-term, current demands and long-term needs for the promotion of innovations, avoiding traps such as "discovering the wheel", insisting on the optimal, to the extent possible, matching of the efforts by the R&D department and its resources, the organized decision making, the tackling of bureaucratic methods and a more flexible consideration of the assumption of risks. The preceding factors are certainly related to strategic planning and orientation, while they are also consistent to the conclusions that are derived with respect to the role of management in the creation and provision of a vision, of the resources and a continuous commitment for innovation (Pearson, 1987). It also reinforces the position by many observes, who suggest that Japanese lead on account of their belief that their own survival depends on the success of programs for the development of new products and thus support them by offering the tangible commitment provided by the resources they invest in them.

DIRECT INVOLVEMENT – INTEGRATION OF OPERATING TEAMS

New product development is a complex, repetitive process that presupposes the contribution of various operating departments, each of which has its own ways of thinking (Dougherty, 1987). Attaining collaboration between these groups and coordinating their efforts is the key to success for successful product development. Roughly 40% of the respondents appeared to agree and suggested the formation and involvement of the operating teams from the initial stages. On a practical level, it was proposed that intradepartmental communication could be promoted via job rotation, regular and scheduled review meetings, joint visits to customers, the development of social relations and the minimization of the physical distance of the facilities where the departments are located. According to Gupta and Wilemon (1990), quick involvement benefits also the determination of the requirements for the product, before money can be wasted and positions/roles may be fixed.

MARKET TESTS AT EARLY STAGES

The rationale behind this shares the same justification with expeditionary marketing. It rests on changes suggested by customer needs and the evaluation thereof. The important role to be played by the active and early involvement of intradepartmental teams must also be stressed here, since each member depending of his or her specialization can contribute to the process, thus attaining a systemic overall contribution by means of the intradepartmental teams he or she belongs to.

Proposed, among other things, is to replace difficult to understand tools for approach and to establish groups which will be voluntary and not imposed upon. Such a process will, as Kidder (1981) suggests, ensure commitment. Volunteer inclusion in groups entails a dedication to the work such individuals will assume.

The authors essentially agree with the research by Wind and Mahajan (1988), who also recommended the redefinition of the entire development process. Additionally, they believe that organizational culture must too move toward the provision of support to innovation. They believe that in order to win the development game and for advantages to be developed, companies must adopt a more integrated approach to procedure, namely, small, self-managed, multifunctional groups; overlap of the development stages; multiple learning; little control; broad inter-corporate diffusion of knowledge; and the inclusion of instability. They, however, consider that a superficial approach to such structural changes will not produce the desired outcome.

They group what contributes to research in four major categories:

1 Support by senior executive management

- Allocation of sufficient resources to efforts for the development of new products
- Allocation of resources and time to non-"scheduled" products
- Maintaining open channels of communication
- Organization of the decision-making process and decentralization of authority
- Regular intradepartmental meetings
- Visits of intradepartmental teams to customers

2 Integration of the special knowledge possessed by operating departments

- Forecast of the environment at the launch of the product
- Understanding of customers' needs, feasibility, manufacturing and demand techniques
- Timely communication of changes to product features
- Trust and commitment between the members of the operating teams and thus facilitation of the interactions among them
- Shorting of response times
- Testing the product before it is being launched
- Avoid false starts
- Intensity/improvement of business learning

3 Accessibility of resources and the management of new product development

- Evaluation of needs in resources from early on
- Identification of the sources for these resources
- Determination of the adequacy of existing technical, design and manufacturing facilities
- Close monitoring of the project

4 Shaping of an organizational environment which promotes group effort

- Training and coaching personnel on the mission for the creation of innovative products
- Use of organizational regulations that embrace and promote group spirit
- Use of bonus to reward and incentivize collective and individual performance
- Encourage groups to identify, safeguard and transfer experience and knowledge from which the organization will benefit as a whole

Provided the preceding items do not remain a wish list, then, according to Gupta and Wilemon (1990), they will contribute the most in terms of speed, cost, flexibility, quality, differentiation, profitability and the increase of value for the consumer.

4 The model

4.1 Variables of the framework

4.1.1 Composition of factors constituting the framework for the activation of High Tech markets

The conditions and constituents defining the critical factors of the framework within which High Tech companies are called to develop their activities were described in previous chapters. It became evident that this is a demanding, "hard to negotiate" and inhospitable environment, via the survey of various viewpoints relating to theoretical and empirical approaches, definitions and logical hypotheses – associations together with their direct and indirect effects on the inherently intrinsic special characteristics of High Tech market on which they acted – on many occasions – as catalysts.

It became clear – independently of the prism adopted on each occasion and of the apperceptions of every theoretical or empirical framework – that the common constituent of all approaches was, or ended up being, the characterization of the activation environment for High Tech enterprises as turbulent, volatile or tumultuous.

The combination of special, to High Tech markets, characteristics creates a dynamic environment which is fertile for the creation of factors generated as the result of the systemic congress of special features which, by means of the systemic augmentation of their qualities, reenter the system and are fed back to it, thus further reinforcing its inherent weaknesses. Via the prism of the dynamic approach, the consequences of the problematic points in High Tech markets reenter (systemically, namely, reinforced as the negative result from the aggregation of the factors that constitute them) in the circuit of characteristics of High Technology and further entrench the specialization (and therefore difficulty) of the factors constituting the High Tech environment. At the same time they also provide the foundations for a complex schema of particular interdependencies between special factors and, therefore, consolidate the dynamic process for the increase in special factors and their qualitative deterioration at the expense of High Tech Enterprises.

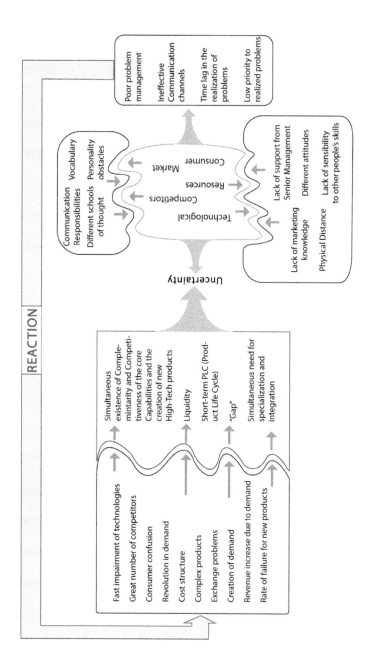

Figure 4.1 Dynamic feedback of the special characteristics composing the landscape for High Tech markets

This is precisely the argument adopted and fully accepted by this work as the best supported logical association of characterizing the features of High Tech markets as "special" and, more specifically, as turbulent and very liquid.

The preceding are in no way, of course, intended to degrade or negate the enormous importance and significance of such markets. Besides their uncontested catalytic role in economic reality, they also, and at the same time, constitute one of the most reliable means for the improvement of living standards while positively contributing to well-being. The threat composed of the rutty landscape of High Tech markets may, with the appropriate handling, become a financially fertile ground for those enterprises which will restructure based on mechanisms for the correct interpretation – analysis and treatment of these "special conditions".

4.1.2 New High Tech products

The importance of new products, especially for High Tech enterprises, is directly connected to the viability of such companies themselves. Despite the fact that the earlier proposition is not contested for almost any product category, the factors that have been suggested as composing the High Tech environment, such as

- the fast obsolescence of cutting-edge technologies,
- the entailed short product life cycle,
- the rapid change in consumers' desires,
- the great number of competitors,
- the intensity of competition,
- problems relating to the exchange of knowledge,
- liquidity,
- constant technological leaps and
- even the rate of failure for new products.

render the development and launching of new High Tech products essentially a mandate and one-way street for the long-term viability and, by extension, profitability. The mandate for the continuous introduction of new products, and, indeed, with the simultaneous decrease of the intervals between their launching, besides being an inviolable clause for survival, it is also expected to be severe (more than 75% of new product launches result to failure, according to Cooper and Kleinschmidt (1991), affected by the special conditions of the High Tech environment. Consequently, also the possibilities for success appear to be (at least) commensurately decreasing with regard to the successful launch of High Tech products.

4.1.3 Time

The almost inviolable citation of Moore's law in many papers and in almost all the books discussing the term *High Technology* introduces the element of time in the web of the complex interrelations of its variables.

According to Roberts (2007), time is that dimension which signifies the dynamics of the demanding High Tech environment. The catalytic effect of time is also underline not only by Takeuchi and Nonaka (1986) but also by Fortune (1987), where the same logic is adopted to stress that the risks of the slow development of new High Tech products are expanded, while Gold (1987) proposes strategies to shorten the time of launching for new products.

Besides the inherent participation of time not only in the intrinsic existing characteristics of the environment but also in the composition thereof, time is put in the foreground as a critical variable for one more reason.

By compressing time, High Tech corporations attempt to transcend and overcome the obstacles and challenges that emerge as a chain reaction of the effects associated with the demanding environment. The traditional one-by-one accessing of the stages of development for new products becomes shorter, and many stages are omitted or abolished, while others are accessed without concern or questioning and expediently.

In the context of a more effective response to the commands of the environment, it is attempted to shorten the time intervening from the conception of an idea for a new product until its commercial launching to the market.

The shortening of the time horizon for the process of launching an innovation – new High Tech product is legitimate and can – under conditions – become a useful tool and a key factor for the successful dealing with competition, the short life cycle of the product and other factors or consequences of factors that act deductively and inhibitory to the mission of the successful launching of new High Tech products (Gupta and Wilemon, 1990; Fortune, 1989; Wall Street Journal, 1988).

On the other hand, time and more specifically the shortening thereof, cannot be considered as the *all-subduer*, or be rendered, without adopting safety valves, conditions and clauses, as the "miraculous cure for all ailments" (Hise et al., 1989; Cooper and Kleinschmidt, 1986) for a successful launch.

The key condition to guarantee the effectiveness of shorting time (without the parallel realization of "discounts" and compromises with respect to the effectiveness of the sequence of processes for launching new products) is the effectiveness of the collaboration and coordination of the entire mechanism of the operating department of the enterprise (Bower and Hout, 1988).

Because of the particularities of the interrelations comprising the High Tech environment, time cannot be unilaterally and one-dimensionally considered as the vehicle which will affect the transition to more efficient management schema with respect to the process for launching new products. It is simultaneously also an index for the effectiveness of the tools adopted and which effectuated the properness of the process. It is, namely, the simultaneous and coexisting variable in a multitude of inherent characteristics of High Tech markets, the intermediate factor that leads to the subsequent effects and a factor that is indicative of the magnitude of the problem, as well as an indivisible ingredient of the systemic synthesis of factors that provide a dynamic (and negatively increasing) feedback to the "primary" factors.

It is only rational that since time is part of the problem (and, indeed, in more than one phases of its structure and evolutionary course), it will also be part of its solution.

However, a more proper conception of time – deemed as such pursuant to the objectives of this work – is to conceive it as a target to be attained, the successful outcome of which directly relates to the effectiveness of the unproblematic intra-departmental communication–collaboration–coordination, while it represents (and presupposes) the "therapy" of inherent problems, or problems entailed by them, irrespective of if it simply participates in the composition of their problematic nature or it poses a self-existing and independent problem itself.

To summarize, the shortening of time is considered a legitimate process, and in the light of this work it is deemed – among other indications and proofs – that it entails and directly depends on the success of the uninterrupted, unhindered and constructive collaboration and, ultimately, integration of the operating departments of marketing and R&D.

4.1.4 Optimization–maximization–intradepartmental integration

In one of his timeless and always topical fables, Aesop talks of a middle-aged man with two mistresses. Due to him having reached the midpoint in life, his head had both gray and black hair. His younger mistress used to pluck the gray hair in order to avoid malicious gossip about their age difference. But his more mature mistress also plucked the black hair, so that he would look more compatible with her and thus avoid ill-intended remarks. The reasons for which this middle-aged man led a double life are obvious: He benefited from the young age of his younger mistress, since youth was something he no longer had, while he benefited from the experience of his mature mistress, since experience usually follows (from) maturity. Of course, if we introduce the element of time to the myth and its plot, we would easily see that in the passage of time our gentleman would end up bald and, consequently, lose the companionship of both ladies, since without any hair on his head he would have forfeited the element which created the vital difference in bridging the age gap between his own age and that of his two mistresses.

Moreover, we could equally safely conclude that the pleasure our man enjoyed in the course of his double relations, despite possibly being double of that he would have had from only one relation, would, in the long run, be less than the magnitude of displeasure brought about by the absolute lack of companion, which would follow the complete loss of his hair. Perhaps, if that gentleman could foresee the turnout of his love life, he could ultimately have chosen instead of maximizing his erotic pleasure for a given period, to optimize his love life for a greater period, having taken account of the limitations that relate to the incompatibility of his two partners' taste and the negative repercussions that these would ultimately bring about.

What lends special value to this myth and in parallel the element which renders it timeless and usable in the contexts of this work is the directness of the parallels that can be drawn with respect to approaching and dealing with multivariate issues. In every scientific field that requires the simultaneous aggregation of many factors in order to attain an objective, commensurate thoughts and considerations take place.

New product development process is not a univocal action. It is a multilevel and multifunctional process (Cooper, 1983) which requires the accord, joining of forces and concurrence of efforts, goals, capacities and capabilities especially by the operating departments of marketing and R&D (Souder, 1987, 1983, 1981, 1977; Gupta et al., 1986a, 1985; Maidique and Zirger, 1984; Shanklin and Ryans, 1984; Millman, 1982; Calantone and Cooper, 1981; Gerstenfeld and Sumiyoshi, 1980; Hopkins, 1980; Souder and Chakrabarti, 1980, 1979, 1978; Cooper, 1979a, 1979b; ACARD, 1978; Rothwell et al., 1974; Gruber et al., 1973; Young, 1973; Lawrence and Lorsch, 1967a; 1967b) and thus entails the unhindered communication and coordination of actions and views, throughout the entire course of the process for the development of a new (innovative) High Tech product.

The previous paragraph essentially captures the concept of integration for the two operating departments, under the light of an integrated and systemic approach of the two departments, namely, their strategic pairing and the synergies entailed by it, as well as the effective use of the specialized operating capacities – capabilities of each department. It constitutes, to put it in other words, the necessary bridge between the specialized parts, which work toward the common direction of the development (and launching) of new innovative products, where both parts share the same goals and priorities (Gupta et al., 1985) and jointly establish the product development schedule.

And while it is evident that Integration, as a concept, acts complementary to specialization, it is also true that extreme specialization approaches (which go as far as to alienate the two departments or turn one against the other), resulting from either inherent obstacles, such as attitudes, schools of thought and so on (Dougherty and Heller, 1994; Griffin and Hauser, 1993; Dougherty, 1992, 1990; Cooper, 1990; Lucas and Bush, 1988; Douglas, 1987; Gupta et al., 1986b; Zeithaml and Zeithaml, 1984; Achrol et al., 1983; Carroad and Carroad, 1982; Block, 1977; Galbraith, 1977; Twiss, 1974; Duncan, 1972; Khandwalla, 1972; Booz and Booz, 1968; Lawrence and Lorsch, 1969; Raudsepp, 1965) or as the result of the factor relating to the bad communication and collaboration that results from any of the directly or indirectly arising special High Tech characteristics, suboptimize the overall result and negatively intensify the difficulties for launching new products.

The lack of communication/collaboration – non-integration – either as the result of the isolated operating effort to attain the – narrowly defined – objectives of one or the other department is a catastrophically destabilizing factor that intensifies uncertainty and exacerbates most of the other factors that compose the environment for the development of novel and innovative High Tech products, while, in a chainlike fashion, it prolongs launch times and drastically contributes to the magnitude of the dynamic negative feedback of the framework within which High Tech products are being developed.

Insufficient/lacking integration decisively deflects from the balance point that must be attained in order to dampen/phase out the adverse environmental conditions and their catastrophic results on the process for introducing a new product.

It ought to be stressed that while operating maximization (under the light of the narrowly and departmental defined attainment of objectives, adoption of practices, culture, etc.) goes against and is an obstacle for the exhaustive approach to optimization and the efficient and rational attainment of the common organizational objectives that is preached by integration. The integration of the departments is not a concept contradicting maximization. It aims at the same result, under the proviso of the specific difference that it treats the issue more spherically and rationally by incorporating in the system of its variables (besides the pursuits of the operational maximization in the sense of the term adopted earlier) other parameters as well. As such a system for conceptualization and treatment is leads more robustly through the "turbulent" and "misty" landscape to the attainment of the objective, namely, the more expedient successful launching of High Tech products.

It is now inconceivable for any operating department of an enterprise to be working toward the direction of attaining the same objectives that constitute subsets of the central goal and not to collaborate with the other departments so as to make the optimization of the central goal of the enterprise attainable (Schneider, 1987; Souder, 1987; Maidique and Zirger, 1984; Millman, 1982; Cooper, 1979b; Souder and Chakrabarti, 1979; Rothwell et al., 1974; Lawrence and Lorsch, 1967a, 1967b).

Communication in such an approach and the safety valves adopted to ensure its effectiveness in such a sector with these special characteristics accentuates business-to-business collaboration as a fundamental condition and improves the margins of the correct and fast management of threats and risks which may arise in course.

4.2 Adopted viewpoint of communication–collaboration– integration

The key variable and constituent factor for success when developing a new product in a High Tech environment, as it has been identified in the majority of both theoretical as well as the models inferring conclusions via empirical research, is intradepartmental collaboration and communication.

The definition of the notion of "collaboration" in the context of this work is not exhausted only in the exchange of information via a system of inflow and outflow mechanisms and the dialectic relation between them. The existence of this needs is nowadays considered self-evident, on account of the modern approaches to enterprises as open systems subject to multivariate influences stemming from their external environment.

But the viewpoint of collaboration and the corresponding documentation of the catalytic need to attain its expansion also inside the boundaries of the organization commences from there.

In the context of the operating competences, marketing is assigned not only with listening to customers' needs, but also with acting as the medium to convey them inside the enterprise. It is thus both the carrier and the joining link that discloses data and inflow inside the organization (Dutta et al., 1999; Griffin and Hauser, 1996; Gupte et al., 1986a; Gruber, 1981; Clarke, 1974).

But it is clear, however, that the utility of this information inflow, besides any typical characteristics it must satisfy (to be accurate, timely and valid) will be judged, ultimately, by the extend by which informing will be heard by the enterprise, namely, the extent by which such informing will be incorporated in the knowledge pool of the enterprise, be filtered and processed via the system of accumulated experiences and will, finally, be introduced and included in the decision-making "algorithm" of the enterprise. An information – the result of efficient and structured efforts by marketing – will be rendered completely useless if it does not influence the direction of the operating alignment toward the objectively and jointly accepted organizational objective.

In the chainlike approach that follows from the acquisition of information inflows as the result of listening to consumers, the next step is to translate and analyze these so as to transubstantiate them to useful products, which will be adopted by consumers as the efficient way to deal with their needs.

Operating competence to translate and interpret these needs to technical specifications and to transubstantiate them to tangible products is, by definition, assigned to the R&D department.

It is rendered clear that the interrelation between the operating departments of marketing and R&D, besides and beyond the symbiotic relation that must distinguish it, is a critical and catalytic factor for the attainment of success when they come together and identify the creation of the product with the need that determines the variables for its composition and birth. This unification of efforts, especially for organizations active in a High Tech environment, is not an optional step toward improving the likelihood of success in launching new products but, rather, a one-way street and prescript for survival.

On account of the fact that many scholarly endeavors recognized and acknowledged the need, the importance and the consequences of approaching and discussing the symbiotic interrelationship of these two departments, the term *integration* as employed by them to describe the operating unification of departmental efforts will be hereinafter adopted.

Before the description of the proposed theoretical mechanism is attempted, it is deemed purposeful to clarify the viewpoint for the adoption and use of the term *integration* in the contexts of this work.

Integration does not aspire to abolish operating department or the role thereof. It is not pursued to create a new, mutant department which will comprise of interdisciplinary scientists or "jacks of all trades" who will have an opinion on everything. This would be neither prudent or legitimate (Schneider, 1987; Souder, 1987; Lawrence and Lorsch, 1967a, 1967b), due to the fact that it is, by definition, unattainable to have specialization in more than one cognitive fields. In other words, it is not deemed legitimate to abolish specialization in favor of integration. What is pursued is to increase the magnitude of specialization but to increase it through integration. Also pursued is to exploit the benefits of both specialization and integration with the simultaneous, to the extent possible, eradication of their disadvantages, via inter-affecting and the effective management of their contact point.

It is proposed to maintain the individuality and nature of part of the two departments so as to maintain the high effectiveness in the use of their capacities and skills and for the attainment of their operating objectives to be effective. In parallel, however, it is imperative that this specialization be included and incorporated in a wider framework for its development and expansion toward the direction recommended by the integration of the departments. The common ground, the section of the two operating wholes is attained by expanding and relating the dividing lines (Galbraith, 1973; March and Simons, 1958) which separate the operating departments. The coming together of a subset of marketing executives with a subset of R&D executives will suggest the common orientation and render clear the direction for targeting the correct goals, while also recommending the proper means for their attainment.

This view, then, pursues

1   the reinforcement, expansion and fortification of the operationally specialized capacities of the departments;
2   the attainment of the preceding toward the direction dictated by the systemic approach of the two departments, so as for the expansion of operational capacities to be incorporated in the framework of integration's objectives. It is, thus, dynamically ensured that extensions of the specialized operating competences will originate as the products (of at least a "partial") integration, and they will simultaneously dynamically and directly affect both the qualitative expansion–reinforcement of integration as well as its consolidation as a fixed state and the long-term viability of the symbiotic relation it represents. Figures 4.2 and 4.3 illustrate this.

4.3 The goals for the proposed framework

The goal of this work is to establish an effective process for the development of new High Tech products, which will incorporate in the mechanisms of its processes, the effective collaboration between the operating departments of (principally) marketing and R&D, and which

•   will contribute toward the integration of the marketing and the R&D department (principal objective) but will also promote an integrated intradepartmental collaboration with the other operating departments.
•   will be market-oriented (consumers and competitors).
•   will facilitate the rational management of the new High Tech portfolio of products of the High Tech enterprise that will adopt it.
•   will contribute toward the improvement of the learning curve of the corporation.

A. Specialization without integration

Common objective

R&D ├────Distancing────┤ MKT

R&D's operational objective

Marketing's operational objective

B. Full integration without specialization

Common objective

Role confusion
Abolishment of individuality
Destruction of core capabilities
Inefficient use of operational capabilities
Abolishment of the ingredients for specialization

R&D   MKT

C. Partial integration and it's dynamic interrelationship with specialization

Ci) Establishment

Marketing Specialization

→ Integration

R&D' Specialization

Figure 4.2 Specialization/integration

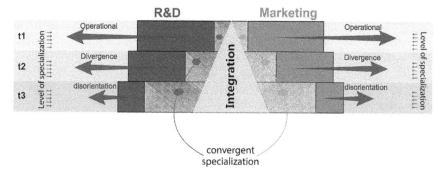

R&D   Marketing

t1   Operational   Operational

t2   Divergence   Divergence

t3   disorientation   disorientation

Level of specialization   Integration   Level of specialization

convergent specialization

Figure 4.3 Positive dynamic intercorrelation of the two departments toward the proper direction for attaining the objective – common organizational goal, positive dynamics

- will contribute to decrease uncertainties.
- will contribute toward the reinforcement of the operating specialization of marketing and R&D departments, toward the direction defined by their common organizational objective and through their integration.
- through the preceding will contribute to time-savings with respect to new High Tech product development.

4.4 Proposed framework

4.4.1 First stage: formation of groups

4.4.1.1 Activities

A. The head of the marketing department will, jointly with the head of the R&D department, designate the executives from the operating departments who will constitute the integration core. As integration core is considered that group of marketing and R&D executives who, by means of the close collaboration, will coordinate its operating capacities and approach the organizational objective by means of the joining of efforts and operating specialization of its executives, correspondingly.

These executives are authorized by their respective heads to come to contact so as to establish a basis, a common ground of understanding and to build a primary communication channel that will function as the herald for integration.

They are tasked with playing the role of the joining link – the communication link between the two departments toward their partial integration. The executives continue to keep contact with their respective operating departments, but at the same time and via the "friction" (that will ensue from the collaboration) and the communication with the corresponding executives from the other department, they gain access to the used work tools, methodology, processes and culture of the other department. This way the capacity to convey useful information to the executives who were not "integrated" under the auspices of the integration core is increased. The non-integrated marketing and R&D executives will continue to perform their respective operationally specialized activities and will constitute, that is, the operating specialization cores.

This integrated group, consisting of the heads of the marketing and R&D departments and the executives appointed for this from the departments shall be hereinafter referred to as the "Core Group" (CG).

The CG will be assigned with the basic responsibility of providing guidance toward the common organizational objective.

B. The CG formed will come to contact with the heads of the other operating departments of the enterprise (not included in the CG), in order to identify possible points (e.g., functions, characteristics of resources, employed procedures, knowledge and skills, relevance, potential areas of contribution) whose relevance to the objective is great and the knowledge of which are necessary for the multi-level and integrated pursuit of the objective. For example, in order for a new High

Tech product (for sake of brevity, NHTP) "X" to be developed, it may be deemed of critical importance to include the financial department of the company in the decision-making process, on the grounds that a great financial investment in capital goods is required or to include the HR department and, indeed, those executives who decide on hiring personnel, the level of specialization and so on since in order to manufacture NHTP "X" more staff may be required, among other issues. After the identification of the critical departments or/and the important areas of contribution to the effective pursuit of the objective or/and the corresponding operating executives who are carriers of skills relevant to the objective has been completed, a wider group enclosing the CG is formed, which will be known as the Basic Group (BG). Besides the principal responsibility of the BG to feed the necessary knowledge, skills and information to the CG, it also assumes the task of identifying individuals, carriers and groups which are located either inside or outside the company and which can operate as carriers for the inflow of information. The duties of the BG include, for example, the identification of an unsatisfied customer (by the company or the competition) and "eliciting" information from him or her or identifying and approach consumer associations and so on. The BG will maintain regular contact with the aforementioned bodies and groups, in a systemic manner, and will systematize the flow of information so as to ensure its utility, the quality level and long-term viability and expansion of the contact, with individuals or carriers who are providers of manifold information.

The potential "informants" are the communication bridge between the BG and all those individuals who can influence the corporation or its decisions, but also those who are the main recipients of its works, namely, senior management, members of the board and shareholders, as well as consumer associations, environmental groups, universities and customers, competitors, salesmen, among others, all those stakeholders, that is, who can influence the decision-making process on each occasion and the identification of its critical parameters.

C. Finally, the Expanded Group (for brevity, EG) is formed from expanding the BG to include senior management and all those individuals or groups cited earlier who the members of the BG and the CG. believe can influence the corporation and/or its decisions. The CG and BG exchange information which either exists as part of the knowledge pool or is derived from the informants or is a combination of the two. The CG determines and designates the strategic coordination of information to and from all departments since it simultaneously operates like an information transmitter (based on the marketing orientation it adopts), for the potential performance and viability of the corporation and as the receiver of individual information coming from other departments and informants and which shape the evaluation of performance and viability. In the stages that follow when there is reference to the members of the BG, then we include the members of the BG–CG, and when there is reference to the members of the EG, then we include the members of EG–BG. An exception to the aforementioned proposed structure of the groupings of members is allowed only for the estimation of the conflict of opinions between the BG and EG where (as it will be seen in stage 4) in the basic group we include also the members of the CG; that is, BG =BG + CG.

Figure 4.4 Three-leveled system for the formation–coordination of groups

It must also be stressed that the members of the marketing and R&D departments who constitute the corresponding operating specialization cores are included in BG, namely, outside of the CG, since under the light of this work, the principal priority is to contribute and develop their specialized operating capacities, under the guidance and directions provided by the CG. Despite the fact that their contact with the part of CG where their executives participate is closer because of the corresponding relevance of their operating subject matters, their principal contribution, however, is not qualitatively differentiated from the contribution of the other operating departments participating in the BG, namely, the provision of specialized knowledge-solutions relating to the cognitive field, under the guidance and common orientation that will ensue from the process of integration of which they are parts of but not the leading ones.

The formation and composition of the groups, the relations between them, can be illustrated as seen in Figure 4.4.

4.4.1.2 Justification of activities

High Tech Products, as John, Weiss and Dutta (1999) observe, essentially constitute an application and realization of a specific know-how and enclose not only the scientific knowledge incorporated in the utility of a product but also the knowledge for its construction and commercial exploitation.

The inability to separate a High Tech product from the technology existing in it (Glazer, 1991; Moriarty and Kosnik, 1989; Capon and Glazer, 1987; Crawford, 1983; Miaoulis and LaPlaca, 1982; Hisrich and Peters, 1978) renders the prominent importance of the operating departments of marketing and R&D clear and places them at the top of the importance hierarchy when creating an NHTP.

Since the role of the marketing and R&D departments carries the most weight (Hatzichronoglou, 1997; NSB, 1996; Moriarty and Kosnik, 1989; Souder, 1987; Jauch and Kraft, 1986; Kotler, 1984; Maidique and Zirger, 1984; Millman, 1982; TIRED, 1982; Cooper, 1979b; Souder and Chakrabarti, 1979; ACARD, 1978; Rothwell et al., 1974) it is rational for their role to be accentuated in the decision-making process relating to the launching of NHTPs and to assume executive status, while these two departments are rendered the essential center for making, checking and evaluating information and decisions, especially in the context of the proposed approach to integration.

The rationale elaborated earlier may be observed both during the procedure for the formation of the CG, namely, from who those designating and checking its composition may be and who will participate in it, as well as from the competences assigned to its members, while it is further reinforced also by the wider framework for definitions/features and particularities that offers the stigma of the vital space and products for High Tech.

High tech products structured and developed based on knowledge about market needs, or which are developed as a response to competition, inherently have a greater likelihood for success than products responding to the challenges of a technological opportunity. The high rate of correlation between being at the technological forefront and the ability for technical and commercial success is documented by research (Souder, 1987). Thus, an orientation with an emphasis on the market, but also the simultaneously ensuing from this, the acceptance of marketing's philosophy (and the practical documentation of the acceptance of their correctness and significance, especially in environments exhibiting activities with respect to High Tech products, by means of the acceptance for the participation of the marketing department, and its upgraded role in the CG) is documented by many of the High Tech factors (and, in parallel, shapes a fertile ground for the development of a competitive advantage by means of the continuous listening to and approaching consumer needs, and the close monitoring of competitors' moves) which affect the activities of High Tech enterprises, such as

- the intensity of competition (Gardner, 1990);
- the great number of competitors (Moriarty and Kosnik, 1989);
- the frequent change and rapid alterations to the terms of the competitive "game" by newcomers or parachute competitors in the sector (Mohr, 2001; Hamel, 1997; Gardner, 1990; Cooper and Schendel, 1976);
- liquidity (Veryzer, 1998);
- emphasis on the competitive side (Clark, 1985);
- the existence of NHTPs developed on the side of offer (Shanklin and Ryans, 1984);
- difficulties in articulating needs by consumers (Mohr, 2001);

- consumers' confusion (Moriarty and Kosnik, 1989);
- consumers' perceptions of technology, use and consumption standards (Ansoff and McDonnell, 1990; Veryzer, 1998; Robertson, 1967);
- the revolutions to demand caused by NHTPs (Moriarty and Kosnik, 1989);
- changes to perception caused by radically innovative NHTPs (Mohr, 2001; Rangan and Bartus, 1995; Abernathy and Utterback, 1978);
- uncertainty stemming from consumers and consumer groups and the entailed uncertainty with respect to the competitive place of the enterprise in the sector (Abell, 1980);
- the fast obsolescence of cutting-edge technologies and the short and tumultuous product life cycle (Moriarty and Kosnik, 1989; Grunenwald and Vernon, 1988);
- the need to effectively and efficiently manage demand;
- the need to acknowledge the mapping and detect the point of the "S"-type technology curve one is at;
- the existence of the "chasm" between the early adopters and the pragmatists and the chaotic consequences this causes to the market (Mohr, 2001; Siegel, 1998; Moore, 1991);
- the complexity characterizing High Tech products (Moriarty and Kosnik, 1989);
- exchange-related issues (John et al., 1999);
- cost/unit, the increasing proceeds on account of demand, the diffusion of knowledge (John et al., 1999);
- the fact that innovative NHTPs can become the protagonists in a "David versus Goliath" scenario (Chandy and Tellis, 1998; Foster, 1986);
- the factors composing market uncertainty (Moriarty and Kosnik, 1989), namely,

  - the needs to be satisfied by high tech,
  - the way such needs will change in the future – over time,
  - whether the market will adopt the industry standards,
  - the rate of expansion for the new technology,
  - the size of the potential market,
  - which compose the acronym FUD (Fear, Uncertainty, Doubt);

- the acceptance of the collection–processing–analysis and dissemination of appropriate information as a critical and catalytic factor for reducing market uncertainty (Moorman and Miner, 1997; Moore, 1991; Ketteringham and White, 1984; Glaser et al., 1983; Marquis, 1982; Baker et al., 1980; Goldhar et al., 1976 Galbraith, 1973; Rothwell and Robertson, 1973; Utterback, 1971) ;
- avoiding the trap that is the unidimensional consideration/treatment of their competitive advantages, that ensues from the until now low attributed significance in the usefulness of mapping consumer needs and delimiting competition (based, for example, on a competitive advantage or the level of competition, etc.) that marketing can offer (Leonard-Barton, 1992; Weick,

1979) (e.g. weakening the marketing department and considering it to be "second class");

- the need to delimit "healthy" cannibalism in the company, the decision or accept or reject it as something legitimate and called for, the need to identify the right moment for cannibalism to begin and end but also the magnitude of the ensuing differential benefit from it (Mohr, 2001; Chandy and Tellis, 1998; Boulding et al., 1997; Hannan and Freeman, 1997; Utterback, 1994; Leonard-Barton, 1992; Chemawat, 1991; Deshpande and Webster, Jr., 1989; Foster, 1986; Kerin et al., 1978; Copulsky, 1976);
- the need to create a vision for the future, which most possibly will include markets not existing or even conceptualized/mapped and which will transcend the confines of the present conception of today's markets (Mohr, 2001; Hamel and Prahalad, 1990);
- marketing's role with respect to the constituents relating to organizational creativity – corporate imagination (Hamel and Prahalad, 1990; e.g., escape from tyranny, offering an array of benefits incorporated in the product and not just technology, change of the price–performance hypotheses, empathetic design); and
- understanding the way by which emerging technologies can allow to satisfy consumers' needs not yet satisfied or to satisfy them more effectively, an understanding that is catalytic for the discovery of new competitive grounds (Hamel and Prahalad, 1990).

On the other hand, the corresponding documentation of the equal participation of the R&D department in the CG, namely, the group that will assume the leading role with respect to the fulfilment of the common and viable organizational vision and goal, emerges as the result of factors such as

- the fact that an NHTP is created on the basis of strong scientific-technical knowledge and its informed application, a process which is by definition associated – if not being completely subsumed – to the operating competences of the R&D department (Veryzer, 1998; Moriarty and Kosnik, 1989; Grunenwald and Vernon, 1988; Rexroad, 1983; TIRED, 1982);
- the multitude of definitions offered by governmental sources or/and international organizations and the criteria they adopt in order to accept considering a company as high tech, which serves to illustrate the catalytic nature of the participation of the skills and activities of the operational R&D department in the development of NHTPs (Hatzichronoglou, 1997; NSB, 1996; Hadlock et al., 1991; Moriarty and Kosnik, 1989);
- the acknowledgment of the constituents of technological uncertainty and their consideration as key ingredients composing the discourse of the singular High Tech environment (Souder and Moenaert, 1992; Abell, 1980);
- the high rate of correlation between innovation and technology (Mohr, 2001; De Meyer, 1985);

- the fact that the scientific-technical skills comprised, as a rule and to a large extent, continue to form the basis of the competitive core of benefits and the differential advantage of many High Tech companies (Wind and Mahajan, 1997; Geroski, 1993; this largely refers to the knowledge and skills possessed by employees and to the techniques – scientific knowledge incorporated in the technical systems); and
- the necessity of the contribution of the knowledge and accumulated experience of the R&D department to the assessment and evaluation – among other things – of whether it is purposeful to cannibalize, when and in which manner.

Especially for High Tech enterprises it is vital to listen to customers' needs and to represent what it articulates appropriately and thus rendering not only that it will be heard loud and clear but also that it would be directly aligned to and in cooperation with the science and knowledge brought by the R&D department (Shanklin and Ryans, 1984). The skills of High Tech enterprises excel in two sectors:

- Their ability to constantly invent new innovations
- Their skill to transubstantiate these innovations to products, which contribute to the satisfaction of (expressed or and not yet realized) consumer needs and preferences

The preceding statements underline the special capacities and a High Tech enterprise must possess, as such may be perceived on the side of offer (Shanklin and Ryans, 1984).

The flip side of the coin describes the capacities of a High Tech company which is demand-oriented (Shanklin and Ryans, 1984) and are

- the skill of listening to needs and to efficiently convey them inside the enterprise and
- their interpretation–transubstantiation to useful, desirable product features.

Either way and regardless of which skill represents a temporally preexisting skill or orientation that triggers the process for the creation of an innovative NHTP, it is clear that an empowered marketing department entails a greater ability to listen and a wider idea pool for the satisfaction of customers, while an empowered R&D department entails a wider range of applications and a greater capacity to establish specifications which will meet consumer needs and will be manifested in the NHTP.

While a combination of the skills will result to a mighty technical-scientific basis with a simultaneous incorporation of marketing's philosophy to it, thus avoiding blunders such as, for example, to opt for a bad launching time (ACARD, 1978), to overemphasize the product's technical features instead of presenting the offer as the product idea's integrated array of benefits (Hamel and Prahalad, 1991) and so on.

The staffing of the CG is deemed purposeful to be carried out under the responsibility and oversight of those in charge of the marketing and R&D departments, since being the operating heads, they will have a universal and encompassing opinion on the executives of their respective departments who report to them and will be (by definition) in a position to know their operational capacities that will render them suitable to staff the CG.

Additionally, those in charge of the marketing and R&D departments come into contact, also in the context of their competences as senior executives, with the senior executives of other operating departments, thus acquiring a more informed and integrated picture of the characteristics required to meet needs and attain the CG's objectives. Besides, the decision-making process for the staffing of the CG by the heads of the marketing and R&D departments (which takes place at the initial stage of the proposed procedure) also contributes toward the reinforcement of communication between them. According to Moenaert and Souder (1990b) the cohesion of such a communications link will contribute more when it occurs during the development stage.

The coming together of marketing and R&D is deemed to be of determinative importance (Calantone and Cooper, 1981), since the successful joint performance of activities (in the contexts of the group) is rendered a particularly important factor to ensure the short- to medium-term product offers and the pairing of product and market. This symbiotic inter-association (Hayes et al., 1988) results to the production of clear benefits which exceed to sum of benefits produced by the two departments with isolated or fragmentary coordinated activities. For the attainment of the preceding, Hofer and Schendel (1978) observe that perhaps the ideal case would be the constant and uninterrupted contact between the two departments. The same authors underline that an obstacle to attaining the collaboration and unification of efforts is the problematic contact between the two departments, or even the lack thereof, and the subsequent ineffectiveness of communication.

Contact between the two departments (which are considered, in the context of this work, keys for the effective attainment of organizational successes via the multitude of benefits that the systemic approach to their capabilities will contribute) and the properly oriented coordination that will ensue from their collaboration are considered critical factors.

An approach between marketing and R&D executives and indeed at the early stages of the development of an NHTP will avert the risk of a gap between the requirements of the environment and the existing Core Capabilities – especially if Core Capabilities originate in a strong scientific basis.

The simultaneous and systematic utilization of marketing's role as the joining link between customers' desires/needs and their conversion to inflows (to the other operating departments of the enterprise, but principally to R&D) and of the R&D department which holds the scientific-technical knowledge to convert these data (the inflows from the other operating departments of the corporation, but principally from marketing) in features of the array of benefits of the products it is called to materialize is a necessary condition for success.

This boils down to reinforcing the process for the uninterrupted and effective contact with the environment and the satisfactory and appropriate transfer of the necessary information flow; it documents the characterization of operating congress and systemic approach for the coordination and collaboration of the two departments as a guarantee for the success of the organizational pursuits. This viewpoint is also consistent with Parry's and Song's view (Quinn and Cameron, 1988) but also other research papers which demonstrate the contact of the two departments as the most critical of variables (Prahalad and Hamel, 1990; Hitt and Ireland, 1985; Snow and Hrebiniak, 1980).

Additionally, by contact in the context of operating collaboration the most powerful conditions are established to break the vicious circle of the renewal and development of the core benefit in a one-dimensional orientation and only toward the direction of the technical supremacy and scientific basis offered by R&D (if not the breaking of the circle itself).

In parallel, the value attributed for the content and the creation of knowledge to the role of the marketing and R&D departments and which is essentially a manifestation of managerial practices accepted (via the establishment of the CG and the selection of its composition), supported and reinforced by the leaders of the enterprise, positively affects the development of NHTPs on many counts. Besides being a tangible rejection of the view suggesting the existence of lower, or lesser operating groups, it offers to both the executives in the CG as well as the operating groups in marketing and R&D an empowerment – an increase, that is, in their faith that they can contribute toward the attainment of the objective. Value is thus ascribed to be the creation of the knowledge to be produced in the context of the approach of the two departments, further reinforced by the company's leadership, and/or which is also included and incorporated in managerial practices.

Parallel to this, the further distancing of the two departments is averted or the chasm is bridged, since it avoids the consolidation–crystallization of accepting the existence of (and correspondingly of attributing) higher status (or operating value) to the up to now considered as the operating "elite" of the enterprise.

The attribution of a higher status to be operating groups will later function as a cell of attraction for talented individuals, who will now be motivated (or at least not deterred) for working both in the R&D but also in the marketing department.

A chainlike – indirect – consequence is also the fact that in the short to medium term the development of the departments' specialization (in parallel to the development of the CG and as the result of proper guidance from it) in the contexts of the proposed process and the results of the attainment of the organizational objective will become a more important pole of attraction then the prior state of ascribing high status (principally to R&D executives) and, naturally, from the attribution of low operating status (principally to marketing executives, but also from other – save for R&D – operating departments).

To summarize, the establishment of the CG and with its recommended staffing will give the starting signal for the retraction and minimization of all forms of incompatibility which may potentially arise from the interrelation of core capacities and innovative creation.

The arguments cited CG can also be considered as indirect effects from reducing the magnitude of dissonance which will gradually and effectively evolve from the contact of the two departments and, indeed, from the inception of the process for the development of an NHTP.

More specifically, the contact of the two departments can become an effective factor for lifting the stereotypes that flourish in operating groups with respect to the others and reduce the magnitude of negative perceptions for the personality differences between them. A reduction of these inhibitory factors hindering communication and the development of trust means to lift the obstacles to their effective communication.

Another, frequently cited, problem (Gardner et al., 2000; Rosen et al., 1998; Veryzer, 1998; Moore, 1991; Ansoff and McDonnell, 1990; Moriarty and Kosnik, 1989; Link, 1987; Samli and Wills, 1986; Ketteringham and White, 1984; Rexroad, 1983; Porter, 1980; Clarke, 1974; Robertson, 1967) to communication and collaboration is the fact of the existence of a different way of thinking between marketing and R&D executives, principally attributed to their different educational background. The dissimilitude in the prism through which they consider the common organizational objectives, the possible difficulties of the two departments to realize the goals, solutions and mutual concessions of one to the other (trade-offs) expand the chasm of lack of understanding with respect to the manner each department perceives and with respect to their perceptions each adopts themselves.

The "friction" and constant contact in the context of the CG as well as the realization of the "kinship" identity attributed to all those included in the CG are considered to be an effective means to structure relations based on mutual understanding, respect and a fertile exploitation of the special abilities of executives, irrespective of whether they belong to marketing or R&D.

Moreover, the contact of the departments and convergence proposed by this framework may have a positive effect on the operating problems relating to the different terminology adopted by each department. The verbal obstacles cease to exist, since the closer contact will disclose and render comprehensible the terms employed by each group to both groups. Simultaneously and since every word will represent and reflect one concept (Glaser et al., 1983; Galbraith, 1973), the corresponding departments will adopt and appropriate the terminology/meaning attributed to words also cumulatively – by the increasingly expanding familiarity – thus appropriating the rationale of the other department. This way, consumer needs and products or services to be developed with the appropriate technical-scientific medium, and which will render the suitable features that will satisfy consumer needs, will cease to be disconnected, due to the establishment of a common ground for understanding – common communication code, accepted and understood by both departments. It is underlines that the lack of contact between the two departments and their separation are factors that distance them from one another. In many cases the key knowledge possessed by R&D for marketing are so alien in nature that they may even go against any efforts. The "twin" obstacles (relating to professionalization and culture) are formed or intensified as the result of the earlier ignorance. The more effective and efficient contact lifts these obstacles and the dividing line, which hinder and obstruct all the way from the birth of an idea to its transubstantiation to a product and its launch in the market (Pavitt, 1991). As it is also pointed out by the Advisory Council for Applied Research and Development (ACARD; Hayes, 1985), the lack of communication acts as an inhibitory catalyst to innovation.

Parallel to the establishment of the CG and the contact between executives, organizational obstacles (usually due to different priorities for goals and responsibilities or different mediums used for comparisons and different perceptions of the purposefulness and "legitimacy" of product development) will cease to exist. Under the auspices of the CG and the mandates of the common objective, but also by means of the properly oriented (toward the attainment of the common goal) specialization, the process will in a chainlike manner lead to a more effective attainment of the objective (which will not be identified, mapped, analyzed and pursued by mutual consent).

Besides the establishment of the CG and based on the logic that although to ensure the honest collaboration (attained, at least partly, by the contact brought about by participation and collaboration in the context of the CG) between marketing and R&D may be a necessary condition for success, it is not in itself sufficient to guarantee it, the CG is expanded.

The expansion of the CG is performed in order to systemically approach and exploit the knowledge and skills from other areas of operational specialization inside the company (namely, toward the integration of the other operating departments).

Besides it would be irrational to the logic of the fairly high significance of the relation and importance of the marketing and R&D departments for the development of an NHTP, for the constituent of the contribution of the other departments to assume a leading role. Something like this would lead to the adoption of a similar shortsighted view and would bring about a commensurate number of problems and obstacles as those of the view this model tries to overcome by proposing the establishment of groups for the more functional symbiotic interrelation between the marketing and R&D departments.

Based on the elasticity and flexibility that is prudent to frame the theoretical model proposed, so that it may be adjusted across a great scope of managerial organizations and structures and/or for a great scope of different operational areas and different staffing thereof, the BG may include or exclude operating departments, depending on the objective pursued, the special conditions and circumstances in the market, the competition, the environment or even the product under development itself. Thus, the proposed theoretical model can be customized or tailor-made to more effectively and efficiently serve the reasons for its existence.

The reason for the participation and organization of those directly interested/involved/affecting the decisions, the stakeholders, and senior management in the EG is that the first, the stakeholders, essentially represent a major piece of the company's external environment (thus the potential informing by them is important) while some of them are recipients of the company's and the development process's decisions and outcomes, and thus their interests are directly related. We avoid to identify stakeholders one by one but, rather, leave their selection to the High Tech enterprise, which will base its decision given the circumstances.

The reason senior management participates in the wider environment of the BG, namely, in the EG, is that it constitutes that internal part of the enterprise which has rights of "life or death" on the potential NHTP (namely, the result of the proposed procedure). Senior management has the final say (in most, if not all, cases) on the critical tactical and strategic decisions for accepting or rejecting the candidate NHTP, to finance it, on the resources that will be made available to it and so on. Additionally, senior management can exercise a multifaceted influence on the process for the establishment of the groups (and, consequently, with respect to the effectiveness of the entire process), reinforcing or abolishing the proposed, by the theoretical framework, viewpoint. Souder and Chakrabarti (1978) feel that senior management can either promote or hinder the development of a productive communication channel, a fact that reinforces the view on its participation in decision making. It was also found (Wind, 1982; Roberts and Fusfeld, 1981; Quinn, 1979; Roberts, 1979, 1978) that the attitude by senior management with respect to the acceptance and the degree of the acceptance of taking risks, has a positive effect on the successful outcome of innovation. Consequently, it is important that it is involved in the process for the identification of variables and decision making so that it can offer a pointer as to the magnitude and orientation of its positions and to get its consent from early on. Gupta, Raj and Wilemon (1985) also feel that senior management can, among other things, contribute to the speed, flexibility, cost decrease, quality, differentiation and increase of the value consumers offer. The factors cited document the role and substance of the participation of senior management in the decision-making process for the development and launch of NHTPs.

4.4.2 Second stage: collection and organization of data in the knowledge pool (KP)

4.4.2.1 Activities

A. An SWOT analysis is to be carried out, assisted by the CG, BG and EG, as well as the "informants". The groups will try to identify factors, in the internal and external environment of the company, which constitute Strengths–Weaknesses–Opportunities–Threats. Identified at this stage will be a large portion of the factors that are critical and whose not only identification and realization but also the joint (by the executives of the groups) analysis and labeling will delimit the field of activation and the terms for action.

B. Then, and based on the collected data and findings of the SWOT, but also the knowledge–experience–informing possessed by the members of the aforementioned groups, a matrix will be jointly filled in on the meeting of all members (of at least the BG and CG), hereinafter referred to as Knowledge Pool (KP). The KP will record information such as the date of the entry, number of participants and their capacity, serial number and so on, which can be used for the fast and easy tracing of the time the entry was submitted, who participated and what his or her contribution was, and so on.

4.4.2.2 Justification of activities

SWOT analysis is a tool that rests on simplicity and its application does not pre-suppose special knowledge pertaining to a managerial background or technical skills. This makes it available to executives who do not necessarily have knowledge on strategy or marketing (Siomkos, 1995).

To fill the SWOT analysis basic knowledge of the industry and the company the planning relates to, suffice. SWOT allows the synthesis and integration–incorporation of different types of information, both qualitative and quantitative. It not only offers the opportunity to organize the necessary information, which may be widely known, but also offers the opportunity to organize very recent information. This is another reason that it constitutes a flexible method (Siomkos, 1995).

Analysis will include, as variables, all the factors that have been identified as Strengths–Weaknesses–Opportunities–Threats (and which, by definition, will originate from the internal and external environment of the company) and which can be labeled, as earlier, depending on their magnitude and their positive or negative influence, both with respect to competitors or consumers, as well as with the factors that constitute the degree or level of attractiveness of the industry and, in general, the remaining factors from the internal and external environment (Siomkos, 1995).

The approach of this framework focuses on the market, namely, both on the competition as well as on customers, and considers this to be the basic dipole which, together intradepartmental coordination, deserves special attention with respect to the realization, detection, identification, recording, analysis and evaluation of data which catalytically shape the orientation of decision making (Narver and Slater, 1990).

In the context of marketing's philosophy and reasonably ensuing from its effort to create a competitive advantage for the business via the process of offering an integrated array of benefits (Hamel and Prahalad, 1990) of the product to the consumer, it would be unimaginable not to attach, to the proposed procedure, factors that also regard competitive-consumer data and which may qualitatively be classified as Strengths–Weaknesses and Opportunities–Threats. Besides the recording of Strengths and Weaknesses by definition, they relate to the internal environment of a corporation, and the basic relations as such are structured in the contexts of its microenvironment (a great subset of which are customers), while a key sector environment where Opportunities–Threats are detected is, among others (such as the economic, technological, political), the competitive environment.

The implementation process for the SWOT analysis will take place, taking account of those variables created from the existence of the special characteristics of High Technology and the conditions shaped by them and, to a large extent, in the light of the combination of such characteristics with the data characteristics of the competition and their consumer orientation, characteristics that will be structured and expressed as Opportunities–Threats–Strengths–Weaknesses. The list of factors that follows and which may subsequently be evaluated (as to the ascription of their characterization as Opportunities–Threats–Strengths–Weaknesses) and then included in the SWOT analysis, although not exhaustive, is adequately sufficient to indicatively offer the mark of the analyzed viewpoint:

- Number of competitors – qualitative composition of competition (existence of "parachuters")
- NHTPs under development by the competition
- Degree of difficulty in the articulation (detection and expression) of needs on the side of consumers
- Easiness of listening to/detecting customer needs (by the corporation and the competition)
- Easiness of converting customers' needs to a given array of product benefits offered to consumers (by the corporation and the competition)
- Degree of uncertainty for customer constituent
- Rate of obsolescence of cutting-edge technology – magnitude of product life-cycle briefness
- Effectiveness in the management of demand (by the corporation and the competition)
- Effectiveness in identifying the point of the S-type technology curve where both the company and its competitors are
- Acknowledgment of the actual size of the "chasm"
- Existing or/and future exchange problems (for the corporation and the competition)
- Cost structure per unit (the corporation and the competition)
- Efficient knowledge dissemination management (business and the competition)
- Standards adoption rate by the market
- Rate of change for needs
- New technology's rate of spread
- Acceptance and incorporation of marketing orientation, adoption of marketing philosophy (the corporation and the competition)
- Cannibalism: existence and magnitude
- Ability to conceive of new markets (the corporation and the competition)
- Existence/quality/magnitude/dimensions of operational creativity (the corporation and the competition)
- Degree and quality of scientific/technical base (the corporation and the competition)
- Ability to conceive of NHTPs (the corporation and the competition)
- Senior management's vision and support
- After-sales support (maintenance/service; the corporation and the competition)
- Observance of delivery times for NHTPs, pursuant to the disclosed in advance launch schedule (the corporation and the competition)

- Existence of ancillary effects from the NHTP (for the corporation and the competition)
- Product offer – the product's array of benefits (by the corporation and the competition)
- Effectiveness of resources allocation (the corporation and the competition)
- Matching of corporate-consumer perceptions on the kind of innovation the NHTP brings (the corporation and the competition)
- Orientation (or the business or/and its competitors) toward demand or offer
- Existence – the degree of complementarity (or competitiveness) relation between Core Capabilities and NHTP (the corporation and the competition)
- Degree of effectiveness in selecting the application of creative destruction by the corporation and the competition
- Knowledge – skills incorporated in techniques and technical systems – work tools (the corporation and the competition)
- Ability to change the performance–price assumptions and hypotheses (the corporation and the competition)
- Promotion of a climate favoring the development of innovation (the corporation and the competition)
- Degree of attainment of the unification of efforts by subdepartments (the corporation and the competition)
- Existence – extend of "twin" culture–professionalization obstacles (the corporation and the competition)
- Ability to find new applications for High Tech products (the corporation and the competition)
- Ability to detect/solve/restore/rehabilitate consumer problems (the corporation and the competition)
- Establishment of long-term research hypotheses (the corporation and the competition)
- Existence of obstacles and size thereof to the integration of marketing and R&D departments (e.g., vocabulary differences, personality differences, differences in perceptions and way of thinking as well as the delimitation of the objectives/data and communicative responsibilities) in the contexts of the enterprise and the competition.
- Difference between the necessary and attained informing
- Ability to develop the optimal combination of the qualitative dimension of information (Accuracy–Compatibility–Utility) and the quantitative one (for the enterprise and the competition)
- Degree of variability – details provided (for the enterprise and the competition)
- Nature of mobilizing – for innovation – force (for the enterprise and the competition)
- Quality of information sources (for the enterprise and the competition)
- Existing organizational structure with respect to formality, concentration and complexity (of the enterprise and the competition)
- Flexibility – adaptiveness (of the enterprise and the competition)
- Sales network (of the enterprise and the competition)

- Identifiability in the market (of the enterprise and the competition)
- Level of offered quality, incorporated in the product (for the enterprise and the competition)
- Mergers–acquisitions
- Market size
- Market evolution and development
- Seasonality – circularity
- Negotiating power of buyers/suppliers
- Obstacles to the entry–exit of new businesses
- Height or necessary investments
- State polity – audits and state intervention
- Social–legal–government trends
- Ability – the size of accumulated trial-and-error experience in dealing with threats and opportunities
- Existence of unusual competences and ensue from access to rare resources or protected markets

A useful test (as a practical technique) to differentiate between strengths/weaknesses and opportunities/threats is to ask if the subject even would have occurred in case the corporation did not. In the case the answer is yes, then the subject or event is classified to the external factors, and, consequently should be viewed as an opportunity or threat.

It is thus clear that SWOT analysis can be structured – completed – and operate under the process described in Figure 4.5.

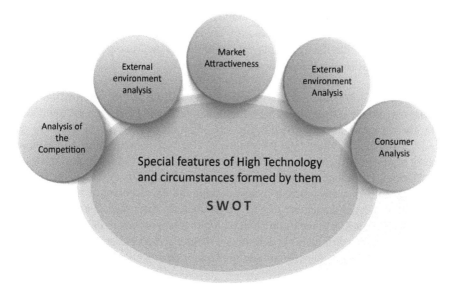

Figure 4.5 SWOT for High Tech

Circles 1 through 5 represent the sets of factors which may affect and feed SWOT analysis. They may affect it either as compounded sets (without, i.e., the combination that follows from the dialectic relation of inter-affect between two sets which is represented as the section of the two sets) or as a combination of all factors in pairs (or even in threes, or fours or all against all) but also with a simultaneous "filtering" influence from all the special characteristics of technology. What is certain is that the size of the special characteristics will play – directly or indirectly – the role of the "filter", the factor for the qualitative and quantitative weighting of the factors, which originate for the environments cited earlier and which will accordingly be classified as Strengths–Weaknesses–Opportunities–Threats before they are (and in order to be) entered into SWOT.

The combination of the supply reservoirs for the external–internal environments, as well as under the provision of the common area of points in them with the features and the special conditions for High Tech shaped by them, as well as the uncompounded contribution of the variables of Strengths–Weaknesses–Opportunities–Threats for any one industry (with a market orientation), contributes all factors which, in light of their qualitative contribution, are entered into the matrix. This ensures the following:

1   The presence of factors inherently participating in the shaping of Strengths–Weaknesses–Opportunities–Threats for all industries
2   That a qualitative approach to the combination of the contribution of factors will take place, for factors that "mutate" (to a greater or lesser extent) and differentiate the composition and qualitative magnitude that shapes them, due to the impact of the High Tech environment
3   That the orientation and direction of the analysis will be largely shaped by consumers and competitors (a mandate for success in High Tech environments too) and will give necessary credence to marketing's philosophy, by the mechanism for recording the multidimensional composition of factors from the different reservoirs they are derived

SWOT can convert this variety in diverseness and the size of information flow from a weakness (especially in the tumultuous and liquid High Tech environment) for the corporation which could negatively affect the process for the design of an NHTP and make it more time-consuming to a key advantage, which will acquire even more weight due to the application of the analysis at the initial design stage.

Besides, High Tech characteristics which were sufficiently described in the previous chambers, from inherent factors making the development of NHTPs more difficult and (simultaneously) being an obstacle to their fast launching can be converted (based on the relevant position logic) to opportunities for the High Tech enterprise which will identify, delimit and diagnose their existence, their qualitative and quantitative dimensions and the web of interrelations that hold between them.

The conversion of an inherent weakness to a strength offers the ability to "match" it faster with opportunities. Of course, it may form the basis for a competitive advantage of that enterprise which will be able to exploit it more expediently.

The fact that such inherent characteristics will continue to influence (or influence to a greater extent) competitive enterprises and the slowdown that may effectively burden them equals a positive, relevant boost to the steps of our enterprise. It is a fact that the first step for solving a problem is to realize and detect its existence, an attitude that condenses and grounds the proof of the benefits offers by this particular tool and, indeed, its use at the appropriate stage and time in the process.

Another important argument for opting to use and attach a SWOT analysis to the mechanism of the proposed framework is that it offers to the members of the group that employs it the ability to uncover their disagreements, through which interesting conclusions and proposals may ensue. The positive contribution of the unveiling of disagreements (and of the rationale – arguments supporting the positions of those who disagree) is but a subset of the benefits that such an analysis contributes. Even in the case where opinions concur, the relevant importance attributed to each factor, the inflows justifying views on each occasion, the manner they are articulated and formulated and the documentation and justification offered for the claims, reveal in a most direct and clear way the perceptions and structure of the way of thinking of those expressing them.

The process of a SWOT analysis will bring together executives from different departments (the role of their collaboration has been stressed on many occasions). In the context of a SWOT analysis process these executives will learn the way of thinking and operation of the other departments, acquire greater ease of communication and contact and expand their own thought-horizon, attaching to it the different levels of cognitive structures and dissimilitude of the cognitive areas of other operating departments.

Succinctly, SWOT Analysis can contribute to the effective attainment of the objective in a twofold manner: On one hand, it is an efficient tool serving the goal for the collection of multisided informing at this stage, while, on the other hand, it effectively positively contributes to the pursued qualitative and wide symbiotic interrelation of the departments, while supporting the benefits from a systemic view to their approach.

Intradepartmental contact is also improved by the KP. The essential arguments formulated in the context of the discussion for its filling-out act also in support of contact–communication. Executives coming from different operating departments share critical information, fill knowledge gaps, bridge or at least realize disagreements and end up in a common space of concurrence or least realize each other's viewpoint. This type of contact promotes communication, which promotes the expression of opinions, the accentuation of contrasts and, ultimately, the legitimate and called-for composition of views and, therefore, good collaboration.

The KP essentially records all of the preceding information, in a systematic manner, while it is easily accessible and its entries are easy to search through. It changes (filled out afresh) as the data from the constant flow of information change in order not only to reflect said data and their evaluation at any time but also to offer a marking of the thoughts and reactions by the group on each occasion. It, thus, permits the dynamic outlook of such changes in the factors over time. Groups can go back at any time to the KP and trace the decision-making process (which grows improved over time because of the attachment to it of acquired experiences) on new products.

Both SWOT analysis and the KP are vehicles for the proper treatment and analysis of the complexity of the factors that constitute the space wherein High Tech Enterprises are active. Groups react to changes by comparing them to the knowledge presently stored in the KP. Every change is entered, and the alternations of circumstances and data that follow, respectively, change the KP while they simultaneously correct the variables of the decision-making algorithm and enrich its experiences. As it is noted by Kolb and Morgan (1986), corporations, like living organisms, possess the ability to learn. The process of organizational learning includes the acquisition, communication and interpretation of knowledge relating to the organization and the use thereof in decision making. Shrivastava's article (Meyers and Wilemon, 1989) shows that a corporation learns also during technological innovation. The same article stresses that before a product is characterized as a failure, one must take account of its contribution in the development of the organization, the formation of the market and the push it gave to technology (inside and outside the confines of the enterprise). New products are largely affected also by the performance and history of the predecessors and, in turn, influence the success or failure of their successors. Experience and expertise acquired during the life cycle of a previous innovation are transferred to the new products that follow each innovation.

4.4.3 Third Stage

This involves the Recording – Graphic representation of Weighted Importance and the attribution of Performance Score by the members of the groups and the weighting of the significance of each one of the three participating groups with respect to the Opportunities–Strengths–Threats–Weaknesses, the constituents of which were detected by the SWOT analysis.

4.4.3.1 Activities

A. The first activity is to build a matrix on which the variables identified in stage 2 are organized and their weighted importance is attributed while their performance is also ascribed, as such factors are perceived by the members of the CG, the BG (CG–BG) and the EG (EG–BG). In addition the product of the sets cited earlier will also be weighted, depending on the group that expresses them.

The variables identified and recorded as critical in the context of the activities in the second stage are organized into horizontal lines. They are recorded and organized as critical variables for Opportunities–Strengths–Threats–Weaknesses. Moreover, opportunities and strengths are groups as variables the magnitude of which shall establish the coordinates of the axes for the linear representation matrix which will immediately follow. Opportunities and Strengths will be depicted on the horizontal axis, while Weaknesses and Threats will be depicted on the vertical one.

(A)₁ The CG for every Strength–Weakness–Opportunity–Threat (namely, for each one of the variables grouped under the label of the aforementioned characterizations of those variables) will proceed with the following activities:

1   Ascribes a relative importance, depending on the perceived magnitude of each variable, from 1 to 10, to all variables that can potentially be characterized as factors constituting an Opportunity (and a Strength–Threat–Weakness). The 1–10 boundaries for ascribing importance are indicative, but the total of the score for Importance ascribed to the factors constituting Opportunities (and Strengths–Threats–Weaknesses) cannot, as an aggregate, exceed the upper boundary of the scoring choices (e.g., for the case of the 1–10 scale, the aggregate score for variables in Opportunities and then the aggregate score for variables in Strengths and so on will not exceed 10) for the weighting to be valid.

2   Scores from 1 to 5 (or any range deemed purposeful) the perceived performance of each variable on the enterprise. Here the weighting proviso (namely, the one regarding the range 1–5, e.g., for the sum of performances to be 5) is not deemed necessary, since the ascription of a performance to each factor with respect to the enterprise may be equally good (or, respectively, equally low), for more than one variables, even for all of them. Of course, perceived performance is ascribed across all variables in Strengths–Weaknesses–Opportunities–Threats.

3   Calculates the product of the two activities above, which essentially reflects the importance of each variable via the perceived magnitude of its influence on the enterprise, depending on the jointly expressed variables that were the outcome of the previous stage

4   Derives the product of the weighted total from the previous action using a (weighted) importance factor signifying the importance of the opinion expressed by the members comprising the CG

(A)₂ Similarly, the BG proceeds with the same actions (without, of course, the participation in the evaluation process of the members of the CG, who deposited their views in the context of that group). The weighted importance factor for views will not necessarily be the same.

(A)₃ The same actions are also undertaken by the EG, without the participation of the members of the BG, for reasons similar to those elaborated in the preceding paragraph. The three weighted totals (with the relative importance ascribed to the views of each group individually), will aggregate at the upper boundary of the range of qualitative measurement selected.

(A)₄ Finally, the weighted sums of the (weighted) totals for all three groups are added horizontally and entered in column "Sum of totals" in the matrix. A vertical addition of the "Sum of totals" for Opportunities and Strengths offers the mark on the horizontal axis while the vertical addition (of the subset of "sum of totals") of

Weaknesses and Threats gives the mark of the vertical axis. These coordinates are entered in the table as the sum of totals of the weighted sums of Opportunities and Strengths and as the sum of the (weighted) totals of Threats and Weaknesses. The vertical column on the sum of totals, thus, represents the following:

1   The sum of weighted totals for each factor participating in Opportunities–Strengths–Threats–Weaknesses, respectively, from all groups
2   The sum of the weighted totals as the addition of the overall evaluation of the factors constituting Opportunities–Strengths–Threats–Weaknesses, respectively, performed by all groups
3   The sum of the total of weighted totals for strengths and opportunities, namely, of the abscissa
4   The sum of totals of weighted sums for threats and weaknesses, namely, the ordinate
5   Additionally, a second column is formed (under the general heading sum of totals), which offers the total of the weighted importance (of the already-weighted variables) ascribed to each group (coefficients α, β, γ for CG, BG and EG, respectively).

B. The deduced outcomes will then be represented on the matrix and on bar diagrams.

(B)₁ A matrix is formed, divided into four quadrants (squares), which follow from the coming together of all possible combinations of high and low levels for the total of the variables depicted on the horizontal axis (after, of course, they are weighted, as was cited earlier), and the low-high levels of the total of the variables depicted on the vertical axis (following their weighting).

(B)₂ The combination of the ordinate and abscissa cited in (III) and (IV) of (A)4, of this action, are given.

(B)₃ A circle is drawn centered on the point on the matrix that was defined and the area of which is the inverse of the difference of the product of the weighted importance and the performance score ascribed by the CG to the critical variables (which have been grouped on the table as Opportunities–Strengths–Threats–Weaknesses) and the product of the weighted importance and performance score ascribed by the BG to the corresponding critical values (alternatively, the area of the circle is proportionate to the agreement between the views expressed by each group). It ought to be stressed that the difference in the products above is always a positive number and where BG is cited, it refers to BG–CG.

The depiction of the difference of products with a circle is performed as follows: Consider a circle with area P, where P is a known number that corresponds to the minimum difference of products, namely the full agreement between CG and BG. However, in order to maintain the proportionality of areas, each respective magnitude of the absolute value of the difference between CG and BG is converted to a respective length of the radius.

This is rendered possible with the following reduction: Consider the area of the circle as given (say α square units where α is arbitrarily defined), which defines the absolute value of the difference of products CG–BG, which gives the minimum difference of opinions (or full agreement) between the two groups. Of course, this area corresponds to a radius on the same circle (since $\Sigma_K = \pi \rho^2$, and $\Sigma_K = \alpha \tau . \mu$, and $\pi = 3.14$), say, ρ_1. Then radius ρ_2 which will be defined (or more accurately will be defined by the area of the circle) to correspond to the difference of views (or, correspondingly to the remainder of the agreement), for example, βo, and will have a length equal to

$$p_2 = \sqrt{\frac{\beta}{\alpha}}.$$

Using this logic, the difference in the area of the circles will represent the difference between the products. Should the absolute value of the two products be the maximum (full discord between the views of the two groups), the second circle will become a point, that is, a circle with a radius equal to zero.

It must be underlined that the proportionality of the area of the circle that represents the maximum agreement between the two groups, and the circle which represents the attained agreement, will determine radius ρ_2 which corresponds to the area of the circle for the attained agreement.

(B)$_4$ An angle is drawn on the aforementioned circle (epicenter), which is the inverse of the difference that follows from the product of the weighted importance and performance score ascribed by BG (where BG = BG – CG) and the product of the weighted importance and performance score ascribed by the EG (alternatively, the greater the degree of agreement – or the smaller the disagreement – is between the BG and the CG and, indeed, as an absolute value), the smaller the epicenter angle will be).

In this case we compare BG to EG and wish to depict the difference of their views, which difference (of the respective products) is an absolute value.

To illustrate the difference as an epicenter angle, the following steps must be followed:

360° correspond to the full agreement of views between the BG and the EG (100% of the circle). For a difference of views with magnitude, say, γ, the formula that gives the degrees is $x^0 = 360\dfrac{\gamma}{100}$.

Magnitude of the difference in opinions expressed in square cm (area)

Figure 4.6 Areas of the circles

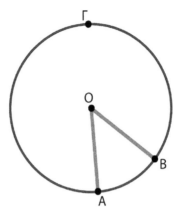

Figure 4.7 Central angle

As the difference of products becomes greater (difference of opinions between the EG and the BG inside the absolute value) the area of the epicenter angle obviously becomes smaller.

Depicted on the matrix is the relative position as a point defined by the perceived ascribed importance of the influence (of all variables ensuing from their labeling as Strengths–Opportunities–Threats–Weaknesses) and the degree of the coincidence of views between the CG and the BG and of the BG. and EG on the aforementioned importance of the influence of variables.

It ought to be stressed that an advantage of the preceding representation on the matrix is the ease of seeing the magnitudes of the factors it describes. Thus, the relative position as the function of Opportunities–Strengths and Weaknesses– Threats is also framed by the description of the coincidence of views between the groups on the critical variables, and all these are easily depicted in a simple manner. The basic advantage, therefore, is the perceptibility of all three criteria of the attractiveness for developing the NHTP, by all participants, independent of their cognitive background, and simultaneously.

Furthermore, the entire process for rating and ascribing a relative importance also promoted the integration of the various departments in the same way that the SWOT analysis also positively contributes toward this.

Besides, using the difference of views as a criterion of attractiveness for the NHTPs in development, namely, as a means to measure the integration of the departments (at least with respect to their expressed views and the manner/rationale/argumentation employed to ascribe the weighted importance and performance score on the critical – and jointly acknowledged as Opportunities–Strengths– Weaknesses–Threats variables), underlines the important role of integration for the development of an NHTP, which, indeed, ensues as the result of processes originating in the enterprise itself.

Another benefit is that if the preceding processes are repeated in their entirety for some other NHTP that is being considered for development, then the attractiveness of the one (with respect to the criteria employed) will be directly and easily comparable to that of the other.

The table used at this stage, as well as the matrix with the series of steps for its completion, can be seen in Figures 4.8, 4.9, 4.10, and 4.11. The numeration on the vertical and horizontal axes of the matrix depends on the boundaries for the weighted scores employed and the scale of the number used to ascribe performance scores.

(B)$_s$ The difference between the weighted (with respect to α, β) products of the weighted importance with respect to the performance rating by CG and BG

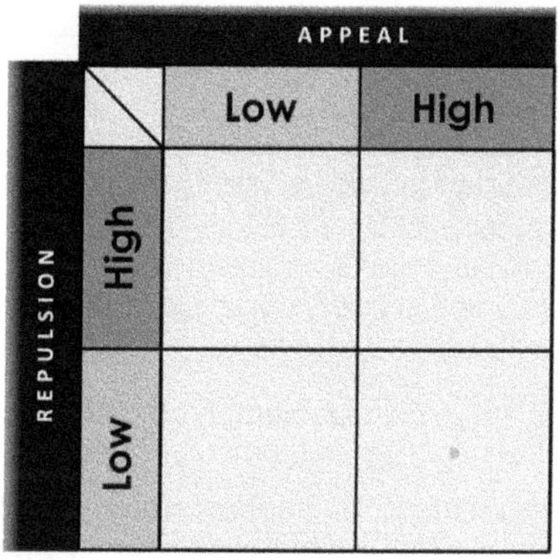

Figure 4.8 Matrix determining the degree of attractiveness and the magnitude of negative influences on the NHTP in development

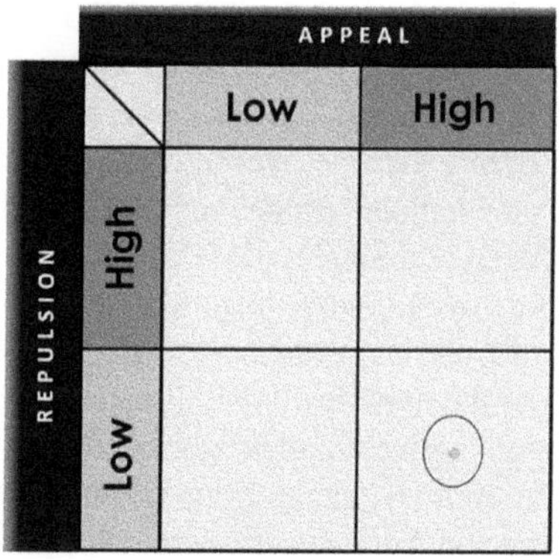

Figure 4.9 Matrix for establishing the degree of attractiveness and the magnitude of negative influences on the NHTP in development, incremented by the degree of coincidence of the views that influence the product, being the variables identified as Strengths–Weaknesses–Opportunities–Threats for the BG (where BG = BG − CG) and the CG

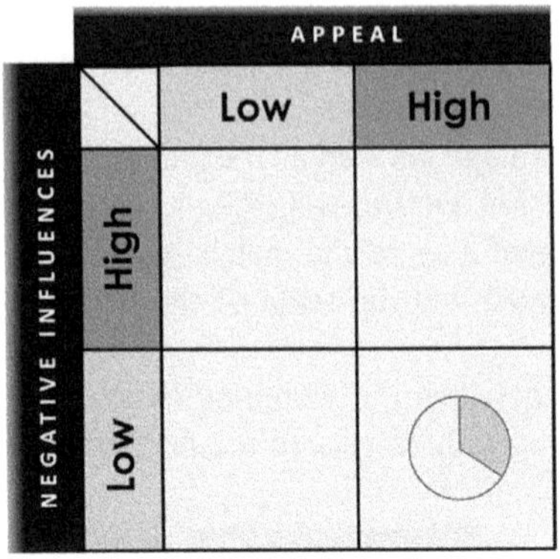

Figure 4.10 Matrix for determining the degree of attractiveness and magnitude of negative
influences for the NHTP in development, increased by the degree of coincidence of views on the effects on the product of the variables identified as
Strengths–Weaknesses–Opportunities–Threats, the views of the BG (where
BG = BG − CG) and the CG augmented by the degree of coincidence of the
views expressed by EG (where EG = EG − BG) and BG

is measured, where BG = BG − CG). Namely, the comparison of views between
CG and BG is repeated, where BG = BG − CG), only now it is weighted by α for
CG and β for BG. Coefficients α, β and γ ascribe the relative weight of opinion
each group carries. The same process is repeated to find the weighted product
difference of weighted importance on performance by the BG and the respective
magnitude for EG. Differences are absolute values in this case as well. What is
needed is to find the weighted (by the special weight carried by each group) difference of views between the CG and the BG and CG + BG and EG. Weighting
factors, α, β and γ (which may fall in the interval 0–1 and must aggregate to 1),
represent the relative importance of the views by each group, pursuant to how senior management views (being the one overall responsible for the final outcome)
the contributions to the development process of the formed groups. Thus, the contingent approach by Moeaert and Souder (1990a), who claim that it constitutes the
most effective way to organize not only technological innovation (the contingent
approach takes account of the level of particularity of development teams) but
also the "arrangement" of the organizational climate (which is the most effective
mechanism, according to Agarwala and Rogers (1976), for preaching harmony,
trust, extroversion and, ultimately, integration) is left to senior management, as is
deemed proper by Rogers and Agarwala-Rogers (1976).

These differences may be illustrated using bar diagrams so that the condition of
linearity (and representational ratio) will also subsist in the representation.

In this way one gains knowledge of the difference of opinions (integration)
and in the light of the relevant weight importance of the views expressed by each
group.

Critical Variables	Core Group 1			Weighting (α)	Core Group 2			Weighting (β)	Expanded Group			Weighting (γ)	Sum of totals (weighting)	
	Fixed Weight A'_1	Rel. Deg. B'_1	$A'_1 \times B'_1$ Γ'_1		Fixed Weight A'_2	Rel. Deg. B'_2	$A'_2 \times B'_2$ Γ'_2		Fixed Weight A_3	Rel. Deg. B_3	$A_3 \times B_3$ Γ_3		Sum of Weighted variables	Sum of Weighted weights of total weighted variables
Opportunity (Horizontal axis)														
Strength (Horizontal axis)													Sum	
Threat (Vertical axis)														
Weakness (Vertical axis)													Sum	

Figure 4.11 Data table (table for ascribing relative weight and influence to Strengths–Weaknesses–Opportunities–Threats by each group [CG, BG and EG] and for weighting the evaluation of each group)

Also underlined must be the fact that it is deemed purposeful to juxtapose the entirety of variables weighted by α, β and γ, respectively, by the CG and BG with EG so as to reveal the difference in opinions between operating departments and senior management and, thus, to indirectly point to the degree of expected support by senior management.

4.4.3.2 Justification of activities

All factors identified by the participants in the groups, as such were structured at stage 1, and were deemed to be an Opportunity–Strength–Threat–Weakness with respect to the NHTP (as such was defined and structured via the Opportunities–Strengths–Threats–Weaknesses) participate as critical variables, under the judgment of all groups.

Every variable is scored by each group as to the weight it carries. Moreover, its performance rate (namely how important the performance of each variable is deemed to be) is assigned to each group. Thus, the product (of each variable) combines the possible effect of each factor on the NHTP, that the High Tech enterprise in question plans to develop together with if such a factor constitutes a Strength–Weakness–Opportunity–Threat for the enterprise.

The reinforcement of a feeling of real participation and involvement by executives in what takes place with respect to the process of the development of an NHTP, is, in parallel, also attained, and an extent of the benefits of integration is realized and gained not only among the marketing and R&D departments but also all those departments/carriers whose participation has been recorded. Besides, the fact that this matrix is jointly completed provides further support for the edifice of intradepartmental integration that is pursued.

The weighting factor ascribed to the perception of the magnitude of influence on the enterprise (depending on the commonly expressed variables that ensued as the outcome of the labelling using the characterizations "Strength–Weakness–Opportunity–Threat" and which were jointly identified by each group and recorded in the KP) reflects the significance and weight each group carries with respect to its opinions. It is employed, that is, to "correct" (weigh) the final total quantitative size of every variable in such a manner so that its final characterization to be performed depending on the special knowledge, involvement and relevant operating relevance of each department contributing to the development of the NHTP.

The sum of the three weighted totals for the corresponding three groups offers the final weighted importance of influence for each variable. The summation of the sums of weighted information totals for variables composing Opportunities and Strengths essentially shows the attractiveness and likelihood for success, as such, are perceived by all the participants of the three groups and indeed, weight such attractiveness in relation to the degree of operating relevance and potential contribution for each department. On the other hand, the sum of the respective totals for Threats and Weaknesses shows the magnitude of difficulties for the negative data with respect to the NHTP development.

Measuring the difference in opinions serves the following objectives. Following extensive contact–communication and exchange of views (in the context of the dialogue to establish the critical variables and survey the manner, magnitude and quality of their influence on the NHTP, the filling-out of the activities and actions in the stages cited earlier) by executive, the convergence of views offers a measure (besides the attained integration) even for the attractiveness (and therefore the likelihood for success) of the NHTP. The difference of opinions to a major extend betrays that the inherent and intrinsic characteristics incorporated in the NHTP development bear a great degree of obscurity between the members of the development team as to the purposefulness and importance for the development. Moreover, the difference of views essentially expresses disagreement (depending on the magnitude of said difference) and is, by necessity, included in the NHTP development while aggregately contributing to the decrease of the likelihood for success of the NHTP. Of course, despite the fact that such difference of views does not necessarily and/or directly entail the failure of the product, the unhindered collaboration and communication between the groups (which establish the objective and will work toward its attainment, if convinced on its properness) is a necessary clause for its success. To put it otherwise, a coincidence of views, to a large extent, on which the critical variables are how, how much and which are their features and also with respect to their positive or negative effected on the product, what hypotheses, limitations, information (and, in general, those factors in the KP) are deemed critical and by how much signifies relevance to the objective and that the goals of the departments coincide (or move, at least, to the same direction) and is a guarantee for the exercise of the collective intradepartmental effort. This constitutes a systemic approach of the skills/capacities/capabilities of each department, the results of which, as a whole, exceed the sum of the results of the efforts made by each department in case the views that were largely contrasting with respect to the variables earlier, and therefore the orientation of goals and hence the orientation of the means for their pursuit, and thus in the use of the means for their attainment.

Moreover, the graphical representation of the preceding in the matrix, and indeed simultaneously, is fully consistent with the limitation–provision posed from the beginning with respect to the model's simplicity. One look suffices to provide a three-level informing:

- The degree of attractiveness depending on the influence of Strengths–Opportunities–Weaknesses–Threats
- The degree of the coincidence (integration) of views between the CG and the BG (which can be viewed as another dimension of the attractiveness of the development of an NHTP)
- The degree of the coincidence (integration) of views between the BG (where BG = BG − CG) and EG. (where EG = EG − BG; which, similarly, can be viewed as another dimension of the attractiveness of the development of an NHTP)

Choosing to measure the difference of opinions between the CG and the BG took place also due to the fact that operating groups outside marketing and R&D play an important role for the development of an NHTP but principally to also measure the perception of the marketing and R&D executives who were not included in the C.G. and to offer a footing for the correlation and to check the degree by which complementarity is utilized and competitiveness is minimized between the concepts of specialization and integration and for the coincidence of the common development orientation toward the same direction., as such was described earlier.

Opting to choose to measure the difference of opinions between the members comprising the BG against the EG took place since both the stakeholders as well as senior management, which constitutes a subset of the aforementioned group, play a determinative role in the support and acceptance of the product. Thus, it is important to take account of the difference of opinions and to measure it. It should be noted that the CG participated in the BG (in the comparison illustrated by the bar diagrams but not in the matrix), thus the difference that will ensue between the BG and EG will also include the view of the CG as an intrinsic variable.

4.4.4 Fourth stage: evaluation–feedback

4.4.4.1 Evaluation

At the end of the three stages one has the following facts:

1 All the variables considered to be Strengths–Weaknesses–Opportunities–Threats
2 The degree of importance for each variable in every group and the corresponding ascribed performance index
3 All the perceived influence (the product of the weighted weight of each variable times the magnitude of its performance) for every variable group, both by the CG as well as by the BG and the EG
4 The perceived (by the members manning each group) influence of each variable, whether said variable has been grouped as an Opportunity, or a Threat, or a Strength or Weakness by the members of the CG, the BG and the EG
5 The total weighted influence of each variable by all groups
6 The total weighted influence for each variable group, both by the CG as well as by the BG and the EG.
7 The degree of attractiveness, namely the weighted sum (with weighting factors α, β and γ, ascribing the weight of the opinion of the CG, the BG and the EG, respectively) of the weighted influences (with weighting factors the relevant weight of each factor, as perceived by the members of the groups) for each variable that belongs to Strengths–Opportunities from the total of the members participating in the groups
8 The degree of negative influences, namely, the weighted sum (with weighting factors the relevant weight of each factor, as perceived by the members of the groups) of influences on each variable belonging to Weaknesses–Threats

9 The combination of the attractiveness, as described earlier, with the negative influences, as they have also been described, as a point on a matrix (graphically)

10 The difference in opinions as to the influence of the variables between the CG and the BG which can be graphically represented as the area of a circle with its point the combination of negativity and attractiveness (where BG = BG − CG)

11 The difference of opinions on the influence of variables between the BG and the EG which is represented as an epicenter angle on the circle defined in 10

12 The weighted (by α, β) difference of views on the influence of variables between the CG and the BG (where BG = BG − CG), which is graphically represented in a bar diagram

13 The weighted (by α, β, and γ) difference of views on the influence of variables between CG + BG and EG which is represented as a bar diagram

It is important to stress that the preceding facts ensued from a process which included the views of all executive who are (directly and less so) involved in the decision-making process on the new product and which essentially via its mechanisms directly contributed to integration – but also indirectly via the erudite way of its participation as a coefficient on the attractiveness of the NHTP.

The evaluation of the factors derived from the NHTP takes place on two levels:

The first level is that of the assessment of the conclusions derived for the NHTP, as these are imprinted either proportionally on the matrix that includes the circle and the epicenter angle, or linearly and proportionally on the bar diagrams.

The second level is to compare the NHTP (with respect to its capabilities for success in the light of the proposed framework) with an alternative (or even more than one) NHTP (after the latter, of course, goes through the same process).

The first level offers a measured by which it will be deemed if it is purposeful for the NHTP to enter the phase of its being launched to the market, with the common denominator being the accentuated role (in the theoretical model) of integration and the systemic benefits of the symbiotic interassociation between the departments that it describes and prescribes. In this light, the framework within which the integration of the departments moves becomes clear, as does the method to measure it.

Via their comparison the fields where one product is superior to another will become apparent and, thus, facilitate the process of making, based on the criteria adopted by the framework, the – on many sides – best choice.

Finally, after making the decision that rested on the mechanism of the proposed theoretical framework and launching the product in the market, the enterprise is in a position to be able to check the validity of the arguments and hypotheses it made and of the rationale it employed in the identification of the SWOT analysis variables. It is also in a position to acknowledge possible errors to the ascribed importance of the variables or/and their possible effects on the enterprise. Answers to the following questions

- "What went well?"
- "What went wrong?"
- "Why?"

feed the documentation of possible changes that must take place on the rationale for completing and ascribing importance to the factors that constitute the variables of the framework's mechanisms.

The fact that to append knowledge and experience ensuing from "pathology" (after the launch has been made) is legitimate notwithstanding, prevention remains the most painless and efficient way to append knowledge and enrich the learning curve of the company. This is the reason why the KP is renewed (with the ensuing changes being systematically and methodically recorded) also during the decision-making process, while this lasts, as well as when it is required by circumstances (unexpected changes to the external or internal environment, changes of conjunctures or interrelations).

4.5 Contribution of the proposed theoretical framework

The proposed theoretical framework contributes to the integration of the operating departments in High Tech enterprises and more specifically of their marketing and R&D departments. Integration, as it has been adopted as a concept in the context of this study, is the systemic approach of the capacities/capabilities of the operating departments of High Tech enterprises. This operating congress and the joint exploitation of specialized operating capabilities contributes benefits to High Tech enterprises that transcend the sum of the benefits ensuing from the disconnected and isolated efforts by the departments (Souder and Chakrabarti, 1978; Lawrence and Lorsch, 1967b).

The theoretical framework works by means of the mechanism for establishing teams and reinforces the union of separate specialized operating capabilities (the union of capabilities is the most cited assumption – a mandate for the smooth and effective launch of NHTPs in the literature; cf., e.g., Dutta et al., 1999; Souder and Moenaert, 1992; Moenaert and Souder, 1990a; Gupta et al., 1986a; Griffin and Hauser, 1986; Maidique and Zirger, 1984; Cheng, 1983; Cooper, 1983, 1979b; Carroad and Carroad, 1982; Millman, 1982; Wind, 1982, 1981; Gruber, 1981; Mansfield, 1981 Gerstenfeld and Sumiyoshi, 1980; Souder and Chakrabarti, 1980; 1979; Galbraith and Nathanson, 1978; Souder, 1987, 1981, 1977; Crawford, 1977; Monteleone, 1976; Dunn and Harnden, 1975; Mansfield and Wagner, 1975; Rothwell et al., 1974; Gruber et al., 1973; Young, 1973; Mansfield et al., 1971; Lawrence and Lorsch, 1969; Ames, 1968; Schön, 1967) and the necessary condition for the success of innovation (Souder, 1987; Maidique and Zirger, 1984; Cooper, 1979b; Souder and Chakrabarti, 1979; Rothwell et al.,

1974) so as to establish the appropriate conditions for the production of additional benefits. It places special gravity on the combination of the competences of the Marketing department with those of the R&D department, without this, however, leaving the other operating departments without responsibilities and, principally, contribution (the interdependence relationship between marketing and other operating departments and the importance of the web of interrelations amongst them despite not having been the subject of extensive research [Hutt and Speh, 1984; Wind and Robertson, 1983] is greatly important [Gupta et al., 1986a]) and other senior executives (whose lack of support constituted 42% of those queried by Gupta and Wilemon [1990]), one of the reasons for delaying the launching of NHTPs) of the enterprise. It does not abolish operating specialization cores, namely, those interdepartmental forces that develop their operating skills. On the contrary, it considers the development of specialization both legitimate and necessary (as it is underlined repeatedly in the literature, departments must have the ability to maintain their individual identity while, on the other hand, they must simultaneously also be encouraged to work by removing the conceptual limits of specialization in order to effectively move toward the attainment of the common objective; (Millman, 1982; Twiss, 1974). It is stressed (Schneider, 1987; Souder, 1987; Lawrence and Lorsch, 1967b) that in order to produce innovation, the existence of both differentiation and integration is necessary. Schneider (1987), Carroad and Carroad (1982) and Lawrence and Lorsch (1967a) have formulated the view that differentiation (due to the specialization of departments) itself is that which creates the need for its integration, within, however, the context of orientations structured on the basis of clearly defined organizational objectives. The nonalignment with and distancing from the direction of the organizational objective act by decreasing the effectiveness of its attainment, as it is stressed by literature (Griffin and Hauser, 1993; Dougherty, 1990; Cooper, 1990; Achrol et al., 1983; Twiss, 1974; Duncan, 1972; Raudsepp, 1965).

Thus, beyond the coordination of the operating capabilities of operating departments, the necessary degree of specialization is both supported but also aligned with the requirements on each occasion, under the guidance of departmental integration. This way one ensures avoiding wasting valuable resources (money, effort) and minimizes the possibility of there being a cost to inexpedient activities (ACARD, 1978; Twiss, 1974; Raudsepp, 1965) (launch of undesirable product, improper launch timing, investment in a technology incompatible with customers' requirements, financial failure, etc.).

Saving on time and resources ensues also as the result of the coordination and more efficient handling of information in a systemic manner. One must underline the fact that both time-saving (which is equivalent to the most expedient launching of the products) as well as the effectiveness in the allocation of resources (which is equivalent with a respective decrease in resource uncertainty) have been stressed on many occasions as characteristics that are critical for the successful outcome of the process for launching High Tech products (Davidson, 1990; Gupta and Wilemon, 1990; Moenaert and Souder, 1990a; Fortune, 1989; Birnbaum, 1988; Wall Street Journal, 1988; Jauch and Kraft, 1986; Takeuchi and Nonaka,

1986). Especially for the efficient transfer, distribution and allocation of inform-ing, in a systemic manner, namely, via the establishment of teams, the manner for coordinating, the creation of the KP, the recording of variables in the table and the completion of their assessment and the evaluation/feedback, it is observed that both SWOT analysis and the organization of the qualitative parameters with relative weight and performance, as well as the KP, besides offering a support framework for integration, they are also carriers for the efficient conveyance of information. By means of the SWOT analysis, as adopted in the present theoreti-cal framework, as well as the KP, but also their completion via the cited mecha-nism, both the quantitative offer of information is increased, as well as the quality thereof. The volume of the perceptible flow of information is increased due to the fact that more information becomes known to more actors (members and the CG, the EG and the BG) simultaneously and on account of the fact that dialogue and the exchange of views at the time the information is recorded gives rise to more informing, by revealing factors (or sources of information) that had not been clearly realized/delimited/mapped until then and since their systematic recording "the moment they are born" precludes their omission or disregard.

The qualitative dimension is improved since their accuracy and compatibility is cross-checked by all members, while the utility of the information depending on the goals it aims to fulfill is also put under scrutiny. Thus, a deep but also wide-ranging enrichment of the "tools" to be employed in decision making is attained together with a decrease in the constituents composing uncertainty (Souder and Moenaert, 1992), and the innovative effort has greater chances to succeed (Tush-man and Nadler, 1978).

Furthermore, via the processes and methodological tools provided by the theo-retical framework, one can attain a decrease of variability (Victor and Blackburn, 1987), since the term refers to the number of special cases a High Tech enterprise needs to confront and as the methodological tool provided by the KP and SWOT record the constituents of the special cases and in the passage of time (via the enrichment of the KP) their potential number (i.e., the number of unknown special cases) is constantly reduced.

Using the same rationale, one can suggest that the analytical scope is also increased since, in the passage of time, the degree by which the processes that determine the sequence of steps to be taken also increases. The process is also improved, since the factors composing the processes (e.g., the process for detect-ing uncertainty and identifying the tools to decrease it, such as effective com-munication and briefing) are recorded and change in parallel to the enterprise's environment.

If one accepts Perrow's (1967) position that the basic challenge on the side of decreasing uncertainty relates to the maximum identification of the relative poten-tial uncertainty (decrease of variability) and the identification of tools to reduce uncertainty (increase of the scope of analysis), then the role of the KP and the SWOT analysis becomes clear.

By decreasing uncertainty (due to the quality/quantity/manner of acquiring and conveying/recording and update of information) one is led, as Souder and

Chakrabarti (1980) observe, to the improvement of decision making and the better implementation of innovative programs.

Critical factors, such as, for example, the (perceived) Opportunities–Threats–Strengths–Weaknesses, are simultaneously disclosed with their designation and are entered as a reference point for decision making. Additionally, the fact that, outside of the direct communication of vital – for the decision – parameters, a number of other variables are also disclosed is of critical importance, since without the proposed methodological tools and the way to use them, these might have never been revealed. Revealed, for example, is the thought process that led to the recognition of a factor as a critical variable. The different cognitive background (to which most of the differences in the cognitive structure of the way of thinking is attributed) becomes, to an extent, common ground or its defining factors become, at a minimum, clear. Through the direct juxtaposition of ideas (from which composition ultimately follows and the necessary conditions for integration are thus created), the fertile ground for a more effective and efficient evaluation and utilization of data are effected.

Furthermore, the fact that this circulation takes place on a systematic basis and not only during periods of crises acts augmentatively to integration and shapes in a dynamic manner continuously improving conditions for the consolidation of the benefits from integration.

Moreover, the participation in the NHTP development of the groups defined, besides that is ensues as the result of a multicompositional process, leaves little room for misunderstandings and/or unilateral or misguided attribution of responsibilities. It reinforces, that is, the climate of cooperation also indirectly, since it removes or does not let arise those conditions (misunderstandings, imposition of views on account of status) which would empower the factors alienating the departments, such as, for example, negative stereotypes, mitigation of the way to perceive/think, ascription of high–low status and so on. Besides, as a method it contributes to the attainment of Millman's (1982) admission, who considers it to be a joint competence of the marketing and R&D departments to become the guardians preserving the good relations between them and that efforts will be made to ensure the resolution of any dispute before it becomes a fixed and permanent characteristic (of their relation and consequently) of the way the corporation operates. Beyond this, it also positively contributes to the decrease of the constituents of dissonance between marketing and R&D that have been cited in the literature (Dougherty, 1992, 1990; Moenaert and Souder, 1990a; Lucas and Bush, 1988; Douglas, 1987; Allen, 1986; Gupta et al., 1986b; Zeithaml and Zeithaml, 1984; Carroad and Carroad, 1982; Block, 1977; Galbraith, 1977). Moreover, as Souder (1987) observes, the allocation and dissemination of knowledge, data and perceptions and the conveyance of information feed mutual understanding on other people's roles and help determine what is expected from everybody. This multicomponent process for taking the decision cited earlier is also associated with the degree of participation or shaping of decisions – with the hierarchy of power and authority. The gathering of decision making increases the higher the level on the hierarchy, inside the organization, responsible for taking the decision becomes and the lower the degree of participation of the other levels in the decision-making process becomes. Zaltman, Dunkan and Holbek (1973) underline the fact that emphasis on the hierarchy of power reduces organizational innovation. Reduced participation in the decision-making process also functions like an "invisible wall" to perceptions and ideas emerging during the course of the development of an innovation. On the contrary, greater participation increases commitment to the completion of the project, since it lends a sense of "ownership". Besides avoiding the ancillary consequences of concentration (decision making only by senior executive levels), the decrease of the reliability and functionality of marketing research findings, which was cited in the empirical studies by Deshpande (1982) and John and Martin (1984), is also averted, as is the problems cited by Wind (1982), namely, that they emerge in centrally oriented structures.

The proposed theoretical framework contributes to the improvement of the learning curve of a company that will adopt it. All critical factors – hypotheses and variables – are systematically recorded, as are their origins. This way at a potential repeat of the process for launching some other High Tech product, besides the fact that a canon of knowledge and hypotheses exist, accessing them will be easy. The contribution of the KP to the improvement of the decision-making "algorithm" is also documented by the continuous renewal of said pool, when variables or the web of their interrelations or conditions, in general, change. The expressed views that have been recorded are compared and assessed under the light of the new data and are adjusted to them. The process of analysis–comparison–evaluation and, ultimately, their change is a par excellence adjustment process which originates as the result of the enrichment of the company's knowledge and experience while simultaneously contributing to it. The union of skills, in whatever form, is the most widely cited assumption-mandate for the smooth and effective launch of NHTPs, in the literature (Dutta et al., 1999; Souder and Moenaert, 1992; Moenaert and Souder, 1990a; Gupta et al., 1986a; Griffin and Hauser, 1986; Maidique and Zirger, 1984; Cheng, 1983; Carroad and Carroad, 1982; Millman, 1982; Wind, 1982; 1981; Gruber, 1981; Mansfield, 1981; Gerstenfeld and Sumiyoshi, 1980; Souder and Chakrabarti, 1980, 1979; Cooper, 1983, 1979b; Souder, 1987, 1981, 1977; Galbraith and Nathanson, 1978; Crawford, 1977; Monteleone, 1976; Dunn and Harnden, 1975; Mansfield and Wagner, 1975; Rothwell et al., 1974; Gruber et al., 1973; Young, 1973; Mansfield et al., 1971; Lawrence and Lorsch, 1969; Ames, 1968; Schön, 1967) and a necessary term for the success of innovation (Souder, 1987; Maidique and Zirger, 1984; Cooper, 1979b; Souder and Chakrabarti, 1979; Rothwell et al., 1974). The decision-making mechanism is improved as the direct result of the enrichment of the learning curve, which it also feeds, thus activating a bidirectional perpetual improvement of one factor (knowledge-experience) via the other (decision making). It is clear that, this way, the cost of possible misfires due to erroneous hypotheses – wrong identification of variables, bad estimate of their weight and so on will be minimized since even errors will contribute positively to the enrichment of the process which, as was cited above, dynamically self-improves via the attachment of additional knowledge and experience to its mechanism (thus also learning and the minimization of the possibility of the same or a similar error to occur again).

The strategic orientation of the model is recommended by the expanded SWOT analysis which helps to, among other things (a) pose objectives-priorities for the new products, (b) give birth to new product ideas, (c) provide information on the competition and (d) provide information on consumers and using the SWOT to fill in the KP.

Besides contributing to the rational decision-making process (for the reasons cited earlier) it also contributes to the rational management of the portfolio of products of High Tech companies. The final stage of the process, provided it is performed for more than one products, is to be able to answer questions regarding the different degree of attractiveness for each product. It is important to stress that the proposed theoretical framework also advocates the criterion of the attained degree of integration and annexes it as an inherent attractiveness variable in its mechanism.

The proposed theoretical framework contributes to the reduction of the constituent factors for uncertainty. More specifically, market, technology, competition and consumer uncertainty are decreased as the result of the systematic pumping and accumulation of information, knowledge and experience by means of the methodological tools developed and which assisted not only the more efficient flow and management but also the quantitative and qualitative improvement of informing.

Resource uncertainty is reduced through the reduction of its ingredients cited earlier.

Moreover, a result of the factors analyzed up to now and which demonstrate the contribution of this theoretical model is considered to be the more effective shorting of time, which ensues as a chain reaction to the effectiveness and efficiency of the process mechanisms and the way these function, as such have been discussed at length earlier.

Bibliography

Abegglen, J. C. and Stalk, G. (1986). "The Japanese corporation as competitor." *California Management Review*, 28(3), 9–27.

Abell, D. F. (1980). *Defining the Business: The Starting Point of Strategic Planning*, Prentice-Hall, Englewood Cliffs, NJ, 87–115.

Abernathy, W. J. and Utterback, J. M. (1978). "Patterns of industrial innovation." *Technology Review*, 80(7), 40–47.

Achrol, R. S., Reve, T. and Stern, L. W. (1983). "The environment of marketing channel dyads: A framework for comparative analysis." *The Journal of Marketing*, 55–67.

Advisory Council for Applied Research and Development (ACARD), Publication, Industrial Innovation, HMSO, December 1978.

Allen, T. J. (1977). *Managing the flow of technology: Technology transfer and the dissemination of technological information*, MIT Press, Cambridge, MA.

Ames, B. C. (1968). "Marketing planning for industrial products." *Harvard Business Review*, 46(5), 100–111.

Ansoff, H. I. and McDonnell, E. J. (1990). *Implanting Strategic Management*, Prentice-Hall, Englewood Cliffs, NJ.

Baker, N. R., Winkofsky, E. P., Langmeyer, L. and Sweeney, D. J. (1980). Idea generations: A procrustean bed of variables, hypotheses, and Implications." *TIMS Studies in the Management Sciences*, 15.

Banerjee, P. M. and Chiu, C. (2009). "Professional biculturalism enculturation training: A new perspective on managing the r&d and marketing interface." *Current Topics in Management: Global Perspectives on Strategy, Behavior, and Performance*, 13.

Basalla, G. (1988). *The Evolution of Technology*. Cambridge University Press, Cambridge.

Beal, G. M. and Rogers, E. M. (1960). "The Adoption of Two Farm Practices in a Central Iowa Community," Special Report 26, Agricultural and Home Economics Experiment Station, Ames, Iowa.

Becker, R. H. and Speltz, L. M. (1983). "Putting the S-curve concept to work." *Research Management*, 26(5), 31–33.

Biller, A. D. and Shanley, E. S. (1975). "Understanding the conflicts between R&D and other groups." *Research Management*, 18(5), 16–21.

Birnbaum, P. H. (1988). "Coping with Environmental and Market Forces Impacting High Technology Industry in the 1990s," In Conference on Managing the High Technology Firm, The Graduate School of Business, University of Colorado, January, pp. 13–15.

Blau, Peter M. (1973). *The Organization of Academic Work*, Wiley-Blackwell, New York.

Block, J. (1977). "Recognizing the coherence of personality," in Magnusson, D. and End-
ler, N. S. (eds), *International Psychology: Current Issues and Future Prospects*, Wiley-
Blackwell, New York.

Booz, A. and Booz, H. (1968). *Management of New Products*, Booz, Allen, and Hamilton,
Inc, Chicago.

Boulding, W., Morgan, R. and Staelin, R. (1997). "Pulling the plug to stop the new product
drain." *Journal of Marketing Research*, 164–176.

Bower, J. L. and Christensen, C. M. (1995). "Disruptive technologies: Catching the wave."
Harvard Business Review, 73(1), 43–53.

Bower, J. L. and Hout, T. M. (1988). "Fast-cycle capability for competitive power." *Harvard Business Review*, 66(6), 110–118.

Brettel, M., Heinemann, F., Engelen, A. and Neubauer, S. (2011). "Cross-functional integration of R&D, marketing, and manufacturing in radical and incremental product
innovations and its effects on project effectiveness and efficiency." *Journal of Product
Innovation Management*, 28(2), 251–269.

Brockner, J. and Rubin, J. Z. (2012). *Entrapment in Escalating Conflicts: A Social Psychological Analysis*, Springer Science & Business Media, New York.

Brown, L. D. (1983). *Managing Conflict at Organizational Interfaces*, Addison Wesley
Publishing Company, Reading, MA.

Brown, R. (1992). "Managing the 'S' curves of innovation." *Journal of Business & Industrial Marketing*, 7(3), 41–52.

Burgelman, R. A. (1983). "Corporate entrepreneurship and strategic management: Insights
from a process study." *Management Science*, 29(12), 1349–1364.

Burns, T. and Stalker, G. (1961). *GM (1961) The Management of Innovation*, Tavistock
Publication, London.

Burrows, Peter. (2000). "Computers and chips." *Business Week*, January 10, pp. 92–93.

Bussey, J. and Sease, D. R. (1988). "Manufacturers strive to slice time needed to develop
products." *The Wall Street Journal*, 17.

Calantone, R. and Cooper, R. G. (1981). "New product scenarios: Prospects for success."
The Journal of Marketing, 48–60.

Calantone, R. and Rubera, G. (2012). "When should RD&E and marketing collaborate?
The moderating role of exploration – exploitation and environmental uncertainty." *Journal of Product Innovation Management*, 29(1), 144–157.

Cameron, K. S. and Quinn, R. E. (1988). *Organizational Paradox and Transformation*,
Ballinger Publishing Co/Harper & Row Publishers, Cambridge, MA.

Capon, N. and Glazer, R. (1987). "Marketing and technology: A strategic coalignment."
The Journal of Marketing, 1–14.

Carey, J. (1990). "The myth that America can't compete." *Business Week*, 15, 44–48.

Carroad, P. A. and Carroad, C. A. (1982). "Strategic interfacing of R&D and marketing."
Research Management, 25(1), 28–33.

Carter, T. (1994). "The Process of Change: Tools for the Change Agent," Report, National
Dairy Development Board, Anand, India.

Chandy, R. K. and Tellis, G. J. (1998). "Organizing for radical product innovation: The
overlooked role of willingness to cannibalize." *Journal of Marketing Research*, 474–487.

Cheng, J. L. 1983. "Interdependence and coordination in organizations: A role-system
analysis." *Academy of Management Journal*, 26(1), 156–162.

Child, J. (1972). "Organizational structure, environment and performance: The role of strategic choice." *Sociology*, 6(1), 1–22.

Christensen, C. M. (1992). "Exploring the limits of the technology S-curve. Part I: Component technologies." *Production and Operations Management*, 1(4), 334–357.

Christensen, C. M. (1997). *The Innovator's Dilemma*, Harvard Business School Press, Boston.

Clark, K. B. (1985). "The interaction of design hierarchies and market concepts in technological evolution." *Research Policy*, 14(5), 235–251.

Clarke, F. (1974). "Three golden rules of contracting." *New Scientist*, Supplement, Contract Research Review, 2.

Cohen, W. M. (1995). "Empirical studies of innovative activity," in Stoneman, P. (ed.), *Handbook of the Economics of Innovation and Technological Change*, Wiley-Blackwell, Cambridge, MA, 182–264.

Coombs, R., McMeekin, A. and Pybus, R. (1998). "Toward the development of benchmarking tools for R&D project management." *R&D Management*, 28(3), 175–186.

Cooper, A. C. and Schendel, D. (1976). "Strategic responses to technological threats." *Business Horizons*, 19(1), 61–69.

Cooper, R. G. (1979a). "The dimensions of industrial new product success and failure." *The Journal of Marketing*, 93–103.

Cooper, R. G. (1979b). "Identifying industrial new product success: Project NewProd." *Industrial Marketing Management*, 8(2), 124–135.

Cooper, R. G. (1983a). "The impact of new product strategies." *Industrial Marketing Management*, 12(4), 243–256.

Cooper, R. G. (1983b). "A process model for industrial New Product Development." *IEEE Transactions on Engineering Management*, EM – 30(1), 2–11.

Cooper, R. G. (1988). "The new product process: A decision guide for management." *Journal of Marketing Management*, 3(3), 238–255.

Cooper, R. G. (1990). "Stage-gate systems: A new tool for managing new products." *Business Horizons*, 33(3), 44–54.

Cooper, R. G. and Kleinschmidt, E. J. (1986). "An investigation into the new product process: Steps, deficiencies, and impact." *Journal of Product Innovation Management*, 3(2), 71–85.

Copulsky, W. (1976). "Cannibalism in the Marketplace." *The Journal of Marketing*, 103–105.

Cordón-Pozo, E., Garcia-Morales, V. J. and Aragon-Correa, J. A. (2006). "Inter-departmental collaboration and new product development success: A study on the collaboration between marketing and R&D in Spanish high-technology firms." *International Journal of Technology Management*, 35(1–4), 52–79.

Cox, W. E. (1967). "Product life cycles as marketing models." *The Journal of Business*, 40(4), 375–384.

Crawford, C. M. (1977). "Product development: Today's most common mistakes." *University of Michigan Business Review*, 29(1), 1–7.

Crawford, C. M. (1980). "Defining the charter for product innovation." *Sloan Management Review*, 22(1), 3.

Crawford, M. C. (1983). *New Products Management*, Irwin, Homewood, IL.

Creativity in Modern Industry. (CMI). *Omni*, March 1981, 6.

Daft, R. L. and Becker, S. W. (1978). *The innovative organization: Innovation adoption in school organizations*, North Holland Publishing Co., New York.

Daft, R. L. and Weick, K. E. (1984). "Toward a model of organizations as interpretation systems." *Academy of Management Review*, 9(2), 284–295.

Dalton, D. R., Todor, W. D., Spendolini, M. J., Fielding, G. J. and Porter, L. W. (1980). "Organization structure and performance: A critical review." *Academy of Management Review*, 5(1), 49–64.

Damanpour, F. (1991). "Organizational innovation: A meta-analysis of effects of determinants and moderators." *Academy of Management Journal*, 34(3), 555–590.

Daniel Sherman, J., Berkowitz, D. and Souder, W. E. (2005). "New product development performance and the interaction of cross-functional integration and knowledge management." *Journal of Product Innovation Management*, 22(5), 399–411.

Davidson, W. (1988). "Technology Environments and Organizational Choice," paper presented at the Conference on Managing the High Technology Firm, The Graduate School of Business, University of Colorado, January 13–19, 1988.

Davies, S. (1979). *Diffusion of Process Innovations*, Cambridge University Press, Cambridge, MA.

De Brentani, U. (1989). "Success and failure in new industrial services." *Journal of Product Innovation Management*, 6(4), 239–258.

De Meyer, A. C. (1985). "The flow of technological innovation in an R & D department." *Research Policy*, 14(6), 315–328.

DeBresson, C. (1991). "Technological innovation and long wave theory: Two pieces of the puzzle." *Journal of Evolutionary Economics*, 1(4), 241–272.

Dentzer, S. (1990). "The coming global boom." *US News & World Report*, 109(3), 22–27.

Deshpandé, R. (1982). "The organizational context of market research use." *The Journal of Marketing*, 91–101.

Deshpandé, R. and Webster Jr., F. E. (1989). "Organizational culture and marketing: Defining the research agenda." *The Journal of Marketing*, 3–15.

Deshpandé, R. and Zaltman, G. (1987). "A comparison of factors affecting use of marketing information in consumer and industrial firms." *Journal of Marketing Research*, 114–118.

Dougherty, D. (1990). "Understanding new markets for new products." *Strategic Management Journal*, 59–78.

Dougherty, D. (1992). "Interpretive barriers to successful product innovation in large firms." *Organization Science*, 3(2), 179–202.

Dougherty, D. and Heller, T. (1994). "The illegitimacy of successful product innovation in established firms." *Organization Science*, 5(2), 200–218.

Dougherty, D. J. (1987). "New Products in Old Organizations: The Myth of the Better Mousetrap in Search of the Beaten Path," (Doctoral dissertation, Massachusetts Institute of Technology).

Douglas, M. (1987). *How Institutions Think*, Routledge & Kegan Paul, London.

Downey, H. K., Hellriegel, D. and Slocum Jr., J. W. (1975). "Environmental uncertainty: The construct and its application." *Administrative Science Quarterly*, 613–629.

Dumaine, B. (1989). "How managers can succeed through speed." *Fortune*, 119(4), 54.

Duncan, R. B. (1972). "Characteristics of organizational environments and perceived environmental uncertainty." *Administrative Science Quarterly*, 313–327.

Dunn, M. J. and Harnden, B. M. (1975). "Interface of marketing and R&D personnel in the product innovation stream." *Journal of the Academy of Marketing Science*, 3(1), 20–33.

Dutta, S., Narasimhan, O. and Rajiv, S. (1999). "Success in high-technology markets: Is marketing capability critical?" *Marketing Science*, 18(4), 547–568.

Easingwood, C. J. (1986). "New product development for service companies." *Journal of Product Innovation Management*, 3(4), 264–275.

Ellinger, A. E. (2000). "Improving marketing/logistics cross-functional collaboration in the supply chain." *Industrial Marketing Management*, 29(1), 85–96.

Emery, F. E. and Trist, E. L. (1965). "The causal texture of organizational environments." *Human Relations*, 18(1), 21–32.

Eng, T. Y. and Ozdemir, S. (2014). "International R&D partnerships and intrafirm R&D – marketing – production integration of manufacturing firms in emerging economies." *Industrial Marketing Management*, 43(1), 32–44.

Englander, A. S. and Gurney, A. (1994). "Medium-term determinants of OECD productivity." *OECD Economic Studies*, 22, 49–109.

Ernst, H., Hoyer, W. D. and Rübsaamen, C. (2010). "Sales, marketing, and research-and-development cooperation across new product development stages: Implications for success." *Journal of Marketing*, 74(5), 80–92.

Ettlie, J. E., Bridges, W. P. and O'keefe, R. D. (1984). "Organization strategy and structural differences for radical versus incremental innovation." *Management Science*, 30(6), 682–695.

Fain, N., Schoormans, J. and Duhovnik, J. (2011). "The effect of R&D-marketing integration on NPD success – the case of SMEs in the growing economy of Slovenia." *International Journal of Technology Management*, 56(1), 92–107.

Fischer, T. and Henkel, J. (2012). "Capturing value from innovation – diverging views of R&D and marketing managers." *IEEE Transactions on Engineering Management*, 59(4), 572–584.

Fisher, J. C. and Pry, R. H. (1971). "A simple substitution model of technological change." *Technological Forecasting & Social Change*, 3, 75–88.

Foster, R. (1986). *Innovation: The Attacker's Advantage*, Summit Books, New York.

Fotiadis, T. and Haramis, G. E. (2002). "Information Systems Maintenance," 7th International Conference on Application of High Performance Computers in Engineering, Bologna, Italy, 23–25 September, 2002.

Fredericks, E. (2005). "Cross-functional involvement in new product development: A resource dependency and human capital perspective." *Qualitative Market Research: An International Journal*, 8(3), 327–341.

Freeman, C. (1974). *The Economics of Industrial Innovation*, Penguin, Baltimore, MD.

Galbraith, J. R. (1973). *Designing Complex Organizations*, Addison-Wesley Longman Publishing Co., Inc., Reading, MA.

Galbraith, J. R. (1977). *Organization Design*, Addison Wesley Publishing Company, Reading, MA.

Galbraith, J. R. and Nathanson, D. A. (1978). *Strategy Implementation: The Role of Structure and Process*, West Pub Co., St. Paul, MN.

Gardner, D. M. (1990). "Are High Technology Products Really Different?/1706," *BEBR faculty Working Paper, no. 90–1706*.

Gardner, D. M., Johnson, F., Lee, M. and Wilkinson, I. (2000). "A contingency approach to marketing high technology products." *European Journal of Marketing*, 34(9/10), 1053–1077.

Garrett, T. C., Buisson, D. H. and Yap, C. M. (2006). "National culture and R&D and marketing integration mechanisms in new product development: A cross-cultural study between Singapore and New Zealand." *Industrial Marketing Management*, 35(3), 293–307.

Gergen, K. J. (1969). *The Psychology of Behavior Exchange*, Addison-Wesley, Reading, MA.

Geroski, P., Machin, S. and Van Reenen, J. (1993). "The profitability of innovating firms." *The RAND Journal of Economics*, 198–211.

Gerstenfeld, A. and Sumiyoshi, K. (1980). "The management of innovation in Japan: Seven forces that make the difference." *Research Management*, 23(1), 30–34.

Ghemawat, P. (1991). "Market incumbency and technological inertia." *Marketing Science*, 10(2), 161–171.

Gibson, J. E. (1981). *Managing R&D*, Wiley-Blackwell, New York.

Gibson, J. L., Ivancevich, J. M. and Donnelly, J. H. (1985). *Organizations: Behavior, Structure, Processes* (5th ed.), Business Publications, Plano, TX.

Glaser, E. M., Abelson, H. H. and Garrison, K. N. (1983). *Putting Knowledge to Use: Facilitating the Diffusion of Knowledge and the Implementation of Planned Change*, Jossey-Bass Incorporated Pub, San Francisco.

Glazer, R. (1991). "Marketing in an information-intensive environment: Strategic implications of knowledge as an asset." *The Journal of Marketing*, 1–19.

Gold, B. (1987). "Approaches to accelerating product and process development." *Journal of Product Innovation Management*, 4(2), 81–88.

Golder, P. N. and Tellis, G. J. (1993). "Pioneer advantage: Marketing logic or marketing legend?" *Journal of Marketing Research*, 158–170.

Goldhar, J. D., Bragaw, L. K. and Schwartz, J. J. (1976). "Information flows, management styles, and technological innovation." *IEEE Transactions on Engineering Management*, (1), 51–62.

Gomes, J. F., de Weerd-Nederhof, P. C., Pearson, A. W. and Cunha, M. P. (2003). "Is more always better? An exploration of the differential effects of functional integration on performance in new product development." *Technovation*, 23(3), 185–191.

Gould, J. and Kolb, W. L. (1964). *A Dictionary of the Social Sciences (Compiled Under the Auspices of UNESCO)*, Free Press of Glencoe, New York.

Griffin, A. and Hauser, J. R. (1993). "The voice of the customer." *Marketing Science*, 12(1), 1–27.

Griffin, A. and Hauser, J. R. (1996). "Integrating R&D and marketing: A review and analysis of the literature." *Journal of Product Innovation Management*, 13(3), 191–215.

Gruber, W. H. (1981), *The Strategic Integration of Corporate Research and Development*, American Management Assn, New York.

Gruber, W. H., Poensgen, O. H. and Prakke, F. (1973). "The isolation of R&D from corporate management." *Research Management*, 16(6), 27–32.

Grunenwald, J. P. and Vernon, T. T. (1988). "Pricing decision making for high-technology products and services." *Journal of Business & Industrial Marketing*, 3(1), 61–70.

Gupta, A. K., Raj, S. P. and Wilemon, D. (1985). "The R&D-marketing interface in high-technology firms." *Journal of Product Innovation Management*, 2(1), 12–24.

Gupta, A. K., Raj, S. P. and Wilemon, D. (1986a). "A model for studying R&D: Marketing interface in the product innovation process." *The Journal of Marketing*, 7–17.

Gupta, A. K., Raj, S. P. and Wilemon, D. (1986b). "R&D and marketing managers in high-tech companies: Are they different?" *IEEE Transactions on Engineering Management*, (1), 25–32.

Gupta, A. K., Raj, S. P. and Wilemon, D. (1987). "Managing the R&D-marketing interface." *Research Management*, 30(2), 38–43.

Gupta, A. K. and Wilemon, D. L. (1988). "The credibility-cooperation connection at the R&D-marketing interface." *Journal of Product Innovation Management*, 5(1), 20–31.

Gupta, A. K. and Wilemon, D. L. (1990). "Accelerating the development of technology-based new products." *California Management Review*, 32(2), 24–44.

Hadlock, P., Hecker, D. and Gannon, J. (1991). "High technology employment: Another view." *Monthly Labor Review*, 114, 26.

Hage, J. (1980). *Theories of Organizations: Form, Process, and Transformation*, John Wiley & Sons, New York.

Hage, J. and Aiken, M. (1967). "Program change and organizational properties a comparative analysis." *American Journal of Sociology*, 72(5), 503–519.

Hage, J. and Aiken, M. (1970). *Social Change in Complex Organizations* (Vol. 41). Random House Trade, New York.

Hage, J., Aiken, M. and Marrett, C. B. (1971). "Organization structure and communications." *American Sociological Review*, 860–871.

Hage, J. and Dewar, R. (1973). "Elite values versus organizational structure in predicting innovation." *Administrative Science Quarterly*, 279–290.

Hamel, G. (1997). "Killer strategies that make shareholders rich." *Fortune*, 135(12), 70–84.

Hamel, G. and Prahalad, C. K. (1991). "Corporate imagination and expeditionary marketing." *Harvard Business Review*, 69(4), 81–92.

Hannan, M. T. and Freeman, J. (1977). "The population ecology of organizations." *American Journal of Sociology*, 82(5), 929–964.

Hatzichronoglou, T. (1997). *Revision of the High-Technology Sector and Product Classification* (No. 1997/2). OECD Publishing, Paris.

Hauptman, O. (1986). "Influence of task type on the relationship between communication and performance: The case of software development." *R&D Management*, 16(2), 127–139.

Hayes, R. H. (1985). "Strategic planning forward – reverse?" *Harvard Business Review*, November–December.

Hayes, R. H., Wheelright, S. C. and Clark,K. B. (1988). *Dynamic Manufacturing Creating the Learning Organization*, Free Press, New York.

Henderson, R. M. and Clark, K. B. (1990). "Architectural innovation: The reconfiguration of existing product technologies and the failure of established firms." *Administrative Science Quarterly*, 9–30.

Hise, R. T., O'Neal, L., McNeal, J. U. and Parasuraman, A. (1989). "The effect of product design activities on commercial success levels of new industrial products." *Journal of Product Innovation Management*, 6(1), 43–50.

Hisrich, R. D. and Peters, M. P. (1978). *Marketing a New Product: Its Planning, Development, and Control*, Addison-Wesley, Reading, MA.

Hitt, M. A. and Ireland, R. D. (1985). "Corporate distinctive competence, strategy, industry and performance." *Strategic Management Journal*, 6(3), 273–293.

Hofer, C. W. and Schendel, D. (1978). *Strategy Formulation: Analytical Concepts*. West Pub Co., St. Paul, MN.

Hopkins, D. (1980). *New-Product Winners and Losers*, The Conference Board. Inc., New York.

Hutt, M. D., Reingen, P. H. and Ronchetto Jr., J. R. (1988). "Tracing emergent processes in marketing strategy formation." *The Journal of Marketing*, 4–19.

Hutt, M. D. and Speh, T. W. (1984). "The marketing strategy center: Diagnosing the industrial marketer's interdisciplinary role." *The Journal of Marketing*, 53–61.

Inoue, M. (1985). "Competition and cooperation among Japanese corporations," in Thyrow, L. C. (ed), *The Management Challenge*, MIT Press, Cambridge, MA.

Itami, H. and Roehl, T. W. (1991). *Mobilizing Invisible Assets*, Harvard University Press, Cambridge, MA.

Jauch, L. R. and Kraft, K. L. (1986). "Strategic management of uncertainty." *Academy of Management Review*, 11(4), 777–790.

Joan, W. (1965). *Industrial Organization: Theory and Practice*, Oxford University Press, London.

John, G. and Martin, J. (1984). "Effects of organizational structure of marketing planning on credibility and utilization of plan output." *Journal of Marketing Research*, 170–183.

John, G., Weiss, A. M. and Dutta, S. (1999). "Marketing in technology-intensive markets: Toward a conceptual framework." *The Journal of Marketing*, 78–91.

Johne, A. and Storey, C. (1998). "New service development: A review of the literature and annotated bibliography." *European journal of Marketing*, 32(3/4), 184–251.

Johnson, R. T. and Ouchi, W. G. (1974). "MADE IN AMERICA-(UNDER JAPANESE MANAGEMENT)." *Harvard Business Review*, 52(5), 61–69.

Kagono, T., Nonaka, I., Okumura, A., Sakakibara, K., Komatsu, Y. and Sakashita, A. (1984). "Mechanistic vs. organic management systems: A comparative study of adaptive patterns of American and Japanese firms." *Annuals of the School of Business Administration Kobe University*, 25, 115–145.

Kahn, K. B. (1996). "Interdepartmental integration: A definition with implications for product development performance." *Journal of Product Innovation Management*, 13(2), 137–151.

Kahn, R. L., Wolfe, D., Quinn, R., Snoeck, J. and Rosenthal, R. (1964). *Organizational Stress*, John Wiley & Sons. Inc., New York.

Kaminski, P., deBresson, C. and Hu, X. (1997). "The clustering of innovative activity in the French economy: An estimation," in DeBresson et al (eds)., *Economic Interdependence and Innovative Activity, An Input-Output Analysis*, Edward Elgar, Cheltenham.

Kang, N., Kim, J. and Park, Y. (2007). "Integration of marketing domain and R&D domain in NPD design process." *Industrial Management & Data Systems*, 107(6), 780–801.

Kanungo, R. N. (1979). "The concepts of alienation and involvement revisited." *Psychological Bulletin*, 86(1), 119.

Karvounis, S. K. (1995). *Διαχείριση τεχνολογίας* και καινοτομίαςαχείριση τεχνολογίας και καινοτομίας (Managing Technology and Innovation), Stamoulis Publications, Athens.

Katz, D. and Kahn, R. (1966). *The Social Psychology of Organizations*, Wiley-Blackwell, New York.

Kay, N. (1988). "The R&D function: Corporate strategy and structure." *Technical Change and Economic Theory*, 283–294.

Kearns, K. P. (1992). "Innovations in local government: A sociocognitive network approach." *Knowledge, Technology & Policy*, 5(2), 45–67.

Kerin, R. A., Harvey, M. G. and Rothe, J. T. (1978). "Cannibalism and new product development." *Business Horizons*, 21(5), 25–31.

Ketteringham, J. and White, J. (1984). "Making technology work for business." *Competitive Strategic Management*, 498–519.

Khandwalla, P. N. (1972). "Environment and its impact on the organization." *International Studies of Management & Organization*, 2(3), 297–313.

Khandwalla, P. N. (1974). *The Design of Organizations*, Harcourt Brace Jovanovich, New York.

Kidder, T. (1981). *The Soul of a New Machine*, Little, Brown and Company, Boston, MA.

Kleinschmidt, E. J. and Cooper, R. G. (1991). "The impact of product innovativeness on performance." *Journal of Product Innovation Management*, 8(4), 240–251.

Kolb, D. A. (1974). "Learning and problem solving," in Kolb, D. A., Rubin, I. M. and McIntyre, J. M. (eds.), *Organizational Psychology*, 2nd ed., Prentice-Hall, Englewood Cliffs, NJ, 27–42.

Kotler P. (1984). *Marketing Management: Analysis, Planning Control* (5th ed.), Prentice-Hall, London.

Kotler, P. and Fahey, L. (1982). "The world's champion marketers: The Japanese." *Journal of Business Strategy*, 3(1), 3–13.

Krishnan, H. A., Tadepalli, R. and Park, D. (2009). "R&D intensity, marketing intensity, and organizational performance." *Journal of Managerial Issues*, 232–244.

Lawrence, P. R. and Lorsch, J. W. (1967a). "Differentiation and integration in complex organizations." *Administrative Science Quarterly*, 1–47.

Lawrence, P. R. and Lorsch, J. W. (1967b). *New Management Job: The Integrator*, Organizational Effectiveness Center and School, 27.

Lawrence, P. R. and Lorsch, J. W. (1969). *Organization and Environment: Managing Differentiation and Integration*, Richard D. Irwin, Homewood, IL.

Lee, T. H. and Nakicenovic, N. (1988). "Technology life – cycles and business decisions." *International Journal of Technology Management*, 3(4), 411–426.

Leenders, M. A. and Wierenga, B. (2008). "The effect of the marketing – R&D interface on new product performance: The critical role of resources and scope." *International Journal of Research in Marketing*, 25(1), 56–68.

Leonard-Barton, D. (1993). "Core capabilities and core rigidities: A paradox in managing new product development." *Strategic Management Journal*, 13, 111–125.

Leontief, W. W. (1993). "Keynote address," 10th International Conference on Input- Output Techniques, Seville, Spain, March.

Leyonard, D. and Rayport, J. F. (1997). "Spark Innovation through Emphatic Design." *Harward Business Review*, (November–December), 102–113.

Lieberman, M. B. and Montgomery, D. B. (1988). „First-mover advantages." *Strategic Management Journal*, 9(S1), 41–58.

Link, A. N. and Zmud, R. W. (1986). "Technical management notes: Additional evidence on the r&d/marketing interface." *IEEE Transactions on Engineering Management*, (1), 43–44.

Link, P. L. (1987). *Marketing of High Technology: An Australian Perspective*, Nelson Wadsworth, Melbourne.

Lipkin, R. (1996). "Fit for a king." *Science News*, 149(20), 316–317.

Lu, L. Y. and Yang, C. (2004). "The R&D and marketing cooperation across new product development stages: An empirical study of Taiwan's IT industry." *Industrial Marketing Management*, 33(7), 593–605.

Lucas, G. H. and Bush, A. J. (1988). "The marketing – R&D interface: Do personality factors have an impact?" *Journal of Product Innovation Management*, 5(4), 257–268.

Luker, Jr., W. and Lyons, D. (1997). "Employment shifts in high-technology industries, 1988–96." *Monthly Labor Review*, 120, 12.

Mahler, A. and Rogers, E. M. (1999). "The diffusion of interactive communication innovations and the critical mass: The adoption of telecommunications services by German banks." *Telecommunications Policy*, 23(10), 719–740.

Maidique, M. A. (1980). "Entrepreneurs, champions, and technological innovation." *Sloan Management Review*, 21(2), 59.

Maidique, M. A. (1984). "Why products fail." *Inc*, 6, 98–105.

Maidique, M. A. and Hayes, R. H. (1984). "The art of high-technology management." *Sloan Management Review*, 25(2), 17.

Maidique, M. A. and Zirger, B. J. (1984). "A study of success and failure in product innovation: The case of the US electronics industry." *IEEE Transactions on Engineering Management*, (4), 192–203.

Mandel, M. J. (1997). "The new business cycle." *Business Week*, 31, 58–68.

Mansfield, E. (1969). *Industrial Research and Technological Innovation: An Economatric Analysis*, Longmans for the Cowles Foundation for Research in Economics at Yale University, New York.

Mansfield, E. (1981). "How economists See R+D." *Harvard Business Review*, 59, November–December, 98–106.

Mansfield, E., Rapport, J., Schnee, J., Wagner, S. and Hamburger, M. (1971). *Research and Innovation in the Modern Corporation*, W. W Norton & Co., New York.

Mansfield, E. and Wagner, S. (1975). "Organizational and strategic factors associated with probabilities of success in industrial R & D." *The Journal of Business*, 48(2), 179–198.

March, J. G. and Simon, H. A. (1958). *Organizations*, Wiley-Blackwell, New York, 262.

Marquis, D. G. (1969). "The anatomy of successful innovations." *Innovation*, 1(7), 28–37.

Mason, C. H. and Milne, G. R. (1994). "An approach for identifying cannibalization within product line extensions and multi-brand strategies." *Journal of Business Research*, 31(2–3), 163–170.

Massey, G. R. and Kyriazis, E. (2007). "Interpersonal trust between marketing and R&D during new product development projects." *European Journal of Marketing*, 41(9/10), 1146–1172.

McKenna, R. (1991). *Relationship Marketing: Successful Strategies for the Age of the Consumer*, Addison-Wesley Publishing Company, Boston, MA.

Meldrum, M. J. (1995). "Marketing high-tech products: The emerging themes." *European Journal of Marketing*, 29(10), 45–58.

Metcalfe, J. S. (1981). "Impulse and diffusion in the study of technical change." *Futures*, 13(5), 347–359.

Meyer, A. D. and Goes, J. B. (1988). "Organizational assimilation of innovations: A multi-level contextual analysis." *Academy of Management Journal*, 31(4), 897–923.

Meyers, P. W. and Wilemon, D. (1989). "Learning in new technology development teams." *Journal of Product Innovation Management*, 6(2), 79–88.

Miaoulis, G. and LaPlaca, P. J. (1982). "A systems approach for developing high technology products." *Industrial Marketing Management*, 11(4), 253–262.

Michalek, J. J., Feinberg, F. M. and Papalambros, P. Y. (2005). "Linking marketing and engineering product design decisions via analytical target cascading." *Journal of Product Innovation Management*, 22(1), 42–62.

Miles, R. E., Snow, C. C., Meyer, A. D. and Coleman, H. J. (1978). "Organizational strategy, structure, and process." *Academy of Management Review*, 3(3), 546–562.

Miller, G. A. and Wager, L. W. (1971). "Adult socialization, organizational structure, and role orientations." *Administrative Science Quarterly*, 151–163.

Milliken, F. J. (1987). "Three types of perceived uncertainty about the environment: State, effect, and response uncertainty." *Academy of Management Review*, 12(1), 133–143.

Millman, A. F. (1982). "Understanding barriers to product innovation at the R & D/marketing interface." *European Journal of Marketing*, 16(5), 22–34.

Mintzberg, H. (1979). *The Structuring of Organization: A Synthesis of the Research*, Prentice-Hall, Englewood Cliffs, NJ.

Moenaert, R. K. and Souder, W. E. (1990a). "An information transfer model for integrating marketing and R&D personnel in new product development projects." *Journal of Product Innovation Management*, 7(2), 91–107.

Moenaert, R. K. and Souder, W. E. (1990b). "An anlysis of the use of extrafunctional information by R&D and marketing personnel: Review and model." *Journal of Product Innovation Management*, 7(3), 213–229.

Mohr, J. J., Sengupta, S. and Slater, S. F. (2009). *Marketing of High-Technology Products and Innovations*, Pearson Prentice Hall, Englewood Cliffs, NJ.

Mokyr, J. (1992). *The Lever of Riches: Technological Creativity and Economic Progress*, Oxford University Press, Oxford.

Monteleone, J. P. (1976). "How R&D and marketing can work together." *Research Management*, 19(2), 19–21.

Moore, G. A. (1991). *The Product Adoption Curve in Crossing the Chasm, Marketing and Selling Technology Products to Mainstream Customers*, HarperCollins, New York.

Moorman, C. and Miner, A. S. (1997). "The impact of organizational memory on new product performance and creativity." *Journal of Marketing Research*, 91–106.

Morgan, G. (1986). *Images of Organization*, Sage, Newbury Park, CA.

Moriarty, R. T. and Kosnik, T. J. (1989). "High-tech marketing: Concepts, continuity, and change." *MIT Sloan Management Review*, 30(4), 7.

Murray, A. and Lehner, U. C. (1990). "What US scientists discover, the Japanese convert – Into Profit." *The Wall Street Journal*, 25, A1–A6.

National Science Board (NSB). (1996). Science and Engineering Indicators- 1996. National Science Foundation. Chapters 4 and 6. Available at: Science & Engineering Indicators 1996.

National Science Foundation (NSF). (1983). *The Process of Technological Innovation: Reviewing the Literature*, NSF, Productivity Improvement Research Section, Washington, DC.

National Science Foundation (USA). (1973). "Barriers to Innovation in Industry,".

Nault, B. R. and Vandenbosch, M. B. (1996). "Eating your own lunch: Protection through preemption." *Organization Science*, 7(3), 342–358.

Nelson, R. R. and Winter, S. G. (1982). *An Evolutionary Theory of Economic Change*, Belknap/ Harvard University Press, Cambridge, MA.

Nieto, M., López, F. and Cruz, F. (1998). "Performance analysis of technology using the S curve model: The case of digital signal processing (DSP) technologies." *Technovation*, 18(6), 439–457.

Noda, K. (1975). "Big business organization," in Vogel, E.F. (ed.), *Modern Japanese Organization and Decision – Making*, The University of California Press, Berkeley, CA.

O'Brien, M. P. (1962). "Technological Planning and Misplanning," In Technological planning at the corporate level: Proceedings of a Conference, Graduate School of Administration, September, 8, 120–133.

Olson, E. M., Walker, Jr., O. C. and Ruekert, R. W. (1995). "Organizing for effective new product development: The moderating role of product innovativeness." *The Journal of Marketing*, 48–62.

Organ, D. W. and Greene, C. N. (1981). "The effects of formalization on professional involvement: A compensatory process approach." *Administrative Science Quarterly*, 237–252.

Ouchi, W. (1981). "Theory Z: How American business can meet the Japanese challenge." *Business Horizons*, 24(6), 82–83.

Palumbo, D. J. (1969). "Power and role specificity in organization theory." *Public Administration Review*, 237–248.

Papageorgiou, P. P. (1990). *Εισαγωγή στο Διεθνές Management* (Introduction to International Management), Stamoulis S.A., Athens.

Parker, J. E. S. (1978). *The Economics of Innovation – The National and Multinational Enterprise in Technological Change*, Longman, New York.

Parry, M. E. and Song, X. M. (1993). "Determinants of R&D – marketing integration in high-tech Japanese firms." *Journal of Product Innovation Management*, 10(1), 4–22.

Pavitt, K. (1991). "Key characteristics of the large innovating firm." *British Journal of Management*, 2(1), 41–50.

Pearson Andrall, E. (1978). "The R+D challenge – getting it out of the lab." *Industry Week*, May 4, 33–36.

Perks, H., Kahn, K. B. and Zhang, C. (2010). "The nature of R&D-marketing integration in Chinese high-tech companies." *International Journal of Innovation Management*, 14(01), 19–40.

Perks, H., Kahn, K. and Zhang, C. (2009). "An empirical evaluation of R&D – marketing NPD integration in Chinese firms: The Guanxi effect." *Journal of Product Innovation Management*, 26(6), 640–651.

Perks, H. and Riihela, N. (2004). "An exploration of inter-functional integration in the new service development process." *The Service Industries Journal*, 24(6), 37–63.

Perrow, C. (1967). "A framework for the comparative analysis of organizations." *American Sociological Review*, 194–208.

Pinchot, G. (1985). *Intrapreneuring: Why You Do Not Have to Leave the Corporation to Become an Entrepreneur*, Harper & Row, Pinchot, New York.

Pinto, J. K. and Covin, J. G. (1989). "Critical factors in project implementation: A comparison of construction and R&D projects." *Technovation*, 9(1), 49–62.

Porter, M. E. (1980). *Competitive Strategy: Techniques for Analyzing Industries and Competition*, Fre Press, New York.

Porter, M. E. (1981). *The Technological Dimension of Competitive Strategy*, Division of Research, Graduate School of Business Administration, Harvard University Press, Cambridge, MA.

Prahalad, C. K. and Hamel, G. (1990). "The core competence of the corporation." *Boston (Ma)*, *1990*, 235–256.

Quinn, James Brian. (1992). *Personal Knowledge: Towards a Post Critical Philosophy*, Harper and Row, New York.

Quinn, J. (1985). "Managing innovation: Controlled chaos." *Harvard Business Review*, 63, May–June, 73–85.

Quinn, J. B. (1979). "Technological innovation, entrepreneurship, and strategy." *Sloan Management Review*, 20(3), 19.

Quinn, J. B. (1980). *Strategies for Change: Logical Incrementalism*, Irwin Professional Publishing, Homewood, IL.

Quinn, J. B., Baruch, J. J. and Zien, K. A. (1997). *Innovation Explosion: Using Intellect and Software to Revolutionize Growth Strategies*, Simon & Schuster, New York.

Rafiq, M. and Saxon, T. (2000). "R&D and marketing integration in NPD in the pharmaceutical industry." *European Journal of Innovation Management*, 3(4), 222–231.

Rangan, V. K. and Bartus, K. (1995). "New product commercialization: Common mistakes," in Rangan, V. K. et al. (eds), *Business Marketing Strategy*, Irwin, Chicago.

Raudsepp, E. (1965). "Conformity and the engineer." *Machine Design*, 14.

Rexroad, R. A. (1983). *High Technology Marketing Management*, Ronald Press, New York.

Roberts, E. B. (1978). "What do we really know about managing R&D?" *Research Management*, 21(6), 6–11.

Roberts, E. B. (1979). "Stimulating technological innovation: Organizational approaches." *Research Management*, 22(6), 26–30.

Roberts, E. B. (1988). "What we've learned: Managing invention and innovation." *Research-Technology Management*, 31(1), 11–29.

Roberts, E. B. and Fusfeld, A. R. (1981). "Staffing the innovative technology-based organization." *Sloan Management Review*, 22(3), 19.

Robertson, T. S. (1967). "The process of innovation and the diffusion of innovation." *The Journal of Marketing*, 14–19.

Rogers, E. M. (1983). *Diffusion of Innovation*, Free Press, New York.

Rogers, E. M. and Agarwala-Rogers, R. (1976). *Communication in Organizations*, Free Press, New York.

Rogers, E. M. and Kincaid, D. L. (1981). *Communication Networks: Toward a New Paradigm for Research*, Free Press, New York.

Rogers, E. M. and Shoemaker, F. F. (1971). *Communication of Innovations: A Cross-Cultural Approach*, Free Press, New York.

Rohlen, T. P. (1975). "The company work group," in *Modern Japanese Organization and Decision-Marking*, University of California Press, Berkeley, CA.

Rosen, D. E., Schroeder, J. E. and Purinton, E. F. (1988). "Marketing high tech products: Lessons in customer focus from the marketplace." *Journal of Consumer and Market Research* (Online 98(6)).

Rosenbloom, R. S. and Cusumano, M. A. (1987). "Technological pioneering and competitive advantage: the birth of the VCR industry." *California Management Review*, 29(4), 51–76.

Rothwell, R., Freeman, C., Horlsey, A., Jervis, V. T. P., Robertson, A. B. and Townsend, J. (1974). "SAPPHO updated-project SAPPHO phase II." *Research Policy*, 3(3), 258–291.

Rothwell, R. and Robertson, A. B. (1973). "The role of communications in technological innovation." *Research Policy*, 2(3), 204–225.

Roussel, P. A. (1983). "Cutting down the guesswork in R & D." *Harvard. Business Review*, 61(5).

Rubenstein, A. H., Chakrabarti, A. K., O'Keefe, R. D., Souder, W. E. and Young, H. C. (1976). "Factors influencing innovation success at the project level." *Research Management*, 19(3), 15–20.

Rubera, G., Ordanini, A. and Calantone, R. (2012). "Whether to integrate R&D and marketing: The effect of firm competence." *Journal of Product Innovation Management*, 29(5), 766–783.

Ruekert, R. W. and Walker, Jr., O. C. (1987). "Marketing's interaction with other functional units: A conceptual framework and empirical evidence." *The Journal of Marketing*, 1–19.

Samli, A. C. and Wills, J. (1986). "Strategies for marketing computers and related products." *Industrial Marketing Management*, 15(1), 23–32.

Saren, M. A. (1984). "A classification and review of models of the intra-firm innovation process." *R&D Management*, 14(1), 11–24.

Schneider, S. C. (1987). "Information overload: Causes and consequences." *Human Systems Management*, 7(2), 143–153.

Schon, D. A. (1967). *Technology and Change: The New Heraclitus*, Seymour Lawrence.

Schumpeter, J. A. (1939). *Business Cycles* (Vol. 1, pp. 161–74), McGraw-Hill, New York.

Shanklin, W. L. and Ryans, J. K. (1982). *Essentials of Marketing High Technology*, Lexington Books, Lexington, MA.

Shanklin, W. L. and Ryans, J. K. (1984). "Organizing for high-tech marketing." *Harvard Business Review*, 62(6), 164–171.

Shibutani, T. (1962). "Reference groups and social control." *Human Behavior and Social Processes: An Interactionist Approach*, 128–147.

Shrivastava, P. (1983). "A typology of organizational learning systems." *Journal of Management Studies*, 20(1), 7–28.

Siegel, M. (1998). "Do computers Slow Us Down?" Fortune, in Landauer, T. K. (ed.), *The Trouble with Computers Usefulness, Usability, and Productivity*, MIT Press, Cambridge, MA, 30 March, 34–38.

Silver, S. D., Cohen, B. P. and Rainwater, J. (1988). "Group structure and information exchange in innovative problem solving." *Advances in Group Processes*, 5, 169–194.

Snow, C. C. and Hrebiniak, L. G. (1980). "Strategy, distinctive competence, and organizational performance." *Administrative Science Quarterly*, 317–336.

Song, L. Z. and Song, M. (2010). "The role of information technologies in enhancing R&D – marketing integration: An empirical investigation." *Journal of Product Innovation Management*, 27(3), 382–401.

Song, M. and Thieme, R. J. (2006). "A cross-national investigation of the R&D – marketing interface in the product innovation process." *Industrial Marketing Management*, 35(3), 308–322.

Song, M. and Xie, J. (2000). "Does innovativeness moderate the relationship between cross-functional integration and product performance?" *Journal of International Marketing*, 8(4), 61–89.

Song, X. M. and Parry, M. E. (1992). "The R&D-marketing interface in Japanese high-technology firms." *Journal of Product Innovation Management*, 9(2), 91–112.

Song, X. M. and Parry, M. E. (1997). "A cross-national comparative study of new product development processes: Japan and the United States." *The Journal of Marketing*, 1–18.

Souder, W. E. (1977). *An Exploratory Study of the Coordinating Mechanisms Between R & D and Marketing as an Influence on the Innovation Process*. School of Engineering, University of Pittsburgh, Pittsburgh.

Souder, W. E. (1981). "Disharmony between R&D and marketing." *Industrial Marketing Management*, 10(1), 67–73.

Souder, W. E. (1983). "Organizing for modern technology and innovation: A review and synthesis." *Technovation*, 2(1), 27–44.

Souder, W. E. (1987). *Managing New Product Innovations*, Lexington Books, Lexington, MA.

Souder, W. E. (1988). "Managing relations between R&D and marketing in new product development projects." *Journal of Product Innovation Management*, 5(1), 6–19.

Souder, W. E. and Chakrabarti, A. K. (1978). "The R&D/marketing interface: Results from an empirical study of innovation projects." *IEEE Transactions on Engineering Management*, (4), 88–93.

Souder, W. E. and Chakrabarti, A. K. (1979). "Industrial innovations: A demographical analysis." *IEEE Transactions on Engineering Management*, (4), 101–109.

Souder, W. E. and Chakrabarti, A. K. (1980). "Managing the coordination of marketing and R&D in the innovation process." *TIMS Studies in the Management Sciences*, 15, 135–150.

Souder, W. E. and Moenaert, R. K. (1992). "Integrating marketing and R&D project personnel within innovation projects: An information uncertainty model." *Journal of Management Studies*, 29(4), 485–512.

Stanley Budner, N. Y. (1962). "Intolerance of ambiguity as a personality variable." *Journal of Personality*, 30(1), 29–50.

Swan, J. E. and Rink, D. R. (1982). "Fitting market strategy to varying product life cycles." *Business Horizons*, 25(1), 72–76.

Tabrizi, B. and Walleigh, R. (1997). "Defining next-generation products: An inside look." *Harvard Business Review*, 75(6), 116–124.

Takeuchi, H. (1985). Motivation and "productivity, in Thurow, L. C. (ed.), *The Management Challenge*, MIT Press, Cambridge, MA.

Takeuchi, H. and Nonaka, I. (1986). "The new new product development game." *Harvard Business Review*.

Technology, Innovation and Regional Economic Development (TIRED). (1982). Washington, DC: U. S. Congress, Office of Technology Assessment, 9 September.

Technology in the National Interest (TNI). (1996). "Committee on Civilian Industrial Technology, Technology Administration," U. S., Department of Commerce, available at www.td.doc.gov/reports/TechNI,INI.pdf

Teece, D. J., Pisano, G. P. and Shuen, A. (1990). *Firm Capabilities, Resources, and the Concept of Strategy: Four Paradigms of Strategic Management*, University of California at Berkeley, Center for Research in Management, Consortium on Competitiveness & Cooperation, Berkeley, CA.

Tellis, G. J. and Crawford, C. M. (1981). "An evolutionary approach to product growth theory." *The Journal of Marketing*, 125–132.

Thomas, L. J. (1984). "Technology and Business Strategy-The R&D Link." *Research Management*, 27(May–June), 15–19.

Thompson J. P. (1967). *Organizations in Action*, McGraw-Hill, New York.

Thwaites, D. (1992). "Organizational influences on the new product development process in financial services." *Journal of Product Innovation Management*, 9(4), 303–313.

Troy, L. C., Hirunyawipada, T. and Paswan, A. K. (2008). "Cross-functional integration and new product success:A n empirical investigation of the findings." *Journal of Marketing*, 72(6), 132–146.

Tsuji, K. (1968). "Decision-making in the Japanese government: A study of ringisei." *Political Development in Modern Japan*, 457–76.

Tushman, M. L. and Anderson, P. (1986). "Technological discontinuities and organizational environments." *Administrative Science Quarterly*, 439–465.

Tushman, M. L. and Nadler, D. A. (1978). "Information processing as an integrating concept in organizational design." *Academy of Management Review*, 3(3), 613–624.

Twiss, B. C. (1986). *Managing Technological Innovation*, Longman Publishing Group, London.

Uttal, B. (1987). "Speeding new ideas to market." *Fortune*, 115(5), 62.

Utterback, J. M. (1971). "The process of technological innovation within the firm." *Academy of Management Journal*, 14(1), 75–88.

Utterback, J. M. (1994). *Mastering the Dynamics of Innovation: How Companies Can Seize Opportunities in the Face of Technological Change*, Harvard Business School Press, Boston, MA.

Vakalios, Ath. (2002). *Τεχνολογία, Κοινωνία, Πολιτισμός* (Technology, Society, Culture), Psifida Publications, Athens.

Vernardakis, N. (1993). "Input-output tables and the location of innovation among small firms in semi-industrialized economy." In *10th International Conference on Input-Output Techniques, Seville*, Spain.

Vernardakis, N., Stephanidis, C. and Akoumianakis, D. (1995). "The use of analytical tools in analysing the demand of assisting technology products: The case of alarm telephones," in Porero, I. and Bellacasa, R. (eds.), *The European Context for Assistive Technology*, IOS Press, Amsterdam.

Veryzer, R. W. (1998). "Key factors affecting customer evaluation of discontinuous new products." *Journal of Product Innovation Management*, 15(2), 136–150.

Victor, B. and Blackburn, R. S. (1987). "Determinants and consequences of task uncertainty: A laboratory and field investigation." *Journal of Management Studies*, 24(4), 387–404.

Vogel, E. F. (1981). *Japan as Number One: Lessons for America*, Harvard University Press, Cambridge, MA.

Walsh, S. T. and Linton, J. D. (2000). "Infrastructure for emergent industries based on discontinuous innovations." *Engineering Management Journal*, 12(2), 23–32.

Weick, K. (1979). *The Social Psychology of Organizing*, Random House, New York.

Wind, Y. (1981). *Marketing and Other Business Functions*. Research in Marketing, Vol. V, Jagdish N. Shet, ed., Jai Press, Greenwich.

Wind, Y. (1982). *Product Policy: Concepts, Methods, and Strategy* (Vol. 8). Addison-Wesley, Reading, MA.

Wind, J. and Mahajan, V. (1997). "Issues and opportunities in new product development: An introduction to the special issue." *Journal of Marketing Research*, 34(1), 1–12.

Wind, Y. and Mahajan, V. (1988). "New product development process: A perspective for reexamination." *Journal of Product Innovation Management*, 5(4), 304–310.

Wind, Y. and Robertson, T. S. (1983). "Marketing strategy: New directions for theory and research." *The Journal of Marketing*, 12–25.

Workman, Jr., J. P. (1993). "Marketing's limited role in new product development in one computer systems firm." *Journal of Marketing Research*, 405–421.

Xu, S., DeBresson, C. and Xu, X. (1996). "The location of innovative activity in China (1992)," in DeBresson et al. (eds.), *Economic Interdependence and Innovative Activity, An Input- Output Analysis*, Edward Elgar, Cheltenham.

Yoshino, M. Y. (1969). "Japan's managerial system: Tradition and innovation." *IMR; Industrial Management Review* (pre-1986), 10(3), 82.

Young, H. C. (1973). "Product Development Setting, Information Exchange, and Marketing-R & D Coupling," (Doctoral dissertation, Northwestern University).

Young, H. C. (1979). "Effective management of research-market teams." *Research Management*, 22(2), 7–12.

Zahra, S. A. (1987). "corporate strategic types, environmental perceptions, managerial philosophies, and goals-an empirical-study." *Akron Business and Economic Review*, 18(2), 64–77.

Zaltman, G., Duncan, R. and Holbek, J. (1973). *Innovations and Organizations*, John Wiley & Sons, New York.

Zarecor, W. D. (1975). "High-technology product planning." *Harvard Business Review*, 53(1), 108–115.

Zeithaml, C. P. and Zeithaml, V. A. (1984). "Environmental management: Revising the marketing perspective." *The Journal of Marketing*, 48(Spring), 46–53.

Index

For Product Safety Concerns and Information please contact our EU
representative GPSR@taylorandfrancis.com
Taylor & Francis Verlag GmbH, Kaufingerstraße 24, 80331 München, Germany

www.ingramcontent.com/pod-product-compliance
Ingram Content Group UK Ltd.
Pitfield, Milton Keynes, MK11 3LW, UK
UKHW020953180425
457613UK00019B/664